A CATALOGUE OF RENAISSANCE PHILOSOPHERS

(1350-1650)

Compiled by

ROBERT A. BAKER
ANDREW J. BAKULA
THOMAS H. BARRY
DAVID E. LA BISSONIERE
LESTER J. LA MOTTE
ARTHUR LUCARELLI
ROBERT T. McGRAW
WILLARD C. McKINNON

WILLIAM H. MILLMANN
GEORGE E. PAPUGA
VELMA C. PRANGE
WILLIAM F. SCHOLL
NORBERT L. SIEWERT
ROSE STERLING
RUTH R. SUESS
ROBERT E. WALTER

THOMAS J. WOODS

Under the Direction of

JOHN O. RIEDL, Ph.D.

MARQUETTE UNIVERSITY PRESS
MILWAUKEE
1940

Second Printing 1961
Third Printing 1982

Copyright, 1940, 1982
by the
Marquette University Press
Milwaukee, Wisconsin

ISBN 0-87462-4347

39

Preface

"A Catalogue of Renaissance Philosophers", first printed in 1940, has been re-printed again due to the revived interest in Renaissance philosophy, theology and religious studies.

As John Riedl indicates in his Foreword:

"The term philosopher has been somewhat loosely interpreted for present purposes. Many scientists, ascetics, theologians and rhetoricans have been included."

And says later:

"No one is more aware, than the compilers, of the limitations of this work. Omissions and wrong emphasis constitute the most serious although perhaps not the most noticeable defect. These are due principally to the lack of sufficient material. Some very .important thinkers are as yet hardly dis-covered much less read and studied, whereas some very insignificant think-ers have been treated with undeserved comprehensiveness by historians."

In view of Dr. Riedls' caveat, we rsepectfully solicit any suggestions for additional Renaissance "philosophers" for editorial consideration as an early supplement and eventual inclusion in this catalog at a future printing.

Robert W. Engbring, Ph.D
Director, Marquette University Press

Editor's Foreword

The Renaissance is so often thought of as a simple movement beginning in the time of Dante and extending to the time of Erasmus and a little beyond, that it would seem to be not merely disillusioning, but positively instructive, to come to appreciate the complexity of the period by seeing the conglomeration of conflicting casts of thought which it embraced. From the birth of Dante in 1265, nine years before the death of St. Thomas Aquinas, to the death of Erasmus in 1536, ten years before the death of Martin Luther, is almost three centuries. And from the death of Erasmus to the birth of Descartes is another half century. Since modern philosophy has usually been thought to begin with Descartes, the period of the Renaissance, intervening as it does between the middle ages and modern times, can hardly be shortened to much less than two and one-half centuries. The present study has set the arbitrary limits of 1350 and 1650. A few people who did their major writing before 1350, and a few who wrote after 1650 are included in order to preserve the continuity.

The term philosopher has been somewhat loosely interpreted for present purposes. Many scientists, ascetics, theologians and rhetoricians have been included. This is partly because some of their writings either were philosophical or had an influence on philosophy, and partly because their inclusion aids materially in the reconstruction of the comprehensive body of knowledge which the first philosophers of modern times received as their inheritance and upon which they erected the structure of modern thought.

In the divisions into schools care has been taken to preserve the unities of time, place and idea. The unities of time and place aid the imagination in reconstructing a philosopher's environment and are usually the means of pointing out his associates or at least the contemporaries whose writings and ideas he had the greatest likelihood of knowing. The unity of idea more properly designates a 'school' of thought, but sometimes develops without the individuals constituting it being aware of one another's existence. In most cases one of the unities had to be sacrificed for the sake of the others. Which one that was to be, was dictated entirely by the desire to put the greatest order into the material.

The original work of compilation had been a project of seventeen undergraduate students comprising a class in the history of modern philosophy, under the direction of the writer who was then assistant professor of philosophy in Marquette University.

No one is more aware, than the compilers, of the limitations of this work. Omissions and wrong emphasis constitute the most serious, although perhaps not the most noticeable defect. These are due principally to the lack of sufficient material. Some very important thinkers are as yet hardly discovered much less read and studied, whereas some very insignificant thinkers have been treated with undeserved comprehensiveness by historians. Although an effort has been made to fill the gaps in history by following the leads which Renaissance writers give when they praise or condemn their contemporaries and by using in some cases even first hand acquaintance with manuscript materials, the very fact that this could be done at all makes more certain that it could equally well be done in dozens of other cases. To serve as the foundation for such study, the names of the persons are often included in a group, even though the lack of information concerning them makes a proper classification impossible. It will also be recognized that the large number of books and their rarity has made impossible more than the most casual, and consequently the most doubtful comments about even recognizably great thinkers. The biographical details selected were usually those that designated the education, teachers, university connections and pupils of a thinker, and such other details as might help to place him in some one or two of the maelstrom of conflicting tendencies in his lifetime. Every effort has been made to achieve uniformity of style of presentation, but the claims of individual personality have had on occasion to be recognized.

John C. Riedl, Ph.D.
Professor Emeritus

Acknowledgements

Special thanks were given, by Dr. John Riedl (now Professor emeritus Philosophy), to Rev. Francis S. Betten, S.J. (deceased) professor of History in Marquette University, for making much useful material available, to Rev. Raphael N. Hamilton, S.J., Ph.D., dean of the Graduate School of Marquette (later University archivist, now deceased) for reading the manuscript; ot J. L. O'Sullivan, B.J., dean of the college of Journalism (later dean emeritus, now deceased), for his very helpful suggestions relative to preparing the material for publication (as Director of the Marquette University Press); to Margaret Lawler, M.A. assistant librarian in Marquette University Library; for innumerable favors and generous assistance, to Donald Gallagher, S.A., instructor in English (later, Ph.D. and associate professor of philosophy and presently a manager with DeRance, Inc. a Wisconsin philanthropic foundation) for information concerning the English College at Doual, to Thomas J. Woods for drawing the map, to Willard C. McKinnon (deceased) for undertaking the making of the index; to Thomas H. Barry for reading the proofs; and especially to Victor M. Hamm, Ph.D. associate professor (professor emeritus, philosophy) for a large amount of material on logic and rhetoric and constant help and criticism throughout the entire work.

The "seventeen undergraduate" students mentioned by Dr. Riedl, above, are listed on the title page.

R.W.E.

TABLE OF CONTENTS

CONTENTS

CONTENTS

A CATALOGUE OF
RENAISSANCE PHILOSOPHERS

I. EARLY ITALIAN HUMANISTS

DANTE ALIGHIERI (1265-1321), Florentine writer, exiled in the political disputes in which he favored the cause of the Guelfs who supported the Holy Roman Emperor against the temporal supremacy of the Pope. Writings:

Divina Commedia, a long poem whose characters include the great philosophers of ancient and mediaeval times. They are made to speak a philosophical language and to pass judgment on the philosophy of their fellow.

De vulgari eloquentia, an essay on linguistics, dealing with the question concerning the origin of language.

De monarchia, in which are discussed, in the first part, the nature of monarchial government and its character as the ideal structure of the state; in the second part, the divine origin of the imperial power; and in the third part, the part the Holy Roman Emperor should play in the union of Italy.

Convito, an incomplete Italian work, which was probably intended to be a handbook of universal knowledge.

Quaestio de aqua et terra, attributed to Dante. A philosophical discussion as to whether water can be higher than the earth at certain places on Earth.

BERNHARD BARLAAM (d. 1348), theologian in a cloister in Calabria where a knowledge of Greek language had long been fostered. He went to Greece whence he was sent as emissary of King Andronicus the younger to the Papal court of Benedict XII at Avignon. (Babylonian captivity of the Popes at Avignon, 1309-1378). There in 1339 he taught Petrarch. Wrote: *Ethica secundum Stoicos composita per D. Barlaamum.*

LEONTIUS PILATUS (d. 1366), a pupil of Barlaam, and in turn Boccaccio's teacher of Greek and literary associate in Florence. Attempted to make a Latin translation of Homer.

FRANCESCO PETRARCA (1304-1374), born at Arezzo of a Florentine notary public who wanted his son to be a lawyer. In 1312 he was taken to Avignon; studied at Montpellier, Bologna and Avignon. In the course of his travel through Italy, France and Germany (and frequently to Rome) he

[1]

discovered manuscripts containing forgotten works of Cicero, Catullus and Propertius. In 1341 crowned poet laureate of Rome, through the influence of Robert, King of Naples. His writings aside from his poems and the great bulk of his letters, include:

De contemptu mundi (1342), a dialogue between Petrarch and St. Augustine.

Epistola ad posteros (ca. 1370), autobiography.

De viris illustribus, a compilation of aphorisms and wise sayings of the ancients.

Contra cuiusdam anonymi Galli calumnias apologia, a pamphlet against a French writer who wanted to prevent the pope from removing the Holy See to Rome.

Against Padua Averrhoists, a pamphlet.

Contra medicum quendam invectivarum libri, a pamphlet directed against a physician in Avignon.

De sui ipsius et multorum ignorantia, a book which grew out of the disputes with the physician and the Averroists.

De vita solitaria (1356), in praise of the life of solitude.

De otio religiosorum (1347), on the monastic life.

De remediis utriusque fortunae (1358/66), a philosophizing on the troubles and transitory happiness of the world.

GIOVANNI BOCCACCIO (1313-1365), disciple and friend of Petrarch; born in Paris of a French mother and an Italian banker of Florence, to which city Boccaccio was soon taken. In 1327 he was sent to Naples to study law, but wasted his time. In 1342 he returned to Florence where in 1348 the Black Death so ravaged the city that, according to some estimates, 60 per cent of the population died and grass grew in the streets. In 1350 his friendship with Petrarch began. His writing besides his love poems and stories notably the *Decameron,* include:

Vita di Dante

Commento sopra la Commedia

De casibus virorum illustrium, begins with Adam.

De claris mulieribus, begins with Eve.

De genealogiis deorum gentilium, a dictionary of classical mythology.

COLUCCIO DI PIERO DE' SALUTATI (Salutato; d. 1406), state chancellor of Florence, friend of Boccaccio. Stoic in his philosophy; interested especially in Cicero and Seneca. Wrote:

[2]

De fato et fortuna, a philosophical poem in hexameters against the astrologers.
De religione et fuga seculi.

II. OCKHAM AND HIS IMMEDIATE FOLLOWERS

WILLIAM OF OCKHAM (ca. 1300-1349/1350), O. Min. Born in Ockham near London in Surrey. Studied at Oxford, 1312-1318. Lectured at Oxford on the *Sentences* of Peter Lombard, 1318-1320. Became 'baccalareus formatus,' ca. 1320. Called in 1324 to Avignon to answer a charge of heresy. Several of Ockham's doctrines were condemned. In 1328 he fled with his fellow-religious Bonagratia and the general of the order, Michael of Cesena, to Pisa where he sought and received the protection of King Louis of Bavaria, until the latter's death in 1348. Wrote a commentary on the first book of *Sentences* of Peter Lombard, and 'reportata' on the other three books. Wrote also:

Summa totius logicae
Summulae in libros Physicorum
Quaestiones super libros Physicorum
Exposito aurea super totam artem veterem; the authenticity of this book is in doubt.
Quodlibeta septem
Centiloquium theologicum
De sacramento altaris et de corpore Christi
De motu, loco, tempore, relatione, praedestinatione et praescientia Dei
Tractatus de dogmatibus papae Johannis XXII, ca. 1333
Contra Johannem XXII, ca. 1335
Tractatus contra Benedictum XII, ca. 1337
Dialogus super dignitate papali et regia, ca. 1338/42
Octo quaestiones super potestate et dignitate papali, ca. 1342
Tractatus de imperatorum et pontificum potestate, ca. 1347

BONAGRATIA OF BERGAMO (d. 1340), O. Min., 'juris utriusque doctor.' Took active part in the controversy concerning the poverty of religious; in this connection he wrote a treatise on the poverty of Christ. Fled with Ockham to Pisa in 1328.

MICHAEL OF CESENA (d. 1342), O. Min. Studied at Paris where he became master of theology. Became general of the order in 1316. Fled with Ockham to Pisa in 1328. Because of his conflict with the pope and his refusal to obey the orders of his superiors, he was dismissed from the order in 1331. His supporters were known as Michaelists.

ADAM WODHAM (Godham; d. 1358). Franciscan teacher in Norwich, London and Oxford. Pupil of Ockham. His commentary on the *Sentences* exists in four redactions. A summary was made by Henry Totting de Oyta (printed in Paris, 1512).

ROBERT HOLKOT (d. 1349), O. P. Born in Northampton. Received his doctorate in theology at the University of Cambridge, where he was later professor. Forsook the Thomist tradition of his order for nominalism and extreme determinism. Wrote:

Super IV libros Sententiarum quaestiones
Praelectiones in librum sapientiae
Explanationes proverbiorum Salomonis
In cantica canticorum
Moralizatio historarium
De origine, definitione et remedio peccatorum

GREGORY NOVELLI DE RIMINI (d. 1358) of the hermits of St. Augustine. Born in Rimini. Studied at Paris. Taught at Paris, Bologna, Padua and Perugia, and then returned to Paris where for four years he lectured on the *Sentences* of Peter Lombard. In 1345 he became master of theology and in 1357 general of his order. Wrote a commentary to the first two books of *Sentences* and a treatise entitled, *De usuris.*

JOHANNES BURIDANUS (ca. 1300-ca. 1358) born at Béthune in Artois. Rector of the University of Paris in 1327 and 1348. Pupil of Ockham. For 25 years he taught logic, physics, psychology, metaphysics, ethics and politics as an Aristotelian, but from an Ockhamist point of view. Modern physics is said to have originated with him and a group of nominalists who carried on his work. To him is attributed the invention of the 'pons asinorum,' the donkey dying of hunger between two bundles of hay of equal size and quality, compared to the human will between two equally good motives. It is, however, not found in his writings and may either have been used by Buridanus in his oral teaching or have been the invention of his contemporaries in order to ridicule his determinism. The 'pons' is to be found in Petrus Tartaretus's *Commentarii in libros totius logicae Aristotelis.* Buridanus wrote commentaries on the *Physics, Metaphysics, Nicomachean ethics* and *Politics* of

[4]

Aristotle. Of the commentary on the *Nicomanchean ethics* there exists a 'reportatio' dated 1372. He also wrote:

Scriptum super Summulas, an elaboration of Ockham's logic. Later commented on by John Dorp, whose work was edited by Johannes Major (1478-1540).

III. PARIS OCKHAMISTS AND THEIR OPPONENTS

JOHN OF MIRECOURT (de Mirecuria), 'monachus albus.' Bachelor of theology. Explained the *Sentences* at the College of St. Bernard at Paris. Influenced by William of Ockham and by the determinism of Thomas Bradwardine. Opposed by Johannes Normannus. Drew up in 1347 a 'declaratio' in his own defense, but shortly thereafter forty propositions taken from his writings were condemned by the chancellor and the faculty of theology of the University of Paris. Wrote a commentary on the *Sentences* of Peter Lombard; this exists in two redactions, the shorter of which may not be his. He also wrote a 'principium.'

JOHANNES NORMANNUS, O.S.B., 'monachus nigrus,' opponent of John of Mirecourt.

NICHOLAS OF AUTRECOURT (de Ultricuria, de Autricuria; d. post 1350), born at Autrecourt on the Meuse. Studied in Paris at the Sorbonne between 1320 and 1327. Became master of arts, bachelor of theology. Entered into dispute with Bernard of Arezzo, O.F.M., against whom he wrote nine letters. Cited by Pope Benedict XII in 1340 before the Roman curia, together with five other students of theology (John the Servite, Elie of Courson, Guido of Veeli, Peter of Monteregali, and Henry the Englishman) to answer for various errors. He alone was severely censured and obliged to retract, 1342. In May, 1346, Pope Clement VI addressed a letter of sympathy and warning to the University of Paris. Nicholas took refuge at the court of Louis of Bavaria, whither many innovators and malcontents had gone. The next year the curia censured a series of 65 propositions taken from his works. He was forced to retract (1347), to have his writings burnt and to give up his mastership of arts. In 1350 he was connected with the Cathedral in Metz. His principal work begins:

Satis exigit ordo executionis.

BERNARD OF AREZZO, O.F.M., opponent of Nicholas of Autrecourt, who wrote nine letters against him.

GILES, a master, who answered the first two letters of Nicholas for Bernard of Arezzo.

JOHANNES DE RIPA (de Marchia), O.F.M., 'doctor difficilis,' master at Paris where he taught in 1357. Started out as a Scotist, but developed his own philosophy in which the 'distinctio formalis' and the 'batitudo, intensio et remissio formarum' play a part. Closely connected with the philosophy of John of Mirecourt. Much thought of by Peter of Candia and John Gerson. Wrote a commentary on the first book of *Sentences* of Peter Lombard.

THEMO JUDAEI, son of a Jewish family from Münster i. W. Master of Arts. Later, physicist at the University of Paris (1349-1360). Colleague of Albert of Saxony, by whom he was influenced. Wrote a commentary on the *Meteora* of Aristotle.

NICHOLAS OF ORESME (ca. 1320-1382). Entered the College of Navarre in Paris, 1348. Became master of theology. Head of the College of Navarre, 1356-1361. Preached before Pope Urban V in Avignon, 1363. Held ecclesiastical positions in Rouen and Paris. Bishop of Lisieux, 1377. Was critical of Aristotle and of the nominalists. Wrote commentaries on the *Politics, De coelo et mundo, Ethics,* and *De Anima* of Aristotle, and on the *Sentences* of Peter Lombard. Wrote also a natural philosophy, a treatise against astrology and the following:
De origine, natura, jure et mutationibus monetarum.
Tractus de communicatione idiomatum, a fragment of the lost commentary on the *Sentences.*
De uniformitate et difformitate intensionum.

JOHN DORP OF LEYDEN, edited and commented on Buridan's *Scriptum super Summulas.* Taught at Paris and later at Cologne.

PETER OF CANDIA (Peter Philargis; ca. 1340-1410), born in Candia in Crete. Became Minorite. Studied at Padua and Oxford; later at Paris where he became master of theology. Became bishop in 1386, and archbishop of Milan in 1402. In 1409 the became antipope Alexander V. Wrote a commentary on the *Sentences* of Peter Lombard, in which he shows himself a Scotistic nominalist. Wrote also four 'principia' or inaugural lectures.

JOHN OF BASLE (d. 1392), a hermit of St. Augustine, lector in Strassburg. In 1371 he became master of theology in Paris, in 1379 general of his order and in 1389 bishop of Lombez. Ockhamist in his philosophy even to the

[6]

extent of defending the articles of Ockham which were under suspecion in 1324. Opposed to the extreme views of John of Mirecourt, and to the determinism of Bradwardine which he regarded as making God the author of sin. Wrote a commentary on the *Sentences*, responses and vespers.

IIENRY OF ODENDORP, a master at Paris. Was one of many Paris masters (Albert of Saxony, Henry of Hainbuch, Henry Totting de Oyta, Gerard of Calcar, Marsilius of Inghen) who, because of difficulties caused by the Great Western Schism, left Paris between 1378 and 1383 for positions in the newly founded German universities.

PIERRE D'AILLY (Petrus de Alliaco, P. Cardinal Camaracensis; 1350-1420), 'Aquila franciae.' Born at Compiègne. Studied theology at the College of Navarre in Paris, 1372. Received his doctorate in 1380. In 1389 he became chancellor of the University of Paris. Was made bishop and later (1411) cardinal. Was a thorough-going Ockhamist. He and John Gerson were known as the 'doctissimi viri nominales.' Wrote works on logic, a commentary on the *Sentences* of Peter Lombard and another on the *De consolatione philosophiae* of Boethius. Wrote also:

De anima

Tractatus de concordantia theologiae et astronomiae (Toul, 1413)

Tractatus de concordia astronomicae veritatis et narrationis historicae (Basel, 1414)

Tractatus secundus de concordia astronomicae veritatis et narrationis historicae.

Tertia tractatus de concordia astronomicae cum theologica et historica veritate (Cologne, 1414).

Apologetica defensio astronomicae veritatis (Cologne, 1414).

Secunda apologetica defensio astronomicae veritatis (Cologne, 1414).

JOHN GERSON (Charlier; 1368-1429), 'doctor christianissimus.' Studied at the College of Navarre in Paris in 1377. Was pupil of Pierre d'Ailly at Paris. Studied theology in 1381. Became Chancellor at the University of Paris in 1395. Two years later made a stay at Bruges; at this time St. Bonaventure was his favorite author. Was won over to mysticism, which he put at the service of the church. From 1401 to 1407 taught once more at Paris and took part in the affairs of the Great Schism. Wrote logical treatises after the mind of William of Ockham, but was more reserved and independent. In his seclusion

at Lyons, where he died, he wrote a great number of mystical works, the chief
of which are:

Centilogium de causa finali
Centilogium de conceptibus
Concordantia metaphysicae cum logica
De reformatione theologiae
Considerationes de theologia mystica speculativa
De theologia mystica practica
Tractatus de elucidatione scholastica mysticae theologiae
Consolatio theologiae
De unitate ecclesiae (1409)
De auferibilitate papae (1409)
De potestate ecclesiastica (1417)
Lectiones duae contra vanam curiositatem
De modis significandi

IV. AUGUSTINIAN FOLLOWERS OF AEGIDIUS ROMANUS

THOMAS OF STRASBURG (d. 1357), born in Hagenau, Alsace; died in
Vienna. Was an Augustinian monk, became a famous teacher at the University of Paris (c. 1341). Was instrumental in founding a university at Verona
in 1351. In his teachings and commentaries he closely adhered to the principles and doctrines of Aegidius Romanus. He taught that there was no formal
distinction between the nature of God and the divine attributes. He believed
that the doctrine of creation could be proved by strict demonstration, but
that without Revelation the human mind could not find if the material world
was created in time, with time, or 'ab aeterno.' He wrote:

Commentary on the *Sentences* of Peter of Lombard (Strasburg, 1490)
Constitutiones Ordinis Sui, a revision of the constitution of his order of which
he was the general.

ALFONSO OF TOLEDO (Alfonso Toletano; fl. 1345), composed in 1345
commentaries on the *Sentences*, in which he refers to Aegidius Romanus
(Giles of Rome) as the 'doctor nostri.'

V. EARLY ENGLISH LOGICIANS

RICHARD SWINESHEAD (Suisset; fl. 1348); was a mathematician. Educated at Merton College, Oxford (1348). Was master of theology. Became
a Cistercian monk at Swineshead in Lincolnshire. Wrote:

Questiones super Sententias.

In Ethica Aristotelis.

In De coelo et mundo.

Descriptiones motuum, or *De motu coeli et similibus.*

Super arte cabalistica.

De intentione et remissione.

De divisionibus.

De insolubilibus inc. Circa finem seu terminum ultimum.

Sophismata logicalia.

Ephemerides.

Mathematicae contentiones.

Liber calculationum. It is of doubtful authorship. Seems to be based on Nicholas of Oresme's *De difformitate qualitatum.*

WILLIAM HEYTESBURY (d. 1380) ; was a logician. Was fellow of Merton College, Oxford, 1370. Was master of theology and chancellor of University of Oxford, 1371. Works printed under the name of Hentisberus or Tisberius. Works:

De sensu composita et diviso de insolubilibus, de scire et dubitare, de relativis, de incipit et desinit, de maximo et minimo, et motu locali.

Regulae solvendi sophismata, commented on by Cajetan of Tiene.

Probationes profundissimae conclusionum regulis positarum

De veritate et falsitate propositionis

Sophismata, a series of 32 treatises, published in 1481 under the authorship of 'Magistri Guliermi Entisberi.'

WILLIAM DE COLYMGAM, Master at Oxford. Wrote *Questiones* to Aristotle's *De generatione et corruptione* and a commentary on the first book of Aristotle's *Physics.*

CLYMETON LANGLEY, Teacher of arts at Oxford, ca. 1350.

JOHN OF DUMBLETON, native of Dumbleton in Gloucestershire. Teacher of arts at Oxford, 1332-1349. He went to Oxford in 1331 where he probably remained the rest of his life. He wrote:

Summa logicae et naturalis philosophiae

De logica intellectuali

Summa theologiae minor

Summa artium

JOHN CHILMARK (Chylmark; fl. 1386), fellow of Merton College, Oxford and a master of arts. Probably lectured in schools belonging to Exeter College. He enjoyed a reputation for his attainment in philosophy but particularly in mathematics. He wrote:

De actione elementorum, perhaps an abridgement of a work by Dumbleton, *Compendium de actione elementorum abstactum de quarta parte J. Dumbletoni.*

De motu

De qualitate propositionis

De alteratione

De augmentatione

De prioritate

De aggregatione

RALPH STRODE (Radulf Strodus). He was a fellow at Merton College, Oxford before 1360, and was famous as a teacher of logic and philosophy, and a writer on educational subjects. He belonged to the 'School of the Middle' which mediated between realists and nominalists. He was acquainted with John Wycliff, yet he attacked his doctrine of predestination. He wrote:

Logica

Consequentiae, a treatise on the syllogism. Commented on by Cajetan of Tiene and Alexander Sermoneta.

Obligationes or *Scholastica militia*, a series of exercises on dialectics. Commented on by Cajetan of Tiene and Alexander Sermoneta.

RICHARD FERIBRIGUS (Ferabrich). He wrote *Consequentiae*, about 1370, which was commented on by Cajetan of Tiene.

VI. OXFORD SCOTISTS AND THEIR OPPONENTS

WALTER CHATTON (of Catton; d. ca. 1344), O.F.M., English critic of William of Ockham and Peter Aureoli; defends Duns Scotus, without entirely following him. His commentary on the *Sentences* of Peter Lombard survives in two redactions.

WALTER BURLEIGH (Gualterus Burlaeus; 1275-1357), 'doctor planus et perspicuus.' Studied at Oxford. Pupil of Duns Scotus. Opposed the nominalism of Ockham. Taught at Paris and at Oxford. Wrote commentaries on the *Ars vetus*, i.e. on Porphyry's *Isagoge*, and on Aristotle's *Categories* and *Perihermenias*, and Gilbert of Poirée's *Liber de sex principiis*, also on Aristotle's

Analytica posteriora, Physics, and *Ethics.* The commentary on the *Ethics* is taken over, in large part word for word, by Albert of Saxony. Wrote also:

De vitis et moribus philosophorum, a history of philosophy from Thales to Seneca, taken mainly from the mediaeval Latin translation of Diogenes Laertius's *Lives of Eminent Philosophers,* from Cicero and from other Latin sources.

Summa alphabetica problematum, an abridgement of Pietro d'Abano's (1257-ca. 1315) commentary on the Aristotelian *Problemata.*

De intentione et remissione formarum

De materia et forma

De potentiis animae

De fluxu et refluxu maris Anglicani

De puritate artis logicae

Obligationes, a treatise on logic.

Sophismata insolubilia

THOMAS BRADWARDINE (ante 1290-1349) 'doctor profundus, magnus logicus'; born at Chichester on the south coast of England. Studied at Oxford, where he was later teacher. In 1325 he became procurator of the University of Oxford. In 1349 he became archbishop of Canterbury. Wrote a commentary on the *Sentences* of Peter Lombard, and the following:

De causa Dei adversus Pelagium et de virtute causarum ad suos Mertonenses (London, 1344). Also called *Summa theologica.*

Placita theologica

De sacra Trinitate

De praemio salvandorum

De praescientia et praedestinatione

Sermones

Meditationes

De quiditate peccati

Ars memorativa

JOHN OF BACANTHORP (d. 1348), O. Carm.; Averroist friend of Bradwardine.

GUIDO (Aegidius of Medonta?, fl. 1354), an adherent of Bradwardine; became a pantheist.

BRINKEL, English Franciscan, follower of Bradwardine.

THOMAS BUCKINGHAM, an Oxford master. Tried to combat Brad-wardine's determinism by holding that the will has power to suspend its acts. He says, however, that God concurs with all human volitions, including sin.

PETER PLAOUL, opponent of Bradwardine.

JOHN WYCLIF (ca. 1320-1348). Born at Wicliffe or Spreswell in York. Studied from 1344-1345 at the University of Oxford under Thomas Brad-wardine. Became master of arts and bachelor of theology. In 1361 he took the parish of Fylingham, and in 1368 was rector of Ludgershall, near Oxford. In 1374 he became pastor at Lutterworth, where he died. Among his many Latin and English writings are the following:

De divino dominio
De civili dominio
De decem praeceptis
De ecclesia
De officio regis
De potestate papae (1378-79)
Trialogus
Diologus sive speculum ecclesiae militantis
Logica
De ente praedicamentali
Summa de ente (Summa intellectualium)

VII. SCOTISTS OF FRANCE

NICOLAS BONETUS (Bonet; d. 1360), O. Min., 'Doctor pacificus' or 'pro-ficuus,' professor of theology at Paris. Made bishop of Malta, 1342. Wrote:
Postilla in Genesim
Comment. in 4 libros Sententiarum
Comment. in Metaphys. Aristotelis
Tractatus de conceptione B. V. M. jussu Clementis V ad modum dialogi.
Formalitates e doctrina Scoti.
Naturalis philosophia

PETRUS THOMAS (Thomasius; 1305-1366), O. Carm., from 1325 in the cloister at Condom. Doctor at the Sorbonne in 1349. Papal theologian at Avignon under Clement VI. Established the faculty of theology at the University of Bologna. Bishop of Patti and Lipari in 1354. Archbishop of Crete

in 1363 and Patriarch of Constantinople in 1364. Wrote:
Formalitates (published at Venice, 1515).

VIII. BRETHREN OF THE COMMON LIFE

GEERT DE GROOTE (1340-1384), Studied at Aachen and later at the Sorbonne and at Prague; taught philosophy and theology at Cologne, where he entered seriously upon the practice of devout life. With his favourite disciple, Florens Radewyns, founded the Brethren of the Common Life, for priests and laymen ca. 1375 at Deventer. The members took no vows, and neither asked for nor received alms; their first aim was to cultivate the interior life, and they worked for their daily bread. The Brethren attempted to obtain for their schools the finest masters in the land. These schools became centers of spiritual and intellectual learning. De Groote was influenced by the writings of Ruysbroeck. Wrote:
Imitatio Christi

FLORENS RADEWYNS (1350-1400) De Groote's successor as head of the Brethren of the Common Life. Studied at Prague. He was converted by De Groote and with him founded the Brethren of the Common Life.

DIERICK MAERTENS; one of the masters of the Brethren of the Common Life.

JOHN A KEMPIS; a member of the Brethren of the Common Life and a brother of Thomas à Kempis.

THOMAS A KEMPIS (1380-1471); born at Kempen in the Diocese of Cologne. At the age of thirteen he set out for Deventer in Holland for his education. His brother John had left Deventer two years previously with five other Brothers of the Common Life to lay the foundations of a new congregation of Canons Regular at Windesheim. John gave Thomas a letter of introduction to Florens Radewyns, the superior of the Brothers of the Common Life at Deventer. After completing his humanities there, Thomas sought admission to the Canons Regular of Windesheim, of which his brother John was prior. Thomas was ordained priest in 1413. He was twice elected superior and was once made procurator at Windesheim. Part of his duties was the training of young religious. Wrote:
De imitatione Christi
Chronicon Montis Sanctae Agnetis
Chronicon Windesemense
Manuale Parvulorum

IX. MYSTICS

JOHN TAULER (ca. 1304-1361). Born at Strasburg; entered the Dominican Order; attended the University of Cologne where he met Meister Eckhart and Henry Suso. From about 1339 to 1347 he lived at Basle where he and Henry of Nördlingen were the center of the society called the Friends of God of Basle. The basis of his mysticism is the doctrine of the 'visio essentiae Dei,' or knowledge of the Divine nature. God lives in every human being, but in order that God might appear in man as a second being, the human sinful activities must cease. The way to God is through love; God replies to its highest development by His presence. The only things attributed to Tauler of which we are sure he was the author are his sermons. The collection of sermons appeared at Leipzig in 1493 and included 84 sermons. The second edition appeared at Basle in 1521-1522, and added 42 more, some of which are doubtful. The third edition appeared at Cologne in 1543, and added 25 more, some of which were also spurious.

HENRY OF NÖRDLINGEN. A Bavarian priest; associate of John Tauler. Acquainted also with Margaretha Ebner, Henry Suso, and other mystics of the time. His writings consist of 58 letters, representing his correspondence with Margaretha Ebner.

MARGARETHA EBNER (1291-1351). Born at Donauworth; entered a Dominican convent in 1332. Henry of Nördlingen was her spiritual guide. The correspondence between them is the first of its kind in German letters. At Henry of Nördlingen's insistence she wrote an account of her revelations and her discourses with the Infant Christ.

HENRY SUSO (ca. 1295-1366). German mystic of the Dominican Order. His principal theme in his writings was the mutual love of God and man. A burning love for Eternal Wisdom dominated his thoughts and action. In the Friends of God he was instrumental in restoring religious observances in the cloisters. He wrote an autobiography of his spiritual life. Wrote also:
Büchlein der Wahrheit
Das Büchlein der ewigen Weisheit (1328). This work has been called the most beautiful fruit of German mysticism.

JOHANNES DER FUSTERER, friend of Suso.

ELSBETH STAGEL, O.P., friend of Suso.

[14]

JOHN OF KASTI (ca. 1399). A Benedictine of the Abbey of Kasti. He was connected with the University of Prague. Wrote:
De adhaerendo Deo

JOHN RUYSBROECK (1293-1381). One of the foremost of the Flemish mystics. Called the Admirable Doctor, and the Divine Doctor. He attacked the false mysticism of Hainault, represented by the Porrettians and Blommardine and his followers. He says that man and God are so closely united they are one, not in essence or nature, but one in love. No complete account of his system of philosophy has been found. He starts with God, comes down to man, and then proceeds to God again. It was not his mysticism so much that was unusual, but rather his manner of presentation, language and style that set him off from the other German mystics. Wrote:
The Seven Degrees of Love
The Ornament of the Spiritual Marriage. This is considered his most important work.
The Treatise on Christian Faith
The Spiritual Tabernacle
Kingdom of Lovers

JOHN OF SCHOENHOVEN. Pupil of Ruysbroeck and his defender against the attack of John Gerson.

X. THE NOMINALIST CONTROVERSY AT THE UNIVERSITY OF PRAGUE

HENRY TOTTING OF OYTA (d. 1397), a nominalist, educated at Paris where he taught arts. Left Paris for a position at the University of Prague, where Conrad of Soltau and Matthew of Cracow were colleagues of his. Left Prague in order to obtain the mastership in theology at Paris (1377), where he became a friend of Henry of Hainbuch. Went later to the University of Vienna at the behest of Henry of Hainbuch who was engaged in its reorganization in 1383. Wrote a commentary on the *Sentences* of Peter Lombard (highly esteemed by John Gerson), and, it seems, an abridgement of Adam Wodham's commentary on the *Sentences*. Wrote also:
Tractatus moralis de contractibus reddituum annuorum
Quaestiones logicae super Porphyrium
Tres libri philosophici de anima (Magistrales tractatus de anima et potentiis eius).

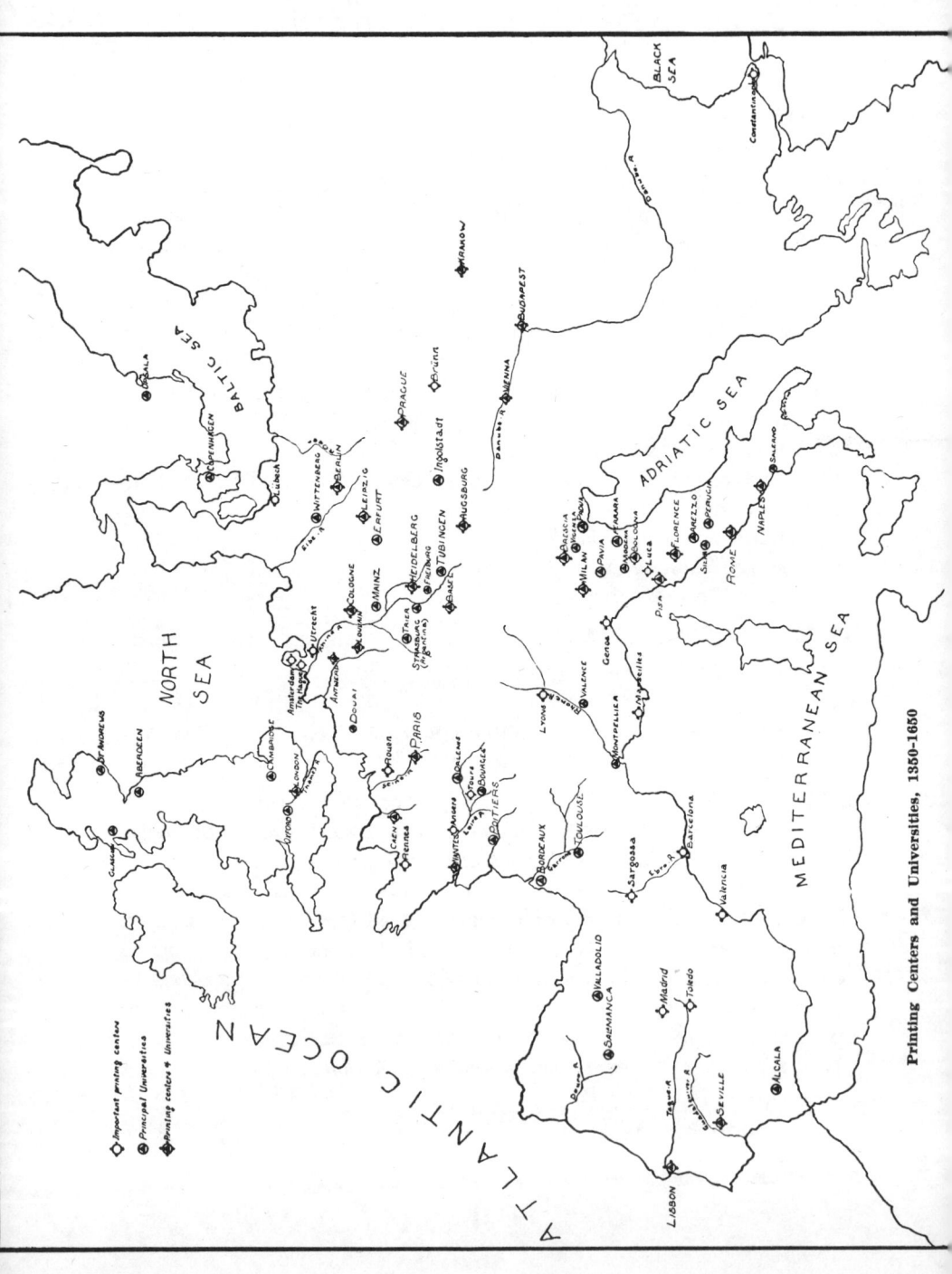

Printing Centers and Universities, 1350-1650

HENRY PAPE OF OYTA, became master at the University of Prague in 1369. May perhaps be found to be the author of some of the works attributed to Henry Totting of Oyta, especially the abridgement of Adam Wodham's commentary on the *Sentences*.

CONRAD OF SOLTAU (Lüneburg; d. 1407). Master of arts in Prague, 1368. Dean of the faculty of philosophy, 1372, and rector of the University of Prague, 1384/85. Entered into the Czech racial dispute and 1387 took a position in the newly established University of Heidelberg. In 1399 was made bishop of Verden. Was influenced in his writings especially by Thomas of Strasburg and Henry Totting of Oyta. Wrote sermons, a commentary of the *Psalms*, and a commentary on the *Sentences*. Also:
Super caput Firmiter, a tractate which deals with the fourth Council of the Lateran.

JOHN HUS (ca. 1370-1415). Born at Husinec in Southern Bohemia. He went to the University of Prague where he became a bachelor of arts in 1393, bachelor of theology in 1394, master of arts in 1396, dean of the faculty of philosophy in 1401-1402 and rector of the university 1402/03. In 1400 was ordained a priest. As a preacher he strove hard to bring about ecclesiastical reforms. In the Czech nationalist dispute he sided with the Czechs. From a philosophical point of view he sided with the realists against the nominalists. The philosophical and national issues combined to drive many professors and students to the German universities of Vienna, and Heidelberg, and led to the establishment of the University of Leipzig. Hus obtained a decree expelling the nominalists from Bohemia. His opposition to the nominalist movement brought down upon him and his associate, Jerome of Prague, the opposition of Peter d'Ailly and John Gerson, the 'doctissimi viri nominales' of Paris. He followed the ideas of John Wyclif, four of whose philosophical tractates and the *Dialogus* he translated into Czech. He was tried for heresy, condemned as a heretic, and burned at the stake in Constance. His writings include
De omni sanguine Christi glorificato (1404)
De ecclesia (1413)
Postylla (1412-1413)

JEROME OF PRAGUE (ca. 1365-1416). Born in Prague. Became bachelor of philosophy in Prague in 1398. Pupil of John Hus. At the behest of Hus, he went to Paris and to Oxford to study, returning with the theological writings of John Wyclif. Travelled in Hus's behalf for several years. Like Hus, he was tried and condemned as a heretic and burned at the stake in Constance. Philosophically he relies heavily on the 'formalitates' of Duns Scotus and on the logical works of John Wyclif.

XI. AT THE UNIVERSITY OF VIENNA

ALBERT OF SAXONY (of Helmstedt, of Ricmerstorp; 1316-1390), Parisian nominalist. Pupil of Johannes Buridanus. Studied and later (1351-ca. 1362) taught at the University of Paris of which he was rector in 1353. Went to Vienna where he played a dominant part in the founding of the University of Vienna, of which he was first rector in 1365. In 1366 he became bishop of Halberstadt. Was Ockhamist in logic. From Johannes Buridanus he took over the impetus theory of cosmic motion. Wrote:

Quastiones super Artem veterem

Quaestiones super Analytica posteriora

Logica. In this work he follows Ockham. Two parts of it: *Obligationes* and *Insolubilia*, are often listed as separate works.

Sophismata

De paralogismis seu fallaciis

Quaestiones super Physicam Aristotelis

Quaestiones meteororum, in which the work of the same name by Nicholas of Oresme was used.

Quaestiones super De caelo et mundo

Quaestiones super De sensu et sensato

Tractatus de proportionibus, in which he follows Thomas Bradwardine. Isidor Isolani made a synopsis of this work.

Demonstrationes de quadrature circuli

Quaestio de proportione dyametri quadrati ad costam eiusdem

Quaestiones super Sphaeram Johannis de Sacrobosco, which was used by Pierre d'Ailly.

Expositio decem librorum Ethicorum Aristotelis, based on the old translation of Robert Grosseteste. Taken in large part from Walter Burleigh.

HENRY OF HAINBUCH, near Langerstein in Hesse (1325-1397). Studied at the University of Paris, where he taught philosophy 1363-1376 and theology 1376-1383. The difficulties arising out of the Great Western Schism caused him to leave Paris for the University of Vienna which he helped to reorganize in 1383/84. Wrote:

Quaestio de cometa (Paris, 1368/69).
Contra astrologos coniunctionistas de eventibus futurorum (Paris, 1374)
Tractatus physicus de reductione effectuum specialium in virtutes communes
De habitudine causarum et influxu naturae communis respectu inferiorum
Tractatus de improbatione epicyclorum et concentricorum
Epistola pacis
Consilium pacis de unione et reformatione ecclesiae
De futuris periculis ecclesiae ex dictis S. Hildegardis
Carmen pro pace
Planctus ecclesiae
Contra fratrem Telesophorum
Quaestiones super libros sententiarum
Commentarii in Genesim; on the first three chapters. Contains much mathematical, physical, astronomical and philosophical material.
Tractatus de contractibus emptionis et venditionis
Epistola de contractibus emptionis et venditionis ad Consules Viennenses
De contemptu mundi (1383)
Speculum animae (De animae conditionibus)

NICHOLAS OF DINKELSBÜHL (Pruntzlein; ca. 1360-1433). Studied philosophy at the University of Vienna where he gave lectures (1390-1398, 1402-1405) on mathematics and physics. From 1398 he studied theology, becoming bachelor in 1405 and master in 1409. He was three times dean of the theological faculty; and rector of the university, 1405-1406. Took part in the disputes occasioned by the Great Western Schism. In 1418 was again at Vienna. From 1422-1424 he gave lectures in the cloister at Melk. His numerous writings are still mostly unprinted, preserved in manuscripts at Vienna, Munich, Melk and Subiaco. Among his writings are:
Quaestiones sententiarum
Postilla evangeliorum dominicalium
Tractatus de dilectione Dei et proximi
Tractatus de praeceptis decalogi

THOMAS OF HASELBACH. Pupil of Nicholas of Dinkelsbühl.

XII. AT THE UNIVERSITY OF HEIDELBERG

MARSILIUS OF INGHEN (d. 1396), 'iniciator nostrae universitatis.' From 1362 he taught in the faculty of arts at Paris, and was rector of the University of Paris in 1367 and 1371. By 1386 he had transferred to Heidelberg where he became first rector of the newly founded university. In logic he accepted the Ockhamist point of view and in physics he followed Johannes Buridanus, Albert of Saxony and Nicholas of Oresme. He wrote a commentary on the *Sentences* of Peter Lombard, and an explanation of the *Ars vetus*, the *Ars nova* and the terminist logic. Wrote also:

Quaestiones in libros de generatione
Abbreviationes libri physicorum

MATTHEW OF CRACOW (ca. 1335-1410) ; born in Cracow. Became master of arts in 1367, bachelor of theology in 1373 and master in 1380. Became professor of theology before 1387 at Prague, where he was associated with Conrad of Soltau, and later at Heidelberg where he was rector from 1396-1397. In 1405 he was made bishop of Worms. Famous also as a preacher. His writings include:

De arte moriendi
De celebratione missae (printed by Gutenberg, 1457/58)
Rationale operum divinorum
De squaloribus curiae Romanae, to which Johannes Falkenberg (d. ca. 1435) answered with his *De monarchia mundi.*

HENRY OF HESSE (of Altendorf; d. 1427). Received degree of master of arts and of theology. Taught at the University of Cologne, 1389-1400; rector at Cologne in 1392. Taught at the University of Heidelberg, 1400-1411; rector at Heidelberg in 1400-1401 and 1411. Joined the Carthusians ca. 1412 in Freiburg i. B. where he was prior, 1417-1424. He was prior also in Mornikhuizen near Arnheim, 1424-1426. He is often confused with Henry of Hainbuch near Langenstein. Wrote commentaries on the Scriptures and on the *Sentences* of Peter Lombard. Wrote also:

Dialogus de celebratione missae

NICOLAUS DE JAWOR, master of Heidelberg; for many years professor of theology and vice-chancellor of the University. Teacher of Johannes Werk of Herrenberg. Wrote:

Tractatus de interdicto

XIII. NOMINALISTS AT THE UNIVERSITY OF COLOGNE

GERARD OF CALCAR (Kykpot), nominalist; studied at the University of Paris where he made his determination in arts in 1365. Later he taught there. Had Peter of Candia as a pupil. In 1383 he went to the University of Vienna, together with Henry Totting of Oyta and others. Went from Vienna to Cologne at the time of the founding of the University of Cologne (1388); on the occasion of its inauguration (1389) he gave a discourse on the harmony between science and the Faith.

JOHANNES BRAMMART (d. 1407), O. Carm. Came from Aachen. Taught ca. 1380 in Paris. Provincial, 1383-1404. Built the Carmelite church in Cologne. Aided in the founding of the University of Cologne, where the Dominicans, Franciscans, Hermits of St. Augustine and Carmelites were incorporated into the theological faculty, each order supplying at most two professors, and lecture rooms in their own buildings for them. Brammart was a nominalist. He wrote sermons and a commentary on the *Sentences* of Peter Lombard.

XIV. AT THE UNIVERSITY OF LOUVAIN

HEIMERICUS DE CAMPO (Heinrich van de Velde; d. 1460). Professor at the University of Cologne where he was leader of the Albertists against the Thomist Gerard Teutegen of Herrenberg. Friend of Nicolaus Cusanus with whom he was invited to the University of Louvain. Cusanus did not go, but Heimericus in 1444 took a position there, where he remained until his death. (The University of Louvain was from its foundation in 1425 opposed to nominalism. Its faculties of arts and theology professed realism; a decision of 1427 required of all those who aspired to the regency an oath 'se numquam doctrinare Buridanum, Marsilium, Ockham aut eorum sequaces.') Heimericus wrote:

Promptuarium argumentorum disputatorum inter lileum Albertistam et spineum Thomistam (printed 1492)

Reparationes naturalis philosophie secundum processum Albertistarum et Thomistarum (printed 1492)

Problemata inter Albertum Magnum et Thomas (printed 1514)

PETER DE RIVO (b. ca. 1420). Born at Assche. Was master of arts at the University of Louvain where he entered into a dispute with a theologian Henry of Zoemeren (Someren) concerning the truth of future contingent propositions. Two parties were formed, but the University officially sided with Peter de Rivo. Cologne and Paris were appealed to. Cologne in 1470 officially decided in favor of Peter de Rivo. Paris did not act officially. The Roman Court was appealed to, Cardinal Bessarion and Francois della Rovere (later Pope Sixtus IV) interested themselves in the matter, and in 1473 Peter de Rivo was impelled by decision of the Roman Court to make a retraction.

HENRY OF ZOEMEREN (Someren). Professor of theology at the University of Louvain, 1437-1470. Entered into a dispute with Peter de Rivo which brought about Henry of Zoemeren's expulsion from the University in 1470.

XV. AVERROISTS

URBAN. A Servite Averroist who taught in Bologna. He wrote:
Urbanus Averroista . . . commentorum omnium
Averroys super librum Aristotelis de Physico auditu expositor clarissimus.
(1334; Venice, 1492)

PAULUS PERUSINUS (a Perusio), O. Carm. Wrote in 1344 a commentary on the *Sentences* of Peter Lombard, in which the influence of John of Baconthorp is to be seen.

JOHN OF BACONTHORP (Johannes Anglicus, John Bacon; d. 1348). Born at Baconthorp in Norfolk. Became a Carmelite and theologian. Received his degrees at the universities of Paris and Oxford. He taught until 1327 when he was made provincial of his order in England. After 1333 he spent the remainder of his life in study. Baconthorp follows Averroes in preference to St. Thomas with whom he disagrees on many points. He adopted a system of realism according to which the universals do not follow but precede the act of intellect. Truth is materially and causally in the external object, formally in the intellect; in the order of generation and perfection, the first subject in itself intelligible, the active intellect is required to render it ultimately intelligible; the conformity of the thing as thought of with the external object constitutes the truth. The final cause of all things is God; but although the first object of our knowledge be the Divine essence, Bacon does not admit that this knowledge comes to us by the light of our natural reason; it is, in his opinion, a supernatural gift of grace. His writings, over one hundred and twenty volumes, are for the most part unprinted, although his commentary (printed in 1510) on the *Sentences* of Peter Lombard became a textbook in the Carmelite Order. He wrote commentaries on Aristotle's *Metaphysics, Ethics, Politics, De anima, De sensu et sensibili, De memoria, De somno et vigilia, De longitudine et brevitate vitae, Physica, Meteora, De caelo et mundo, De generatione et corruptione, Sophistici Elenchi, Topica, Analytica priora,* and *Analytica posteriora.* He wrote also:
Quodlibeta
Compendium legis Christi

De potentiis animae
De astrorum scientia
Contra artes magicas
De sphaera iudiciali
De multiplicatione specierum
De aeternitate Dei

PAUL OF VENICE (Paulus Venetus; ca. 1368-1429). Born at Udine and died at Venice. He was a theologian of the Hermits of Saint Augustine. He studied at Oxford in 1390 and finished his courses at the University of Padua, where he later lectured. He was called to Rome in 1427 by Pope Martin V to hear the charges brought against St. Bernardine of Siena, occasioned by the preaching of the 'new devotion' to the Holy Name. Paul was a follower of John of Jandun, (fl. 1315) who was the recognized leader of Parisian Averroism in his day. He wrote commentaries on works of Aristotle, particularly on the *Physics*. Wrote also:

De conceptione B. Mariae Virginis
De quadratura circuli
De circulis componentibus mundum
Summulae logicae
Logica parva et logica magna (Logica duplex), which was used largely as a textbook during the fifteenth and sixteenth centuries. Bartholomaeus Marzolus, O.P. attacked Paul of Venice's logic in his *Dubium super logicam P. Veneti.*

XVI. JEWISH COMMENTARIES ON ARISTOTELIAN PHILOSOPHY

LEVI BEN GERSON (Gersonides; 1288-1344). Mathematician and astronomer, wrote super-commentaries on Averroes's commentaries on Aristotle. He attempts to reduce prophecy to a psychological phenomenon. Philosophers have nothing to do with prophecies; prophecy as he sees it is a supernatural power. The gifted intellect of the prophet interprets the illusion. In theology he refers to God as the 'unmoved mover.' Reason, theory, science, explanation are the considerations most important in things philosophical as well as things religious. Theory is more important than practice, and belief stands higher than mere conduct. Gerson, as did his predecessors, read the Bible through the Aristotelian view. He is a disciple of ibn Daub and Maimonides. Wrote:

Milhamot Adonai (The War of the Lord) wherein he undertakes to solve in a thoroughly scholastic manner the problems in theology and philosophy which Maimonides left somewhat incomplete.

Treatise on Astronomy, a scientific treatise dealing with an astronomical instrument which he had discovered. It was translated into Latin by order of Pope Clement VI.

MOSES OF NARBONNE. Jewish writer of fourteenth century; called 'Master Vital.' He has left us an account of *The Hermit's Guide* written by Avempace (Ibn Badsha) in the eleventh century, which supplements Averroes's unsatisfactory allusion to that work. It shows how men can attain a union with the Active Intellect. Wrote a commentary to the *Moreh Nebuchim* of Moses Maimonides.

HASDAI BEN ABRAHAM CRESCAS (1340-1410), Spanish-Jew born in Barcelona. Crescas admitted determinism. In opposition to the general trend of his period he tried uprooting the Aristotelian authority in Judaism. Crescas substituted the will and emotion for rationalism and logical inference. Love of God, not the knowledge of God, is the highest aim of man according to his theory. His philosophy is based on the spiritual and emotional side of man. In proving the unity, existence, and incorporeality of God, Crescas objects to all of Maimonides's proofs; he says the Bible alone may be trusted. He deals with the six fundamental dogmas of Judaism: God's knowledge of existing things, providence, power, freedom, prophecy, and purpose; he treats them in an anti-intellectual manner. His most original contribution to philosophy was his idea on the freedom of the soul; he declares that determinism is not fatalism. Wrote:

Or Adonai, (Light of the Lord)

SHEMTOB BEN JOSEPH IBN SHEMTOB (ca. 1440); greatly opposed to Greek science and philosophy; he is not content with assailing Gersonides, but goes back to the very beginning and blames Maimonides for all the heretics that had crept into the Jewish camp.

JOSEPH BEN SHEMTOB, (d. 1480), contrary to the ideas of his father, he shows a great admiration for Aristotle and Maimonides. But he is enabled to do so by lending credence to a legend that Aristotle in his old age recanted his heretical doctrines, in particular that of the eternity of the world. He claims it must have been a misunderstanding when Maimonides and others make Aristotle deny the special Providence. Like his father he realizes the danger of studying too much Greek science and philosophy. He says however that true science is not opposed to Judaism. He wrote:

Commentary on Aristotle. He endeavors to show that the Stagirite's ethical doctrines had been misunderstood: that the highest good of man and his ultimate happiness are to be sought according to Aristotle not in this world but in the next.

SHEMTOB BEN JOSEPH (fl. ca. 1461-1489), son of the above, followed in his father's footsteps. He wrote:

Commentary on the Guide of the Perplexed, in which he defends Maimonides against the attacks of Crescas.

JOSEPH ALBO (1380-1444), a Jewish philosopher who set out to show that Judaism was the true religion and Christianity spurious. Also had three principles of religion; they are as follows: (1) existence of God, (2) revelation, (3) reward and punishment hereafter. He reduced Maimonides' principles to six: God's knowledge, providence, power, prophecy, free will, purpose. In the field of law he says: natural law is universal, conventional law is prescribed by reason, and Divine law is ordered by God through a prophet. Albo says every follower of the Mosaic law must believe in creation 'ex nihilo,' superiority of Moses to all other prophets, immutability of law; human perfection attainable by obeying the commandments of the law; resurrection; the Messiah. Wrote:

Book of Roots (Sefer Ikkarim). The philosophical discussion in the last three sections gives the impression of an eclectic compilation in the interest of a moderate conservatism. The style is that of the popularizer and the homilist; and to this he owes his popularity, which was denied his more original teacher, Crescas.

ABRAHAM BEN ISAAC OF GRANADA. He declares that he who does not acknowledge God in the manner of the Kabbalah sins unwittingly, is not regarded by God, has not his special providence, and like the abandoned and the wicked is left to fate. Wrote:

The Covenant of Peace, (1391-1409) in which he discusses the mysteries of the names of God and the angles, permutations, commutations, and vowel points and accents.

MOSES BOTAREL (Batorelo). He praises philosophy, speaks of Aristotle as of a prophet and maintains that philosophy and the Kabbalah propound exactly the same doctrines, and that they differ only in language and technical terms. He was the teacher of the Christian scholar Maestro Juan. He shows also the method by which dreams could be interpreted as prophecies of the future. He wrote a commentary on the book *Jetzira* (ca. 1409).

ISSAC BEN MOSES ARAMA (1420-1494). He was interested in the Kabbala and placed Jewish revelation above philosophy. He tried to explain the relation between philosophy and theology. He wrote:
Akedat Yizhak, a philosophical-homiletical commentary on the Pentateuch.

ABRABANEL ISSAC (1437-1508), the distinguished Jewish statesman who went with his brethren into exile at the time of the expulsion of the Jews from Spain in 1492, was a prolific writer on Biblical exegesis and religious philosophy. He defends Maimonides against the attacks of Crescas and Albo, he is nevertheless an outspoken opponent of the rationalistic attitude and has no phrases strong enough against such men as Gersonides. Later in life he adopted Kabbalistic views along with philosophic doctrines.

JUDAH BEN YECHIEL MESSER LEON OF MANTUA (1450-1490)

ELIZAH DELMEDIGO (1460-1497). Philosopher who taught in several Italian centers of learning. Translated some of Averrhoes' commentaries into Latin at the instigation of Pico della Mirandola. Wrote:
Behinath ha-Dath (Investigation of Religion). In this work he attempts to depart from the traditional attitude in which religion and philosophy were identified.

JUDAH LEO ABRABANEL (1470-1530), the son of Abrabanel Issac, more mild than his father, and some believe he may have been a convert to Christianity. He wrote:
Dialoghi di Amore, (Dialogues of Love), a philosophical work in Latin, which breathes the spirit of the Renaissance of the fifteenth and sixteenth centuries. It is under the influence of Plato and Plotinus and identifies God with love, which is regarded as the essential principle of all life and activity in the world, including even the inorganic natural processes. There is no attempt made to construct a Jewish philosophy.

JOSEPH SOLOMON DELMEDIGO (1591-1655). Pupil of Galileo. Wrote many books on science and philosophy. Bore a considerable part in initiating the critical movement in Judaism and belonged to the sceptical school.

XVII. THE SCHOOL OF MANUEL CHRYSOLORAS

MANUEL CHRYSOLORAS (d. 1415). Pupil of Plethon; the first native Greek who appeared as a public teacher of the Greek language and literature in Italy (at Venice and afterwards at Florence.)

JOHANNES CHRYSOLORAS. Nephew and pupil of Manuel Chrysoloras.

LEONARDO BRUNI ARETINUS (i.e. of Arrezo, birthplace of Petrarch; 1369-1440). The most important pupil of Manuel Chrysoloras. In recognition of his literary achievements, he was made a citizen of honor in Florence, and freed from taxes. For a while he was secretary to the pope.

FRANCISCUS BARBARUS. Pupil of Manuel Chrysoloras.

GUARINUS OF VERONA. Pupil of Manuel Chrysoloras.

HERMOLAUS BARBARUS (Ermolao Barbaro; 1454-1493). A nephew of Francis Barbarus and pupil of Guarinus; translated works of Aristotle and Themistius's commentaries on Aristotle. Wrote also:
Compendium Scientiae Naturalis ex Aristotle (printed in 1547)

FRANCISCUS PHILELPHUS (Francesco Filelfo; 1398-1481). Born at Tolentino; died at Florence. Studied at Constantinople under Johannes Chrysoloras and at Padua; appointed professor at 18. Taught moral philosophy at Venice, 1417-19. Married Johannes Chrysoloras' daughter Theodora.

MARIUS PHILELPHUS (1426-1480). Son of Franciscus Philelphus and Theodora Chrysoloras.

XVIII. RAYMOND OF SABUNDE

RAYMOND OF SABUNDE (d. 1342). Born at Barcelona, Spain. Taught theology, philosophy, and medicine at University of Toulouse from 1340 to 1342. Taught a kind of theosophy which maintained that since man is a connecting link between the natural and the supernatural, it is possible to arrive at a knowledge even of the most profound mysteries of Faith by a study of human nature. This tendency of thought is similar to that of Raymond Lully. Montaigne has a long essay on him in the *Essais*. He apparently wrote several works on theology and philosophy, only one of which remains: *Theologia Naturalis*, first written in Spanish, translated into French by Montaigne, and into Latin.

XIX. THOMISTS IN SOUTHERN EUROPE

JOHN CAPREOLUS (1380-1444), 'princeps Thomistarum.' Born at Rodez where he received early education. Finished studies at Paris, went to Toulouse and finally to Rodez where he died. Defended St. Thomas against Scotus, William of Ockham, and other nominalists. Wrote:
Libri defensionum theologiae divi Thomae de Aquino

ANTONINUS OF FLORENCE (1379-1459). Became Dominican in 1406. First prior of St. Marks in 1439 and held this office until created Bishop of Florence in 1446. Studied production of wealth, its distribution and utilization. Believed wealth should serve all but condemned luxury and extravagance. Wrote:
Summa theologica, his chief work, in which he proclaims himself the convinced disciple of St. Thomas.
Chronica or *Summa historialis*, a kind of encyclopaedia of universal history.

XX. THOMISTS OF COLOGNE

HENRY OF GORKUM (Gorrichem; d. 1431). Became master of arts at the University of Paris in 1418. Went to the University of Cologne where he became professor and rector (1419-1431) of that division of the faculty of arts known as the Schola Montana. (The other divisions of the faculty of arts at Cologne were the Laurentiana; Korneliana, disbanded in 1520; and Kukana, which became the Tricoronatum when the Jesuits took it over in 1556, and which more recently has been known as the Dreikönigsgymnasium.) Under Henry of Gorkum the Thomist tendency, which later was set in opposition to the 'schola Albertistarum,' was developed. He wrote:
Conclusiones in libros magistri Sententiarum
Compendium Summae theologiae S. Thomae (printed in 1473)
Tractatus consultatorii, a collection of treatises including: *De divinis nominibus, De praedestinatione, De justo bello* and others.

GERARD TEUTEGEN OF HERRENBERG (de Monte; d. 1480). Leader of the Thomists at Cologne. Wrote a commentary on the *De ente et essentia* of St. Thomas Aquinas. Wrote also:

Apologetica . . . qua ostensorem concordiae inter S. Thomas et venerabilem Albertum magnum impugnat opprobriis, auctoritatibus et rationibus ommissis.

LAMBERTUS DE MONTE (d. 1499). Pupil of Gerard Teutegen of Herrenberg.

JOHANNES VERSOR (d. 1485). Wrote commentaries on the *De ente et essentia* of St. Thomas Aquinas, and on the *Summulae* of Petrus Hispanus. Wrote also:
Quaestiones super veterem artem
Super omnes libros novae logicae

GERARD OF ELTEN (d. 1484), O.P. Thomist leader at the University of Cologne. Taught in the faculty of arts, and later in the faculty of theology, 1447-1461. Was rector of the University, 1458 and 1463/64. Joined the reformed Dominican cloister in Cologne, ca. 1467; professor there. Head of the Dominican house of studies in Heidelberg, 1474. Wrote a commentary on the first part of the *Summa theologica* of St. Thomas Aquinas.

DIONYSIUS THE CARTHUSIAN (1402/03-1471), 'doctor ecstaticus.' Born in Rickel in the diocese of Lüttich. Received the doctorate of theology at the University of Cologne before he was 21. In 1423 he joined the Carthusians in Roermonde. Accompanied Cardinal Nicolaus Cusanus on his visitation journey through North and West Germany in 1451. Wrote commentaries on the *Sentences* of Peter Lombard, the *De consolatione philosophiae* of Boethius, and all the works, including the letters, of Pseudo-Dionysius the Areopagite. He also made commentaries on the *Gospels*, the *Epistles* of St. Paul and several books of the Old Testament.

XXI. HEIDELBERG GRADUATES IN ARTS

JODOCUS AICHMANN OF CALW (Jost Eichmann). Came from Calw in Württemberg. Became master of arts in Heidelberg in 1444. Taught arts at Heidelberg. In 1452 he and his colleague, Marcellus Geist of Atzenheim, were dismissed from the faculty for having criticized several members of the faculty and their methods of teaching. In 1463 he was professor of theology in the University of Heidelberg, and had already served as dean of the faculty and as rector of the University. In 1479 he, Nicolaus of Wachenheim and Herwich of Amsterdam were called to Mainz as theologians for consultation.

In 1486 he was doctor of holy scripture and preacher in Heidelberg. Wrote an abstract entitled:

Conclusiones Alberti Magni extracte ex libro divisionum Bohecii.

MARCELLUS GEIST OF ATZENHEIM (d. 1469). Studied arts at Heidelberg, 1445-1447. Became bachelor of arts in 1447 and master in 1448. He was on the faculty of arts, 1448-1452, during which time he studied theology at Heidelberg. Pupil of Johannes Wenk of Herrenberg. In 1452 he and his colleague Jodocus Aichmann of Calw were dismissed from the faculty for having criticized several members of the faculty and their methods of teaching. The nominalist controversy seems to have made his reinstatement and further stay at Heidelberg undesirable for him. He and several others had already been attracted to the religious life. In 1454 he joined the Carthusians. During his novitiate (1454-1455), he copied many writings of Nicolaus Cusanus, notably, *De querendo Deum, De filiacione Dei, De dato patris luminum, De coniecturis,* and the Latin version of Cusanus's commentary on the *Pater noster.* He copied also many works of Pseudo-Dionysius the Areopagite, Albertus Magnus and Aristotle. He was made prior of the Carthusian cloister at Portaceli near Bern, 1459-1469. Also appointed prior of the Carthusian cloister at Mainz, but died on a visit to Naples the same year. His own writings, preserved in great part formerly in the Carthusian library at Mainz and now in the Mainz Stadtbibliothek include:

De spiritu bono et malo
Sermones epistolares pro defunctis in epistolas in ordine Carth. legi consuetas.
Quaedam dicta et opuscula
De universali natura
Super canonem misse et alia ipsius dicta
Ad infirmum

SIXTUS OF DONAUWÖRTH (de Werdea). Studied at Heidelberg, 1442-1450. Pupil of Johannes Wenk of Herrenberg. Became bachelor of arts in 1450. Was schoolmaster in Wimpfen am Berg in 1453. Perhaps joined the Carthusians with Marcellus Geist of Atzenheim in 1454. He copied the *De docta ignorantia* of Nicolaus Cusanus and the *Super veterem artem* of Albertus Magnus, and made extracts from writings of Johannes Wenk.

JOHANNES JUFF BUTZBACH (d. 1495). Studied at Heidelberg, 1452-1454. Became bachelor of arts in 1454; master, 1457; and dean, 1460. Between 1458 and 1463 copied many manuscripts dealing with the arts. Joined the Carthusians. Died in Mainz.

XXII. THE DE DOCTA IGNORANTIA CONTROVERSY

NICOLAUS CUSANUS (Nicolas Chrypffs, Krebs; 1401-1464). He was born at Berncastel-Kues. As a boy he was educated in the classics by the Brethren of the Common Life at Deventer. From 1416 to 1417 he attended the University of Heidelberg and from 1417 to 1423 he studied at Padua. He stayed a while in Rome and in 1425 went to Cologne to complete his theological studies. At Cologne he became acquainted with the Albertist professor, Heimericus de Campo, O.P. He attended the church council of Basle (1432-1437) and later went with the Pope's ambassador to Constantinople. He became a cardinal in 1449, and was made Bishop of Buxen (Tyrol) in 1450. He returned to Italy in 1460 and died at Todi in Umbria. He did not believe that scholastically educated reason could demonstrate the fundamental propositions of theology. This belief is based on the proposition that the soul in the state of ecstacy has power to transcend all finite limitations. In love of God, man becomes one with God. Cusanus defines God as the unity without otherness. Of generated things the world is the best. God is the absolute maximum, and the world which God created is the unfolded maximum. Wrote, besides numerous sermons, the following:

De docta ignorantia (1440), in which he says that his wisdom was the knowledge of his ignorance.

De coniecturis (1440), a sequel to the *De docta ignorantia*. In it he states that all human knowing is mere conjecture.

De querendo Deum (1445)

De filiatione Dei (1445)

De dato Patris luminum (1446)

De genesi (1447)

Apologia doctae ignorantiae (1449)

Idiota (1450) Includes: *De sapientia, De mente* and *De staticis experimentis*

De novissimis diebus (1453)

De visione Dei (1453)

Complementum theologicum, figuratum in complementis mathematicis (1454)

De pace seu concordantia fidei (1454)

De beryllo (1458)

De possest (1460)

De cribratione Alchoran (1461)

De non aliud (1462)

De venatione sapientiae (1463)

De apice theoriae (1464)
De ludo globi (1464)
Compendium (1464)

JOHANNES WENK OF HERRENBERG (Wenck; d. 1460). Master of arts in Paris. Priest in the diocese of Speyer in 1426. Studied theology at Heidelberg, 1427-1432. Had Nicolaus de Jawor as teacher. Became professor of theology at Heidelberg, and rector of the university in 1435, 1444, and 1451. Was teacher of Marcellus Geist of Atzenheim and Sixtus of Donauwörth. Attended the council of Basle in 1439. Was conservative in his philosophy. Followed a Thomist-Albertist path. Opposed Nicolaus Cusanus. Wrote collations, sermons, and commentaries on *Genesis, Exodus, Jeremias* and the *De coelesti hierarchia* of Pseudo-Dionysius the Areopagite. Wrote also:

De ignota litteratura, directed against the *De docta ignorantia* (1440) of
  Nicolaus Cusanus. Cusanus replied with his *Apologia doctae ignorantiae*
  (1449)
Memoriale divinorum officiorum
De oratione domini Jesu Christi in Monte Oliveti
De oratione dominica
Sedicim regule predicatoris
De consequenciis
Paradigmata ingeniorum artis
Liber de anima

JOHANNES DE GELNHAUSEN (Geilhusen). Jurist. Occupied governmental positions first in Kuttenberg in Bohemia, then (1380) in Brunn, and later (1400-1407) in Iglau. Exchanged letters with Johannes Wenk of Herrenberg concerning the *De docta ignorantia* of Nicolaus Cusanus. Wrote:
Collectarius perpetuarum formarum

BERNARD DE WAGING (ca. 1400-1472) O.S.B. Native of Waging (Waching) near Salzburg. Received bachelor's degree at the University of Vienna. Joined the Benedictines at Melk when he was very young. Went later (1446) to the monastery at Tegernsee of which he was prior. He was the chief protagonist of monastic reform within the Benedictine order in Southern Germany. Close friend of Nicolaus Cusanus with whom he exchanged letters concerning mysticism and monastic reform, and of the abbots Ayndorffer and Ayrinschmolz. Wrote:

Laudatorium Doctae ignorantiae (1451), in which he shows that Cusanus's work differs from the mystical theology of the monks at Melk in the greater use, in the former, of learning as a means of union with God. This work was opposed by Caspar Ayndorffer.

Defensorium Laudatorii Doctae ignorantiae, an answer to Caspar Ayndorffer, to which the Carthusian, Vincentius de Aggsbach, replied with his *Replicatio contra Defensorium Laudatorii Doctae ignorantiae* (1459)

Tractatus de cognoscendo Deo, containing a commentary on the last chapter of the *Itinerarium mentis in Deum* of St. Bonaventure

Remediarius pusillanimarum

De spiritualibus sentimentis

Avisamenta reformationis ordinis S. Benedicti (1464) sent to the Archbishop of Salzburg.

Speculum mortis.

CASPAR AYNDORFFER (1401-1461) O.S.B. Born at Munich. Joined the Benedictines at Tegernsee where he instituted a reform modelled on that of Melk. He was responsible for great progress in art and learning, the effects of which continued until the closing of the monastery in 1803. Opposed Bernard de Waging's defense of the *De docta ignorantia* of Nicolaus Cusanus, by an appeal to the *De triplici via* of Hugo de Palmis

HUGO DE PALMIS. Carthusian writer on mystical theology. Wrote:
De triplici via, which was much appealed to in the Cusanus controversy.

VINCENTIUS DE AGGSBACH. Member of the Carthusian cloister at Aggsbach near Melk in Southern Austria. Opponent of Nicolaus Cusanus and Bernard de Waging regarding their notion of mystical theology. Wrote:
Replicatio contra defensorium Laudatorii Doctae ignorantiae (1459), an answer to Bernard de Waging's *Defensorium Laudatorii Doctae ignorantiae.*

JOHANNES SCHLITPACHER (of Weilheim; 1403-1482), O.S.B. Grew up in Schlitbach near Weilheim. Studied at the humanist school at Ulm, 1421-1423. Master of arts at the University of Vienna. Joined the Benedictines at Melk where he was master of studies in 1434, superior, and prior. Prior of several other houses. Took an important part in religious reform. Made excerpts from Nicolaus Cusanus's *Apologia doctae ignorantiae*. He has a note on the origin of the Cusanus controversy which begins:
Sequitur occasio premissi in hoc sexterno libelli. In it is recorded the dispute

between Bernard de Waging and Vincentius de Aggsbach. Johannes
Schlitpacher later acted as mediator in the dispute between Bernard de
Waging and Marquard Sprenger on the one side and Vincentius de Aggs-
bach on the other.

MARQUARD SPRENGER, of Munich. Wrote:

Elucidatorium mysticae theologiae, the answer to a request from the monks
for his opinion on the Cusanus controversy. In it he sides with Cusanus,
using St. Thomas Aquinas as his authority.

JOHANNES OF KASTL (Castellensis), O.S.B. Entered the Benedictine
abbey of Kastl, near Ralisbon in Bavaria. Kastl is not far from Tegernsee and
Melk; with these houses the monks of Kastl exchanged books and ideas.
Wrote:

De fine religiosae perfectionis et de modo fruendi Dei in praesenti vita (ca.
1410), which used to be listed as a work of St. Albertus Magnus under
the title, *De adhaerendo Deo.*

De natura, gratia et gloria ac beatitudine in patria. The last chapter is on the
vision of God.

XXIII. EARLY ANTI-ARISTOTELIANS

LAURENTIUS VALLA (Lorenzo della Valle; 1407-1457); born in Rome;
educated at the University of Pavia where he later (1431-1433) taught
rhetoric. 1442-1447 at the Court of the Muses which had been founded in
Naples by Alfonso ('the Magnanimous,' d. 1458), King of Naples and
Sicily. Later became papal secretary and canonist. Translated the *Iliad,*
Herodotus and Thucydides into Latin. Opposed to the philosophy of Aristotle. Much more inclined to follow the philosophy of Cicero and the
later Greek ethical schools. Openly proclaimed his sympathy for the Epicurean ethics. Among his works are:

De elegantia, a scientific analysis of the rules of Latin grammar and style.

De voluptate ac de vero bono (1431), a diologue presenting in turn the Stoic,
Epicurean and Christian ethical systems. The Christian is allowed to pre-
vail, but the Epicurean is treated with favor.

Declamatio de falso credita et ementita Constantini donatione

Dialectricae disputationes contra Aristotelicos (first edition, 1499)

De libero arbitrio, dialogues on the subject of free choice in its relation to the knowledge and power of God.

Apologia

RUDOLPH AGRICOLA (Rolef Huysmann; 1442-1485) ; born at Balfo near Groningen, Holland. Studied first at the University of Louvain; then at Paris under Heynlin von Stein. At Paris he formed a close friendship with Johannes Reuchlin. Stayed seven years in Italy, chiefly at Ferrara where he attended the lectures of Theodorus Gaza. Then he went to Heidelberg where he became professor in 1482 at the invitation of John of Dalberg, Bishop of Worms. Influenced by Laurentius Valla. During the last few years of his life he took up the study of theology. Works:

De studio formando, a pedagogical treatise which he sent to his friend Barbarianus.

De inventione dialectica; lists physics, ethics and logic as the three parts of philosophy; states that the primary function of logic is the formation of speech, and that there is no difference between dialectics and rhetoric.

XXIV. THE PLATONIC ACADEMY

COSIMO DE MEDICI (1389-1464), was so deeply attracted by Gemistus Pletho's enthusiasm for Plato's philosophy that he decided to have young Marsilio Ficino trained in philosophy and Greek in order to make a Latin translation of the complete works of Plato. Through Ficino he founded the Platonic Academy at Florence in 1459. Cosimo died at the age of seventy-five while engaged in listening to the reading of one of Plato's dialogues.

GEORGIUS GEMISTUS PLETHO (1355-1450), was born in Constantinople. He aided in expounding Platonism, and was himself a humanist. According to Höffding, *History of Modern Philosophy,* he held that God who is an absolute single substance gave origin to spiritual beings or ideas by emanation and that these ideas in turn gave off human souls. The souls by contemplating the ideas gained their intellectual knowledge. God created matter from nothing, but it was the ideas that infused forms into matter and so constituted the bodily universe. Wrote:

Compendium of the Dogmas of Zoroaster and Plato, in which the theosophic tendency of Platonism is exalted in opposition to the tendency of Aristotelianism towards naturalism.

MARSILIO FICINO (1433-1499), was born at Florence. He was a pupil of Pletho and the first head of the Platonic academy. He translated the works of Plato as well as the complete works of Plotinus into Latin. It is hard to separate his philosophical from his astronomical studies. Works:

De voluptate, which attempts to point out the agreement of Plato and Aristotle.

Theologia Platonica. De immortalitate videlicet animorum ac aeterna felicitate libri XVIII (1474) ; dedicated to Lorenzo de Medici (1448-1492).

JOHANNES ARGYROPOLUS (ca. 1416-1486), a Greek humanist born at Constantinople. He taught at Padua in 1434; later made rector of the University. About 1456, he was invited to Florence by Cosimo de Medici and was there appointed professor of Greek in the University. Among his scholars were Angelus Politianus and Johann Reuchlin. His principal works were translations of the following portions of Aristotle: *Categoriae, De interpretatione, Analytica posteriora, Physica, De caelo, De anima, Metaphysica, Ethica Nicomachea* and *Politica.* He also wrote:

Expositio Ethicorum Aristotelis

CRISTOPLE LANDINUS, teacher of Angelus Politianus.

ANGELUS POLITIANUS (Angelo Poliziano, 1454-1494), born in Tuscany. He taught at the University of Florence. Among his pupils were Reuchlin, Grocyn, and Linacre. He himself was a pupil of Johannes Argyropholus and of Christople Landinus.

XXV. LATE SCOTISTS

WILLIAM OF VAUROUILLON (de Valle Rullonis; d. 1463), O.F.M., A bachelor of theology at Paris in 1429, and master in 1448. Wrote a commentary on the *Sentences* of Peter Lombard (1429/30) and a *vademecum* or *collectarium* of the *Opus oxoniense* of Duns Scotus. Both of these books were used as manuals in the schools.

NICOLAS DE ORBELLIS (Dorbellus; d. 1472/75), O. Min., master of theology in Poitiers. Wrote a commentary on the *Sentences* of Peter Lombard; and also on the *Nicomachean Ethics* of Aristotle, in which the inspiration of Albert of Saxony is evident. Wrote also:

Super sententias compendium singulare, extracts from Duns Scotus's commentary on the *Sentences.*

Declarationes quorundam terminorum theologiae.

Super Summulas Petri Hispani.
De scientia mathematica, a commentary on Aristotle.
Compendium mathematicae.

JOHANNES MAGISTRI (1432-1482). Wrote:
Dicta introductoria in doctrinam doctoris subtilis.

LOUIS OF PRUSSIA (Johann Wohlgemuth), O.F.M., came probably from Heilsberg in East Prussia. Studied at Cologne. Directed studies in Posen and Thorn. Wrote among other things:
Trilogium animae (Nürnberg, 1498), a handbook of knowledge for religious. Significant historically for its frequent references to a large number of mediaeval writers.

ANTONIUS SIRECTUS, who between 1470 and 1475 treated of the *formalitates* of Duns Scotus.

STEPHEN BRULEFER (Pillet; d. ca. 1500). Born at St. Malo in Brittany. Teacher and preacher in Paris, Mainz and Metz. Wrote:
Formalitates in doctrinam Scoti (Paris, 1490)
In IV B. Bonaventurae Sent. libros (Basel, 1501)
Opuscula (Paris, 1500)

PAUL SCRIPTORIS (Schreiber; d. 1505), O.F.M., from Weilderstadt in Württemberg. Studied under Stephen Brulefer in Paris. From 1494 he gave lectures in a cloister in Tübingen on mathematics, astronomy, geography and theology. Appointed professor of theology at Toulouse, but died enroute at Kaysersberg in Alsace. Wrote a commentary on Duns Scotus's commentary on the first book of *Sentences* (1498, the first book printed in Tübingen.)

NICHOLAS TINCTOR of Gunzenhausen; taught in Paris and in Ingolstadt. Wrote:
Dicta Tinctoris super Summulas P. Hispani (1486). Used as a manual in Tübingen.

ANTONIUS TROMBETA (d. 1518). Wrote:
In Scoti formalitates.
Quaestiones quodlibetales.
De animarum humanarum plurificatione, against the Averroists.

JOHANNES FABER DE WERDEA
THOMAS BRICOT. Wrote:

Quaestiones on the *Posterior analytics* of Aristotle.

Textus abbreviatus logices (Basle, 1492). Commented on by George of Brussels, the commentary being completed by Bricot himself.

GEORGE OF BRUSSELS, began a commentary on the *Textus abbreviatus logices* of Thomas Bricot, published in Lyons, 1503. Wrote also a commentary on the *Summulae* of Petrus Hispanus.

SAMUEL DE CASSINES. Wrote:

Liber isagogicus ad doctrinam Scoti et ad Aristotelica logicalia.

Liber isagogicus ad physicos apices assequendos.

Expositio triplex in VIII libros Physicorum.

PETRUS TARTARETUS, a secular professor in Paris; in 1490 was rector of the University of Paris. Wrote commentaries on first six books of the *Metaphysics*, on the *Organon*, on the *Physics* and on the first six books of the *Ethics* of Aristotle. Of great importance are his expositions of Duns Scotus's *Quodlibeta* and commentary on the *Sentences*, as well as the following in which he defends Scotist realism against Ockhamist nominalism:

Commentarii in libros totius logicae Aristotelis, a commentary on the *Organon* in which is to be found the logical figure known as the 'pons asinorum,' the invention of which, it seems, is falsely ascribed to Buridanus.

Expositio in Summulas Petri Hispani.

Clarissima singularisque totiusque philosophiae necnon metaphysicae Aristotelis expositio.

Commentationes in Aristotelem secundum subtilissimi doct. Scoti sententiam.

MAURITIUS A PORTU (Fildäus, O'Fihely; 1463-1513), O. Conv., 'flos mundi,' Irish Scotist, studied at Oxford, and later, after entering the religious life, at Padua. Made archbishop of Tuam in 1506. He made critical editions of several writings of Duns Scotus and of the *Quodlibeta* and the commentary on the *Sentences* of Mayron (Franciscus Maironis, d. 1327), who was the outstanding pupil of Duns Scotus. He wrote also:

Expositio in quaestiones dialecticas J. Scoti super Porphyrium (Venice, 1500, 1519).

Epitomata in Scoti formalitates (Venice, 1514, 1522).

[38]

FRANCISCUS LYCHETUS (d. 1520), O.F.M.; born at Lovario near Bergamo; died in Budapest. Teacher of theology at Naples. Wrote very important commentaries on the first three books of the *Sentences* of Peter Lombard, and on the *Quodlibeta* and the *Quaestiones in metaphysicam* of Duns Scotus (printed in Brescia, ca. 1517).

XXVI. ITALIAN OCKHAMISTS

OLIVIERI, Sienese doctor of arts and of medicine. Wrote:
Tractatus rationalis scientiae (ca. 1491).

ALLESANDRO SERMONETA, physician and teacher at the University of Pisa, 1473; disciple of Olivieri.

BENEDICTUS VICTORIUS FAVENTINUS, disciple of Olivieri.

GIACOMO RICCI, physician.

BERNARDINUS PETRI DE LANDUCIIS, physician.

PAULUS NICOLETTUS, Augustinian hermit, Venice.

PAULUS PERGULENSIS (d. 1451), Augustinian hermit, Venice.

PETRUS MANTUANUS

MARCUS DE BENEVENTO, A Celestine monk, introduced nominalism at Bologna ca. 1496; in same year he edited the works of Ockham.

XXVII. THE PLATO-ARISTOTLE CONTROVERSY OF PLETHON

BASILIUS BESSARION (1403-1472), was a pupil of Gemistus Plethon, and defended him against Theodorus Gaza. He translated works of Aristotle into Latin. Bessarion was a temperate admirer of Plato's philosophy and considered it more in accord than Aristotelianism with Christian dogma; however he rejected the Platonic doctrines concerning the pre-existence of the soul, the plurality of gods, and a world soul. He became Archbishop of Nicola in 1436 and in this capacity tried to effect a union between the Greek and the Roman churches. He himself became a cardinal in the Roman church under Pope Eugene IV. Philosophically he tried to divide the territory of knowledge between Aristotle and Plato so that Plato should be the authority in theology and Aristotle in the philosophy of nature. He contributed greatly to the extension of speculative thought in the department of theology. He wrote:
Adversus calumniatorem Platonis, in which he tries to find a common ground between the doctrines of Plato and of Aristotle, and states that the two

differ in the form rather than in the content of their teaching. The treatise is directed against the *Comparatio Aristotelis et Platonis* of Georgius Trapezuntius.

GEORGIUS SCHOLARIUS GENNADIUS (d. 1464), born in Constantinople. He was a Patriarch under Sultan Mohammed for a time, beginning in 1453. He was an opponent of Plethon. He took part in the Council of Florence, which dealt with the union of the Greek and Latin church. He wrote commentaries on Porphyry's *Isagoge* and on the logical works of Aristotle. He translated among other things, Gilbert of Poirée's *Liber de sex principiis* into Greek. He wrote also:

Against the Doubts of Plethon Concerning Aristotle, in Greek.

VITTORINO DA FELTRE, teacher of Theodorus Gaza and Georgius Trapezuntius.

GEORGIUS TRAPEZUNTIUS (1396-1484), pupil of Franciscus Barbarus, Guarinus of Verona, and Vittorino da Feltre. He was active in the Council of Florence. Taught rhetoric and philosophy at Venice and Rome. Wrote several works on Aristotle and also commentaries on them. In his studies of Aristotle he found definite and tenable philosophical theorems, given in systematic form and suitable for teaching. He was anti-Platonistic and sided with the partisans of Aristotle in the controversy raised by Plethon. He wrote:

Comparatio Platonis et Aristotelis, in which he censures the doctrine of Pletho as unchristian, and says that Pletho intended to found a new religion, neither Christian nor Mohammedan, but neo-Platonic and heathen.

THEODORUS GAZA (ca. 1400-ca. 1473), pupil of Plethon; came to Italy in 1444; studied under Vittorino da Feltre; joined the Roman church. In 1447 he became professor of Greek language and literature in the newly founded University of Ferrara. About 1450 he was professor of philosophy under Pope Nicholas V (1447-1455) in Rome. In 1476 he gave lectures on Aristotle in Ferrara where he was heard by Rudolph Agricola. He was an opponent of Plethon, but still a friend of Bessarion. He translated numerous works of Aristotle, Alexander of Aphrodisias, and Theophrastus into Latin. He also translated Cicero's *De senectute* and *Somnium Scipionis* into Greek. Among his works are:

That Nature does not Deliberate (1461), a writing directed against Pletho, which Bessarion in his *De natura et arte* answers.

Antirhetikon, an answer to Bessarion which incited Michael Apostolius to come forth in defense of Plethon.

A Dialogue between Theodorus and Plethon concerning the Philosophy of Aristotle, in which the knowledge of substance is discussed.

Concerning Voluntary and Involuntary Actions, a defense in Greek against the attack of Apostolius.

MICHAEL APOSTOLIUS, defender of Plethon, opposed by both Bessarion and Callistos.

ANDRONICUS CALLISTOS, friend of Gaza; answered the attack of Apostolius.

XXVIII. THE PADUA AVERROISTS AND THEIR OPPONENTS

CAJETAN OF THIENE (Cajetanus Thienaeus; 1387-1465). One of the principal Averroists at the University of Padua; later abandoned Averroism because of certain doctrines which were irreconcilable with the Catholic faith.

NICOLETTO VERNIAS of Chieti. Taught at Padua from 1471 to 1499. In 1499 he taught that if a heavy body fell it was in consequence of the motion of the air surrounding it. Later in life, he admitted the plurality and immortality of human souls. Wrote:

Quaestio an dentur universalia realis
De unitate intellectus

AUGUSTINUS NIPHUS (Suessanus Agostino Nifo; 1473-1538). Pupil of Nicoletto Vernias; labored in a strange reaction against Ptolemaic astronomy, in a work that has not come down to us. Edited (1495-1497) the works of Averroes. Wrote in 1518 for Pope Leo X a work against Petrus Pomponatius's *De immortalitate animae,* in which he opposes Alexander of Aphrodisias's interpretation of Aristotle by an appeal to that of St. Thomas Aquinas. Pomponatius, under the protection of Cardinal Bembo, answered with a *Defensorium contra Niphum.* Niphus wrote also:

De intellectu et daemonibus. In this book he holds that there are no immortal beings besides the intelligences of the spheres and the numerically single intellect for men. In 1492 the work was revised.

NICHOLAUS LEONICUS THOMAEUS (b. 1446). Born in Venice; taught at Padua from 1497; influenced by Marcellus Ficinus and Pico della Mirand-

ola. Defended the immortality of the soul. Wrote:
Dialogi which are entitled:

Trophonius, sive, De divinatione
Bembus, sive, De animorum immortalitate
Alverotus, sive, De tribus animorum vehiculis
Peripateticus, sive, De nominum inventione
Sannutus, sive, De compescendo luctu
Severinus, sive, De relatitvorum natura
Sadoletus, sive, De precibus
Phoebus, sive, De aetatum moribus
Bonominus, sive, De alica
Samnutus, sive, De ludo talario

ALEXANDER ACHILLINI (1463-1512). Taught at Bologna and Padua. Philosophical adversary of Pomponatius and an uncompromising Averroist and strong opponent of the theory of impetus and of all Parisian doctrines. He was the first to describe the small bones of the ear, mention the orifices of Wharton's ducts, and described somewhat in detail the ileocaecal valve and other hitherto not well-known portions of the intestines. Wrote:

De orbibus (1498). This treatise is a strange reaction against Ptolemaic astronomy. He maintained the principle that in air, or any fluid whatever, ten equal stones fall with the same velocity as one of their number; and if all were combined they would still fall with the same velocity. Therefore in a fluid two stones, one of which is ten times heavier than the other, fall with the same velocity.

MARCUS ANTONIUS ZIMARA (died 1532). Born in Naples. Travelled to Rome and later to Padua. Wrote commentaries on works of Aristotle and of Averroes in which he attempted to reconcile Averroism with the Christian dogma. The unity of the human intellect he interprets to mean the unity of the principles of knowledge.

PETRUS POMPONATIUS (Pietro Pomponazzi; 1462-1524). Born and educated at Mantua; education completed at Padua, where he became a professor of philosophy. Later lectured on the *De Anima* at Ferrara, and finally taught at Bologna. In opposition to the Averroists, Pomponatius denied the immortality of the soul on the basis that as the soul is the form of the body (as St. Thomas Aquinas also asserted) it must by hypothesis perish with the body, that form apart from matter is unthinkable. Virtue, therefore, can no longer be viewed solely in relation to reward and punishment in another existence, but rather there must be a new criterion, 'virtue for virtue's sake.' In spite of these views he remained a Catholic contending that religion and philosophy, faith and knowledge, may be diametrically opposed and yet coexist for the same thinker. Wrote:

De immortalitate animae (1516). This work gave rise to a storm of controversy between the orthodox Thomists of the Catholic church, the Averroists headed by Agostino Nifo, and the so-called Alexandrist school.

Apologia (1517)

Defensorium (1519). This pamphlet explains his paradoxical position as Catholic and philosophic materialist.

De incantationibus (1520). This work tries to establish the non-existence of demons and spirits on the basis of the Aristotelian theory of the cosmos, although the author as a believing Christian asserts his faith in their existence.

De fate (1523)

THE FIFTH LATERAN COUNCIL (1512-1517). This council declared that the immortality of the soul can be proved by reason. In its eighth session, December 19, 1513, it declared against the 'New Aristotelians' that the rational soul 'non solum vere per se et essentialiter humani corporis forma exsistat, sicut in canone felicis recordationis Clementis Papae V praedecessoris nostri in (generali) Viennensi Concilio edito continetur; verum et immortalis, et pro corporum, quibus infunditur, multitudine singulariter multiplicabilis, et multiplicata, et multiplicanda sit.' Cf. H. Denzinger and Cl. Bannwart, *Enchiridion symbolorum* (Freiburg i. B.: Herder, 1922), 738.

J. A. MARTA. Platonist upholder of the immortality of the soul.

GASPARO CONTARINI (1483-1542). Platonist upholder of the immortality of the soul; Italian cardinal under Pope Paul III.

ANTON SIRMOND. Platonist upholder of the immortality of the soul.

SIMON PORTA (died 1555). Pupil of Pomponatius.

BARTHOLOMAEUS SPINA OF PISA, O.F. (ca. 1475-1546). Opponent of Pomponatius. Became a Dominican in 1594. Appointed to chair of theology at Padua in 1536. As Master of the Sacred Palace for four years (1542-1546) he rendered great services to the Holy See and to the Fathers of the Council of Trent regarding many difficult and mooted questions. Following 1518,

Spina was engaged in controversy with his famous confrère, Cardinal Cajetan. He was also opposed to Ambrose Catharinus, whom he denounced as guilty of heresy to Paul III in 1546. Wrote:

Tutela veritatis de immortalitate animae contra Petrum Pomponatium (1518)
Flagellum in tres libros apologiae Pomponatii de immortalitate animae (1518)
De conceptione B. Mariae Virginis (1533). In this treatise Spina opposed the doctrine of the Immaculate Conception.

XXIX. ROMAN ACADEMY

POMPONIO LETO (Giulio Sanseverino; 1425-1497), born in Calabria, died in Rome. He and several others founded a semi-pagan academy, which is known as the Roman Academy. He was looked upon by Pope Paul II as a scorner of Christianity and conspirator. Later imprisoned because of his actions, but defended himself, reminding his capturers that he had maintained the immortality of the soul, a belief often discussed by his fellow humanists. Released by Pope Sixtus IV. He wrote:

De magistratibus, sacerdotiis et legibus Romanorum
De romanae urbis antiquitate
Compendium historiae romanae ab interitu Gordiani usque ad Justinum III

BARTOLOMEO PLATINA (Sacchi; 1421-1481), born at Piadena, died at Rome. Elected a member of the College of Abbreviators (1463) under Pope Pius II, but was deprived of this privilege with the accession of Pope Paul II. Imprisoned on various charges along with Leto, but he did not deny that members of the Roman Academy were found guilty of immorality. Appointed Vatican librarian by Pope Sixtus IV, and also instructed to make a collection of the chief privileges of the Roman Church. His most important work is:

Vitae Pontificum Platinae historici liber de vita Christi ac omnium pontificum qui hactenus ducenti fuere et XX, (Venice, 1479), this is the first systematic papal handbook, and is an attack on Pope Paul II.

FILIPPO BUONACCORSI (Callimachus; 1437-1496), born at Gimignano, died at Cracow. Came to Rome where he was associated with Pomponio Leto. As a result of the controversy with Pope Paul II he fled to Greece, and from there to Egypt and other lands. He wrote: .

Historia rerum gestarum in Hungaria et contra Turcos

XXX. THE HUMANIST CIRCLE OF POPE LEO X

POPE LEO X (Giovanni de'Medici; 1475-1521), born at Florence, died at Rome. He was pope from 1513 to the day he died. At an early age he received numerous appointments in Church offices, and was given the title of cardinal at the age of thirteen. He was involved in several disputes with the kings of various countries, notably Louis XII of France, and Holy Roman Emperor Maximilian I. Leo was troubled throughout his reign with heresy and schism. He excommunicated Martin Luther after the latter had posted his famous 95 theses. He had difficulty in remedying this religious turmoil, but this can be explained by the political complications of the time. The death of the emperor Maximilian I seriously affected the situation, and Leo had to decide on a successor to the throne. As a patron of learning Leo X deserves a prominent place among the popes. Although he attempted and carried out a few reforms, nevertheless he did not recognize sufficiently the need of reform within the Church.

PIETRO BEMBO (1470-1547), born in Venice. Accompanied Giulio de' Medici to Rome, where he was appointed secretary to Pope Leo X in 1513. Made cardinal in 1539 by Pope Paul III, and then devoted himself to theology and classical history. Before his entrance into the priesthood, he was a student of the classics under Lascaris at Messina. He closely imitated the classics in his style of writing. He wrote:
History of Venice (1551)
Gli Asolani

JACOPO SADOLETO (1477-1547), born at Modena. He spent most of his time in the studies of humanism and acquired reputation as a Latin poet. Leo X chose him as his secretary along with Pietro Bembo, and in 1517 made him bishop of Carpentras. His great aim in life was to win back the Protestants by peaceful persuasion and by putting Catholic doctrine in a conciliatory form. He wrote:
Commentary on Romans, which gave great offense to Rome and Paris.
Epistles (1533), a treatise on education.
Phaedrus (1538), a defense of philosophy.

BERNARDO ACCOLTI (1465-1536), born at Arezzo. His works were read by many distinguished prelates of the age, most notable of these being Cardinal Bembo who left on record a testimony to his extraordinary talent. He wrote:

Virginia (Florence, 1513)

Comedia (Florence, 1513)

Capitoli e Strambotti de Messer Bernardo Accolti Atetino (Florence, 1513)

MARCO GIROLAMO VIDA (ca. 1489-1566), born at Cremona, died at Alva. Entered the order of the Canonici Regolari Lateranensi, and later sought to be admitted to the Papal court in Rome because that was the high seat of learning of his time. Pope Leo X bestowed on him the priory of St. Sylvester at Frascati. Clement VII raised him to the rank of apostolic protonotary, and appointed him bishop of Alba in 1532. Vida attended the Council of Trent and recorded the conversations of many of the luminaries at that gathering. His works include:

Christiad, a Latin poem on the life of Christ.

Art of Poetry

De Republica, the conversations at the Council of Trent (1545-1563).

GIANGIORGIO TRISSINO (1478-1550), born at Vicenza, died at Rome. He had a good humanistic training studying Greek under the famous Demetrius Chalcondylas at Milan and philosophy under Nicolò Leoniceno at Ferrara. Leo X sent him to Germany in 1515, as his nuncio. Later on Clement VII employed him as ambassador. Around him were gathered the most cultured men of the time. He wrote:

Sofonisba (1515), an Italian tragedy to show deference to the classic rules.

Italia liberata dai Goti, (1547-8) dealing with the campaigns of Belisarius in Italy.

Castellano (1529)

XXXI. KABBALISTS

R. JOCHANAN ALEMAN, a Jewish Kabbalist who came to Italy from Constantinople. Teacher of John Pico della Mirandola.

ELLA DEL MEDIGO (b. 1450). Professor of philosophy at University of Padua and teacher of Pico della Mirandola. Wrote:

An Examination of the Law

GIOVANNI PICO DELLA MIRANDOLA (1463-1494). Famous philosopher and classical scholar. Studied in Italy and France, principally at Bologna, Ferrara, and Padua. He was tutored in the Kabbalah by R. Jochanan Aleman

and interwove some of its teachings in his philosophical theories. His aim was to conciliate religion and philosophy. As a result of his Kabbalistic studies, he published in 1486, at the age of 24, 900 theses and undertook to defend them in the presence of all European scholars whom he invited to Rome at his expense. Among these theses was the following: 'No science yields greater proof of the divinity of Christ than magic and the Kabbalah.' The disputation was prohibited. He devoted his later life to a defense of Christ against Jews, Mohammedans and astrologers. Also wrote:
Heptaphus
De ente et uno

JOHANNES FRANCISCUS PICO DELLA MIRANDOLA (ca. 1469-1533). Nephew of Giovanni Pico della Mirandola. Like his uncle, he devoted himself to philosophy but made it subject to the Bible. Wrote:
De studio divinae et humanae sapientia
Examen doctrinae unitatis gentium

CORNELIUS AGRIPPA VON NETTESHEIM (1486-1535). Born in Cologne. Studied at Cologne and Paris. Taught Hebrew at Dole and also taught in England. Later studied medicine, alchemy, theology and finally devoted himself to Kabbalism under the influence of Reuchlin. His works have a strong tendency toward occultism. Lived and died a Catholic, but was sympathetic toward some of Luther's doctrines. Wrote:
De occulta philosophia
De incertitudine et vanitate scientiarum
De nobilitate et praecelentia feminei sexus declamatio
Libellus de sacramento matrimonii

GEORGIUS VENETUS (Francesco Giorgio Zorzi, 1460-1540), O.F.M. Born in Venice. Joined the Franciscans in 1480. Died in Asalo. Wrote:
De harmonia mundi totius cantica tria, his principal work, in which he subscribed to a neo-Pythagorean, Kabbalist theosophy.
In scripturam sacram et philosophos tria millia problemata (1536), which was opposed by Sixtus of Siena, Bellarmine, Possevino and Mersenne. The latter included it in his list of atheistic books.

CASPAR SCHWENKFELD VON OSSING (1490-1561). Born in Silesia. Studied at Cologne. Moved from place to place because of persecutions arising out of his criticisms of carnal conceptions of the sacraments of some Catholics and Lutherans. He sought to spiritualize Lutheranism. Maintained that Luther had fallen back to an historical view of faith, whereas the faith which saves can never consist in the outward acceptance of an historical fact. He who makes salvation dependent on preaching and the Sacrament, confuses the invisible and the visible Church. The layman is his own priest. Wrote:

Letter on the Eucharist
On Prayer
On the Office of Teacher of the New Testament
Two Responses to Melancthon

SEBASTIAN FRANCK (1500-1545). Studied at Heidelberg. Lived for a time at Nürnberg where he is associated with Schwenkfeld. He believed that according to the true philosophy of the children of God, God is the biggest, highest the only good whom none can either hurt or help and who by his own word or wisdom and spirit created things. Apart from God things are nothing; He is in everything, and constitutes the being of everything. Man is free in will though limited in act. Wrote:

Paradoxa
De arbore scientiae boni et mali
Chronica
Germaniae chronicon
Cosmographia

MOSES CORDOVERO (b. 1522). Studied the Kabbalah under his learned brother-in-law Solomon Aleavez. Was chiefly concerned with the scientific speculations of the Kabbalah. Wrote:

A Sombre or Sweet Light (1587)
The Book of Retirement (1543)
The Garden of Pomegranates (1591)

VALENTIN WEIGEL (1533-1588). Studied at Leipzig and Wittenberg; spent rest of life as pastor of a church at Zschopau. Follower of Franck and German mystics and borrowed much from them. Escaped Franck's fate by subscribing to the public formulas of agreement and developing his mystical doctrines in the presence of trusted friends only. Believed that true wisdom has its foundation in self-knowledge—knowledge of our origin and destiny. Man is the microcosm; in him are united soul, spirit and body originating respectively in the divine, the celestial and the earthly worlds. By his soul (only) he is an image of God and is immortal. God is one and self-sufficient; man is dependent, and contains in himself alterity, has self-existence not of necessity, but by grace or favor. True Christianity, true resurrection and consciousness of God, are contained in 'death to self.' Doctrine contained in oft-repeated saying, 'If I am free from myself I am free from the foul fiend, for every man is his own worst foe.' Wrote:

Studium Universale
Know Thyself
Kurzer Bericht vom Wege und Weise, alle Dingen zu erkennen
Christliches Gesprach vom wahren Christentum
Libellus de vita beata (1609)

ISAAC LURIA (Loria; b. 1534). Taught the ascetic and miraculous phases of the Kabbalah.

CHAJIM VITAL (1553-1620). Disciple of Luria; his works gave an extraordinary impetus to the Kabbalah and gave rise to the new school and separate congregation in Palestine. Produced the gigantic and famous system of the Kabbalah entitled *The Tree of Life*. Another one of his works, that of *Etz Chajim* is one of the two bibles of the Kabbalah.

ESAJAS STIEFEL (d. 1627). Follower of Weigel.

EZECHIEL METH (d. 1640). Nephew of Esajas Stiefel, follower of Weigel.

LEO DE MODENA (1571-1648). Was the most daring of the opponents of Kabbalah. Wrote:
Ben David (1635-36)
The Roaring Lion (1639)

JOSEPH SOLOMON DEL MEDIGO (1591-1637). Contemporary of Leo de Modena.

JOSEPH DE VOISIN (fl. 1635). Translated some extracts of the Sohar which treat of the nature of the human soul for those Christians who did not understand the Aramaic in which this Thesaurus is written.

XXXII. LATER TERMINISTS

JOHN WESSEL (Wessel Gansfort; 1420-1489), Dutch theologian, born and died in Gröningen. He was educated at Zwolle, and lived with the Brethren of the Common Life. Although a layman, he spent many years studying in monasteries. From 1449 he studied at the University of Cologne, and graduated with his masters degree. In 1456 he was professor of arts at the University of Heidelberg. He lectured at Paris. He was converted to formalism, and then adopted nominalism. In 1474 he was at Venice and then returned home to spend the rest of his years in quiet study. He never thought of separating from the church and died a Catholic. In the sixteenth century however his wrtiings were placed on the *Index* of forbidden books because of their errors. He wrote:

Farrago rerum theologicarum (1521)
De sacramento Eucharistiae et audienda missa
De oratione et modo orandi
De causis incarnationis

HENRY GREVE at Leipzig

MICHAEL OF BRESLAU at Cracow

STEPHANUS DE MONTE (fl. 1490) at Padua

ANTONIUS SILVESTER (d. 1515)

JUDOCUS ISENACENSIS (d. 1519)

HENRY BEBEL (1472-1518), born in Justingen in Württemberg. Studied in Cracow, 1492 and Basel, 1495. From 1496 professor in Tübingen, where he had Johannes Altenstaig of Mindelheim as a pupil. Famous principally for his humanistic studies. Wrote:
Triumphus Veneris (1509), a poem.
Ars versificandi
Facetiae (1508-1509)

JOHANNES ALTENSTAIG OF MINDELHEIM (d. after 1525). Born in Mindelheim. Studied at the University of Tübingen, 1497-1509, where he joined the 'moderni' or nominalists. Pupil of Henry Bebel there. Professor of philosophy and theology at the Augustinian house in Palling, 1509-1512. From 1512 assistant priest in Mindelheim. Wrote a commentary on Henry Bebel's *Triumphus Veneris*. Wrote also:
Vocabularius vocum (1508)
Opus pro conficiundis epistolis (1512)
Dialectica (1514)
Vocabularius theologiae (1517)
Isokrates von dem Reich (1517)
Opusculum de amicitia (1519)
De felicitate triplici (1519)

Ain nutzlich vnnd in hailiger geschrifft gegründte vnderricht, was ain Christen mensch thun oder lassen sol (1523).

Von der Füllerey ein müter aller vbel vnd laster (1525).

CONRAD OF BUCHEN (d. 1531)

BARTHOLOMAEUS ARNOLDI, (Usingen; ca. 1465-1532). Born in Usingen in Nassau. Attended the University of Erfurt in 1484-1491. In 1491 became master of the free arts. Taught philosophy for thirty years. Joined the Hermits of St. Augustine in 1512. In 1514 became doctor of theology, without, however, giving up his place on the faculty of philosophy. Teacher of Luther, and later his opponent. In 1522 became preacher at the cathedral. Wrote:

De sacramentis, an extract from which goes under the title of *Polemica de SS. Eucharistiae sacramento.*

XXXIII. THE SCHOOL OF CONSTANTINUS LASCARIS

CONSTANTINUS LASCARIS, (1434-1501); born at Constantinople and died at Messina. Was said to have spent about seven years in Corfu. At Rhodes he acquired manuscripts, and finally settled at Milan as a copyist of manuscripts. He taught Greek to Princess Hippolyta Sforza. He gave to the city of Milan his seventy-six manuscripts. He was the teacher of Cardinal Bembo. Author of:

Erotemata (1476), a grammar in which he follows Choeroboscus; the first book printed in Greek.

JOHANNES LASCARIS (Rhyndacenus; 1445-1535); born at Rhyndacus; died at Rome. When still a youth he went to Venice, where he met Bessarion, who sent him to study Latin at Padua. Late, after the death of Bessarion, Lorenzo de Medici asked him to go to Florence. Here he gave lectures on Thucydides, Demosthenes, Sophocles, and the Greek Anthology. Lorenzo sent him to Greece in quest of manuscripts. On his second trip he acquired two hundred from Mount Athos but, in the meantime, Lorenzo had died. He then became ambassador for France at Venice, (1503-1508), at which time he joined the Greek Academy of Aldus Manutius (1449-1515). He then aided King Louis XII of France in forming the Library of Blois. He later had charge of it with Bunde after Francis I had it removed to Fontainebleau. He is credited with the publication of the first editions of the Greek Anthology (1494), four plays of Euripides, Callimachus (ca. 1495), Apollonius,

Lucian (1496), the scholia of Didymus (1517) and the scholia of Porphyrius on Homer (1518).

MARCUS MUSURUS (1470-1517); born at Retimo, Crete; died at Rome. Was the son of a rich merchant, and when quite young went to Florence where he studied Greek under John Lascaris. Marcus almost became his equal in classical scholarship. In 1503 he became a professor at Padua where he taught Greek successfully. Later he became a member of the Aldine Academy of Hellenists at Venice. Musurus gave valuable assistance to Aldus Mantius in his preparation of the earliest printed editions of the Greek authors. So great was his reputation as a teacher that the students came from many countries to hear him lecture. Erasmus testifies to his exact knowledge of Latin. To his guidance the editions of Aristophanes, Plato, Pindar, Hesychinus, Athenaeus, and Pausanias owed their critical correctness. In 1516 he established a Greek printing press in Rome under Pope Leo X who appointed him Bishop of Malvasia in the Morea, but he died before he could reach the diocese. His works include:

Etymologicum Magnum (1499), the first Latin and Greek lexicon; printed by Zacharias Callierges of Crete.

Elegy on Plato which, together with several epigrams of his, was published in the Aldine edition of Plato (Venice, 1513).

XXXIV. ALBERTISTS

GERHARD HARDEWYK (d. 1503). Wrote commentaries on the Nova logica and on the Summulae logicales of Petrus Hispanus.

ARNOLD OF LUYDE (of Tongres; d. 1540). Wrote commentaries on the Organon and on the Summulae logicales of Petrus Hispanus.

XXXV. GILES OF VITERBO

GILES OF VITERBO (died 1532). Theologian and humanist; born at Viterbo, Italy; entered Augustinian Order; delivered famous ecclesiastical discourse at Fifth General Council in 1512 at the Lateran; became cardinal and in 1523 received title of Patriarch of Constantinople; desired to reform ecclesiastical conditions. Wrote:

Historia viginti saeculorum per totidem psalmos conscripta. This work deals with a philosophical and historical history of the world before and after Christ's birth.

Libellus de ecclesiae incremento
Informatio pro sedis apostolicae auctoritate contra Lutheranam sectam

XXXVI. LEONARDO DA VINCI

LEONARDO DA VINCI (1452-1519) ; born at Vince, near Florence; died at Cloux. Was the son of a notary and a peasant woman. Became a painter, sculptor, architect, engineer and scholar, and one of the greatest minds of the Renaissance. There are three periods in Leonardo's biography: the Florentine period (1469-1482) ; the Milanese period (1483-1499) ; the Normandie period (1500-1519). He regarded the soul as the principle of perception, memory and thought. He held that experience is necessary for knowledge. His writings include: a large collection in the Ambrosian Library of Milan called the *Codex Atlanticus* consisting of 393 folio pages on which are pasted more than 1600 leaves of notes; at Paris in the library of the Institute twelve manuscripts numbered from A to M; at London, three volumes at South Kensington, a manuscript of 566 pages at the British Museum, and at Windsor anatomical plates and drawings.

XXXVII. MACHIAVELLI

NICCOLO MACHIAVELLI (1469-1527) ; born in Florence. At 29 he started his public life. He was open-eyed, close-mouthed and industrious. He rarely agreed with his more accomplished contemporaries. He was appointed to office of First Secretary to the Signoria and later assumed charge of the Second Chancery. It was his philosophy that it was of no use to have an end, however noble, without the necessary means to attain it. By this he implied that there was a system where everything depends on the determination of power by ends. He saw human nature as the foundation of ethics and politics. In certain instances his philosophy approaches that of Aristotle. He wrote two books which dealt with political theory and technique in statecraft:

Il Principe, in which he outlined the means by which a ruler may acquire and maintain power.

Discorsi, in which he tells rulers to employ any means, however lawless and unscrupulous, to gain political ends.

[53]

XXXVIII. LATER BRETHREN OF THE COMMON LIFE AND THEIR FAMOUS PUPILS

ALEXANDER HEGIUS (ca. 1433-1498); humanist, influenced by his teacher, Rudolph Agricola. Was ordained a priest at a mature age. In 1469 he became rector of the school at Wesel and soon afterwards was made head of the monastic school at Emmerich. In 1474 he assumed direction of the school at Deventer. Hegius was the teacher of Erasmus.

GABRIEL BIEL (1425-1495); born at Speyer, Germany and died at Tübingen. He pursued his studies at Heidelberg and Erfürt. In 1460 he became a preacher at the Cathedral of Mainz and eight years later joined the Brethren of the Common Life. He became superior of this society at Bützbach, and in 1479 was appointed provost of the church in Urach. At this time he gave his aid to Count Eberhard of Würtemburg in the foundation of the University of Tübingen. In 1484 he was appointed first professor of theology in the new university. In thought Biel was a nominalist, follower of William of Ockham. Among his works are:

Sacri canonis Missae exposito resolutissima literalis et mystica
Epitome et collectorium ex Occamo super IV libros sententiarum
Tractatus de potestate et utilitate monetarum

DESIDERIUS ERASMUS of Rotterdam (1467-1536), humanist theologian; born at Gouda. He had Alexander Hegius and Lorenzo Valla as teachers. He became an Augustinian canon and was ordained in 1492. In August, 1495, Erasmus entered the "domus pauperum" of the college of Montaigu, then under the rule of Jan Standonck, a leader of the 'devotio moderna,' the Dutch movement for the reformation of the monastic orders. Erasmus had the ear of the educated class. The general ardour for the restoration of the arts and of learning created an aristocratic public, of which Erasmus was supreme pontiff. Among his writings are:

Adagia (1500), a compilation of proverbs and anecdotes.
Moriae Encomium (*Laus Stultitiae*; 1509)
De ratione studii (1512); contains an educational program along humanist lines.
Colloquia familiaria (publ. 1518)
De conscribendis epistolis
Enchiridion militia christiani; a plea for a return to the source of Christianity in its primitive simplicity.

Diatribe de libero arbitrio (1524) ; influenced by St. John Fischer's *Assertionis Lutheranae confutatio* (1523) ; Martin Luther's *De servo arbitrio* (1525) was written in answer to it.

XXXIX. REUCHLIN AND HIS ASSOCIATES

JOHN REUCHLIN (Capnion; 1455-1522). Studied in Freiburg i. B., Paris and Basle. Became master of arts in 1477. Studied law at Orléans and Poitiers beginning in 1478. In 1481 he received his licentiate in law in Poitiers, and in 1481 his doctorate of law in Tübingen. About 1485 he began the study of Hebrew, and eventually of the Kabbalah. Became the adviser of Graf Eberhard whom he accompanied to Rome in 1482. Held similar positions in other places. In 1520-21 he was professor of Greek and Hebrew at the University of Ingolstadt which he forsook so as to escape a plague. He went to Tübingen where he taught grammar until he died. Wrote:

Vocabularius breviloquus (1475)

De verbo mirifico (1494)

Liber de arte praedicandi (1504)

Rudimenta linguae hebraicae (1506)

Augenspiegel (1511) in answer to the *Handspiegel* (1511) of Pfefferkorn, a converted Jew, who answered with *Brandspiegel* (1512).

Defensio contra calumniatores Colonienses (1513), an answer to Pfefferkorn's *Brandspiegel.*

Clarorum virorum epistolae (1514), in which he published the letters of his humanist friends, B. Adelmann, H. v. d. Busche, W. Pirkheimer and others.

De arte cabbalistica (1517)

De accentibus et orthographia linguae hebraicae (1518)

JOHANN VON DALBERG (1445-1503) ; was the Bishop of Worms and in 1496 invited Reuchlin to Heidelberg which was the seat of the Rhenish Society.

KONRAD CELTES (1459-1508) ; was a German humanist, who was born at Wipfeld and studied at Heidelberg. As a teacher at various universities he established learned societies on the model of the academy of Pomponius Laetus at Rome. Among these was the Sodalitas literaria Rhenana or Celtica at Mainz (1491).

JOHANN TRITHEIM (Thithemius; 1462-1516); was the abbot of Span-
heim, as well as a reputéd magician. In a letter to Johann Winburg he refers
to Faust as a fool rather than a philosopher.

XL. CHURCH AND STATE IN ENGLAND

KING HENRY VIII (1491-1547). Born at Greenwich. First English king
to be educated under the influence of the Renaissance. He became an accomplished scholar, linguist, musician, and athlete. On taking the throne he
proved himself a devoted Catholic and acquired the title, 'defender of the
Faith.' But after he had been married eighteen years to Catherine of Aragon,
he wished the Pope to annul his marriage so that he could remarry. The refusal
of the Pope to King Henry's wishes brought about a breach between church
and state. Henry VIII declared the supremacy of the King of England in
matters of religion. In a controversy between Catholicism and Lutheranism the
king sided with Catholicism, but in spite of this, Henry VIII no doubt laid
the foundation for Protestantism in England. He wrote:
Assertio septem sacramentorum contra M. Lutherum.

ST. THOMAS MORE (1477/78-1535). He was born in London and educated at Oxford. He prepared to study law; but entered a political life. He
developed from Platonic principles highly ideal schemes of state organization
and government. Became successively speaker of the House of Commons, and
treasurer to the exchequer, and Lord Chancellor under Henry VIII. He
later opposed Henry VIII, was imprisoned in the Tower of London, and
suffered martyrdom for his faith. He wrote:
Utopia. It describes an imaginary republic so governed as to secure universal
   happiness. From the title of that work the present meaning of the word
   'Utopia' is derived; that is, an imaginary condition of life beautiful in
   theory, but impossible in practice. It is believed that Plato was the source
   for his political 'Utopia,' which described an ideal island with community
   of goods, national education, and a philosophy in which the good of the
   individual is sacrificed for the good of the state.
The Dialogue of Comfort Against Tribulation
A Treatise on the Passion
Four Last Things
A Dyalogue of Syr Thomas More, Knt., a work against Luther and Tyndale.
The Apologye of Syr Thomas More (1533), a work in defence of his own
   polemical style and of the treatment of heretics by the clergy.

ST. JOHN FISHER (ca. 1469-1535), humanist and a political theorist. He was a contemporary of More. He was educated at Cambridge; became cardinal and bishop. Fisher was the champion of the rights of conscience and the only English bishop to resist the wishes of the King. He died the death of a martyr. He wrote:

Sacri sacerdotii defensio contra Lutherum
Assertionis Lutheranae confutatio (1523)
Defensio assertionis regis Anglici (1525)
De Eucharistia (1527)
A Spiritual Consolation

THOMAS WOLSEY (1475-1530). Educated at Magdalen College, Oxford; graduated with a B. A. at fifteen. Was at one time master of the College and had under his charge three sons of Thomas Grey. Received the cardinalate from Pope Leo X in May 1514. Wolsey was made chaplain by Henry VII, and in 1509 dean of London. Wrote:

Anglica Historia

JOHN COLET (1466-1519). Dean of St. Paul's Cathedral and founder of St. Paul's School. Studied at Oxford and travelled in Italy and France. He was ordained a priest in England in 1496. Professor of the New Testament in the University of Oxford, 1496-1504. Lectured at Oxford on St. Paul's *Epistles,* stressing the personality of the Saint. In London he became the intimate friend and spiritual adviser to Sir Thomas More. Spurred Erasmus to write. He devoted his inherited fortune to the foundation of St. Paul's School, in which Greek was given equal value to Latin. In 1512 he was accused of advance views, but Archbishop Warham dismissed the charges as frivolous. He wrote commentaries on St. Paul's *Epistles* and on works of Pseudo-Dionysius the Areopagite. Wrote also:

Convocation Sermon of 1512
A righte fruitfull admonition concerning the order of a good Christian man's Life
Joannis Coleti Theologi olim Decani Divi Pauli Æditio (1527)
Opus de sacramentis ecclesiae
Absolutissimus de octo orationis partium constructione libellus

STEPHEN GARDINER (1483-1555). Took his doctorate of law at Cambridge and then became Thomas Wolsey's secretary. In 1527 became the emissary of King Henry VIII to Pope Clement VII in the problem of the King's marriage. In 1531 he was given the great bishopric of Winchester. At the death of Henry in 1547, Gardiner was deprived of his bishopric. Mary Tudor later took him from his confinement in the Tower and made him her Chancellor. He wrote:

De vera obedientia oratio (1535), in which he favors the supreme authority of the King.

Conquestio ad M. Bucerum de impudenti ejusdem pseudologia (1544)

A Detection of the Devil's Sophistrie wherein he robbeth the unlearned people of the true byleef in the most blessed Sacrament of the Aulter (1546)

Epistola ad M. Bucerum (1546)

A Declaration of suche true Articles as G. Joye hath gone about to confute as false (1546)

An Explication of the true Catholique Fayth touching the blessed Sacrament (1551)

Confutatio cavillationum (1551)

Palinodia libri de vera obedientia (1552)

Contra convitia Martini Buceri (1554)

Exetasis testimoniorum quae Bucerus minus genuine e S. Patribus non sancte edidit de coelibatus dono (1554)

Epistolae ad J. Checum de pronuntiatione linguae graecae (1555)

THOMAS CRANMER (1489-1556). Sent to Cambridge at fourteen. Became a fellow of Jesus College in 1510 or 1511. Ordained a priest in 1523. In taking his oath of office he said he wanted to retain allegiance to the Pope only in so far as was consistent with his supreme duty to the King. He became the first Protestant Bishop of Canterbury. He wrote:

Defence of the True and Catholic Doctrine of the Sacrament (1550)

An Answer to Doctor Richard Smith

XLI. VIVES

JUAN LUIS VIVES (Ludovicus Vives Valentinus; 1492-1540). Spanish humanist and electic philosopher. Born at Valencia, died at Bruges. He studied at the University of Paris. In 1512 he settled in Bruges. In 1519 he was appointed professor at the University of Louvain, and attached to the college of the Castle. During his stay at Louvain he was associated with Erasmus. His attitude in his commentary on St. Augustine's *De civitate Dei* made him an object of suspicion during the wars of religion. The works of

Vives are very numerous and deal with piety, teaching and education, political economy, and philosophy. He wrote:

Exercitatio linguae latinae
De initiis, sectis et laudibus philosophiae (1518)
Censura de Aristotelis operibus (1519)
De ratione studii puerilis (1523)
De institutione feminae christianae (1523)
Satellitium animi (1524)
Introductio ad veram sapientiam (1524)
De causis corruptarum artium (1531)
De tradendis disciplinis (1531)
Colloquia
De prima philosophia (1531)
De instrumento probabilitatis
De censura veri (1531)
De ratione dicendi (1532)
De communione rerum ad Germanos inferiores (1535)
Exercitationes animi in Deum (1535)
De anima et vita (1538)
De veritate fidei christianae (published in 1543)

XLII. COPERNICUS WITH HIS FRIENDS AND OTHER LATER FOLLOWERS

NICHOLAS COPERNICUS (Koppernigk; 1473-1543). Polish priest born at Thorn. Studied the Humanities at Bologna, Rome and Padua Universities. He belonged to that group of philosophers called Naturalists and is said to have been a strong Aristotelian. By his reading of Ptolemy and by studies of the heavens with the naked eye, he had become convinced that the Ptolemaic astronomy was incorrect. He believed in the simplicity of nature and said, 'The wisdom of nature attains its end by the simplest ways, without circumlocutions, and by means of a harmonious interaction between all the elements involved. She seeks to bind many effects to one single cause, rather than to increase the number of causes.' He was convinced that the sun is the central point and source of light of the world. Round it move the planets, fixed in concentric spheres, in a series in which the earth takes its place between Venus and Mars. The earth turns on its own axis. The whole universe is comprehended within the firm and immovable heaven of the fixed stars, which is its outermost limit. The sphere of the fixed stars is the absolute place in respect of which every other place and every other motion is determined. Heaven is the most honorable part of the universe, hence immovability beseems it. During his entire lifetime he wrote four books on the revolutions of heavenly bodies. Two of them are:

Narratio prima de libris revolutionum, which explained the Copernican theory.

De orbium celestium revolutionibus

TIDEMANN GIESE (1480-1550). Born in Danzig; Vicar general of Frauenburg, 1523-1527; Bishop of Rulm, 1537, and of Ermland, 1549-1550. So vehement an opponent of Protestantism that Hosius spoke of him as 'horrendas haereses.' Bishop Dantiscus and Rheticus urged him to publish his works. He died in Heilsberg. Wrote:

Antilogikon flosculorum Lutheranorum (Cracow, 1525), an answer to Briesmann's *Flosculi*.

De regno Christi (1536), in 3 books, now lost, which in 1538 he sent for criticism to Melancthon and to Erasmus through the good offices of his nephew Rogge, a pupil of Melancthon.

ERASMUS REINHOLD (1511-1553). Studied at Wittenberg. Wrote:

Tabulae Prutenicae (1551), which was a calculation upon Copernican principles and represented celestial movements far better, although large discrepancies were still apparent. He stated that it was possible to apply the principles set forth to terrestial objects, though he applied them only to the sun.

TYCHO BRAHE (1546-1601). Danish astronomer; studied at Copenhagen, Leipzig, Rostock and Augsburg. Delivered lectures in Copenhagen by royal command in 1574. He was given an observatory at Herritzvad. Johannes Kepler joined him in 1600, for whom he furnished accurate observation materials. Brahe perfected the art of pre-telescopic observation as means of ascertaining the true form of the universe. Wrote:

De novâ stellâ (1573) a work on his observation of a new star in Cassiopeia.

De mundi aetherei recentioribus phaenomenis (edited by Kepler, 1588). This gives an account of the Tychonic plan, in which a via media is sought between the Copernican and Ptolemaic systems. The earth retains its mobility, and the five planets revolve around the sun.

Epistolae astronomicae (1596)

Astronomiae instauratae mechanica (1598), which describes his instruments and gives an account of the moon's variation.

Astronomicae instauratae progymnasmata (edited by Kepler, Prague, 1602-1603), which treats of 777 fixed stars and the motion of the sun and moon.

RHETICUS (George Joachim; 1514-1576). A German astronomer and mathematician whose original name was George Joachim. Studied at Tiguri with Oswald Mycone; appointed professor of mathematics at Wittenberg in 1537. Attracted by the new Copernican theory, he resigned the professorship, and in 1539 went to Frauenburg to study under Copernicus. It was through his enthusiasm that Copernicus was persuaded to complete his *De orbium celestium revolutionibus*. Died at Caesovica in Hungary. Wrote:

Opus Palatinum de triangulis (1576). Rheticus worked on this treatise until his death, giving the world the first detailed information on the new system. It was published by the mathematician Valentine Otho in 1596.

Narratio de libris revolutionum Copernici (1540)

Ephemerides (1551)

B. PITISCUS (1561-1613). Wrote:

Thesaurus mathematicus (1613) in which the sine table calculated to 15 places, which had been begun by Rheticus, was completed.

XLIII. PARACELSUS AND HIS SCHOOL

PARACELSUS (Theophrastus Bombast von Hohenheim; 1493-1541), born at Einseideln, died at Salzburg. Studied medicine in Germany, Italy, and France; and in 1526 became a professor and town physician at Basel. In 1528, he fled from Colmar because of a dispute in which he was concerned, and spent his time as an itinerant physician in southern Germany, Kärnten, and Salzburg. He builds his philosophy upon the neo-Platonism of Marsilius Ficinus. He wrote:

Naturphilosophie, a theosophical work in which the world is viewed as a living being, a macrocosm, as opposed to man, the microcosm. There are really three worlds: the earthly world of the elements, the heavenly world of the stars, and the spiritual or divine world.

Mensch, in which he shows how man reduplicates, on a smaller scale, the three worlds, in that man has a visible body of elements, an invisible astral body, or 'spiritus,' and a divine soul which comes from God and has its seat in the heart.

Medizin, in which he opposes Galen and Avicenna whose medical works he burned.

A. ELLINGER (d. 1582), professor at Jena

LEONARD THURNEYSSER (1530-1595)

PETER SEVERINUS (1542-1602), of Denmark. He wrote:
Idea medicinae philosophiae, (published in Hague, 1603)
Epistola scripta Theophrasto Paracelso, in qua ratio ordinis et nomina totiusque philosophiae adeptae methodus ostenditur.

JOHANNES BAPTISTA VAN HELMONT (1577-1644), born at Brussels, died at Vilvorde. Educated at Louvain, and took his doctor's degree in 1599. He was a disciple of Paracelsus and a mystic with strong leanings towards the supernatural; yet, on the other hand, he was touched with the new learning that produced such men as Harvey and Bacon. He was a careful observer of nature and an exact experimenter. He was the first to understand that there are gases distinct in kind from atmospheric air. He introduced a complicated system of supernatural agencies like the 'archei' of Paracelsus, which preside over and direct the affairs of the body. He wrote:
De magnetica vulnerum curatione (1621), in which van Helmont incurred the suspicion of some churchmen since it was thought to derogate from some of the miracles.

SEBASTIAN WIRDIG (1613-1687)

FRANZ MERCURIUS VAN HELMONT (1618-1699), born at Vilvorde, died at Berlin. He was a mystical theosopher and alchemist; son of Johannes Baptista van Helmont. Wrote:
Ortus medicinae, vel opera et opuscula omnia, (Amsterdam, 1668), the collected works of his father.
Cabbalah denudata (1677)
Opuscula philosophica (1690)

XLIV.   THE CUSANUS SCHOOL OF JACOBUS FABER

JACOBUS FABER (Faber Stapulensis, Jacques Lefèvre; 1455-1537). Born in Etaples in Picardy. Died at Nérac. Studied in Italy where he learned humanism. He received his master of arts degree from the Sorbonne, where he taught from about 1500 to 1517. Until 1520 he made an extensive study of the Bible at the monastery of St. Germain-des-Prés which was then just outside the southern walls of Paris. In 1520 he went to Meaux to his friend Guillaume Briçonnet II (1472-1534) who was abbot of St. Germain-des-Prés (from 1507) and bishop of Meaux (from 1516), and who had at first showed friendly interest in the protestant reformation. In Meaux he became associated with Wilhelm Farel, who became his pupil and later a reformer of western Switzerland. In 1525 the Sorbonne condemned 48 sentences taken from his *Epitres et evangiles des cinquante et deux dimanches de l'an* (1525). He fled to Strassburg where he became associated with Wolfgang Capito. King Francis I made him tutor of the king's son Charles at Blois. Later he went to Nérac where John Calvin visited him in 1534. He never separated from the Catholic Church. Among his writings are a French translation of the New Testament (1523), of the *Psalms* (1525) and of the remainder of the Old Testament (1528) ; Latin commentaries on the *Ethics* (Paris, 1496) and the first six books of the *Metaphysics* (Paris, 1505) of Aristotle, on the *Epistles* of St. Paul (1512), on the Catholic Epistles (1527) and on the Gospels (1522) ; and Latin translations of the Greek Fathers, notably Dionysius the Areopagite (1498) and John Damascene (1507). He also edited the works of Nicolaus Cusanus (Paris, 1514). He wrote also:

Theologia vivificans (Paris, 1498)

Quincuplex Psalterium, gallicum, romanum, hebraicum, vetus, conciliatum (Paris, 1509).

Propriorum recreatione (Paris, 1510)

Liber trium virorum et trium virginum (1513)

Accurata recognitio trium voluminum operum N. Cusae (Paris, 1514)

De Maria Magdalena et triduo Christi disceptatio (Paris, 1517)

De tribus et unica Magdalena disceptatio secundo (Paris, 1519)

Epitres et evangiles des cinquante et deux dimanches de l'an (Meaux, 1525).

JOSSE CLICHTHOVE OF NIEUPORT (Jodocus Clichtoveus; ca. 1472-1543). Born in Nieuport in Flanders. Began his studies at Louvain. Went to Paris for philosophical and theological studies, where he received his doctorate in theology in 1506. Was a disciple of Jacobus Faber. Appointed professor at the Sorbonne in 1506. In 1515 he began to direct the studies of Louis Guillard, bishop-elect of Tournai, first at Paris, then at Tournai. In 1527 he went with Guillard to Chartres whence the latter had been transferred. He became preacher in the cathedral there. His writings include commentaries on many Aristotelean treatises: logic, natural philosophy, ethics, arithmetic and geometry. He commented on several books of Scripture, and on some of the Fathers and Doctors of the Church. He wrote also:

De vera nobilitate opusculum (Paris, 1512)

Elucidatorium ecclesiasticum (Paris, 1516)

De vita et moribus sacerdotum (Paris, 1519)

Antilutherus (Paris, 1524)

Propugnaculum ecclesiae adversus Lutheranos (Paris, 1526)

De Sacramento Eucharistiae contra Oecolampadium (Paris, 1526)

Compendium veritatum ad fidem pertinentium contra erroneas Lutheranorum assertiones ex dictis et actis in concilio provinciali Senonensi apud Parisios celebrato (Paris, 1529)

Sermones (Paris, 1534)

Convulsio calumniarum Ulrichi Veleni quibus S. Petrum nunquam Romae fuisse cavillatur (Paris, 1535)

CAROLUS BOVILLUS (Charles Bouelles or Bouillé; ca. 1470-ca. 1553). Born in Sancourt in Picardy. Pupil of Jacobus Faber. Died at Noyon. Was one of the chief spreaders of the philosophy of Nicolaus Cusanus in France. He followed the mystical tendency of Cusanus, the concomitant theosophical rationalism, and the tendency in the Renaissance to view man as a microcosm. He wrote many mathematical, philosophical, philological and theological works, among them:

Liber de intellectu, de sensu, de nihilo, ars oppositorum, de generatione, de sapiente, liber aliquot epistolarum philosophicarum, published together in Paris, 1510.

Physicorum elementorum libri decem (Paris, 1512)

Libellus de constitutione et utilitate artium humanarum

JOHANNES STURM (1507-1589). Born in Schleiden in the Eifel. Attended the school of the Brethren of the Common Life in Lüttich, and later the University of Louvain. Went to Paris where he studied under Jacobus Faber. In 1529 became teacher in Paris, where he had Peter Ramus as a pupil and where he became protestant. Through Martin Bucer he was invited in 1537 to Strassburg as professor of classical languages. Wrote:

De literarum ludis recte aperiendis (Strassburg, 1538)

De emendatione ecclesiae (1538)

Partitionum dialecticarum libri IV (Strassburg, 1539), written before the principal works of Peter Ramus appeared.

Epistola apologetica (Newstadt, 1581), written against Jacobus Andreas.

XLV. THE SCHOOL OF JOHN MAYOR

JOHN MAYOR (Johannes Scotus Major; 1496-1550), born at Gleghornie in Scotland, died at St. Andrew's. He studied at Oxford, Cambridge, and Paris, and graduated as master of arts in the College of St. Barbe in 1494, and as doctor of theology in the College of Montaigu in 1505. He was professor of logic and theology at the University of Paris (1505-18), University of Glasgow (1518-23), University of St. Andrew's (1523-25), and again at the University of Paris (1525-1530). In 1530 he returned to St. Andrew's and was made provost of St. Salvator's College until his death. Among his pupils were the Scotch reformers, John Knox, Patrick Hamilton, and George Buchanan. He was the chief exponent of the nominalistic or terministic tendency, and, as a canonist, held that the chief ecclesiastical authority does not reside in the pope, but in the whole Church. He also held that the source of civil authority lies with the people who transfer it to the ruler and can wrest it from him, even by force, if necessary. Besides the Scotch reformers, his pupils included David Cranston of Glascow, Antonius Coronel and Gaspar Lax of Spain, and John Dullaert of Ghent. He wrote commentaries on the *Sentences* of Peter Lombard (1508) and on the *Physics* and *Ethics* of Aristotle (1526). Wrote also:

Historia majoris Britanniae, tam Angliae quam Scotiae (Paris, 1521), in which the author's spirit of independence is faithfully portrayed.

Introductiorum (Paris, 1508) a commentary on Aristotle's dialectics.

Questiones logicales (Paris, 1528) a commentary on the four Gospels.

JOHN DULLAERT (ca. 1471-1513), the Aristotelian commentator of whom Juan Luis Vives had such unpleasant recollections.

JOHN KNOX (ca. 1505-1572), born at Gifford, died in Edinburgh. He was educated at the University of Glasgow, being taught there by John Mayor. The time of his schooling and his earlier life is extremely vague, and no certain date is known of him until he registered under the Archbishop of St. Andrew's as a priest in 1543. A few years later, after he defended George Wishart, the reformer, he was teaching Protestantism in St. Andrew's. In 1547, St. Andrew's was captured by the French fleet, and Knox was interned for about two years. He was released under the influence of Edward VI of England, and in 1551 was made royal chaplain. Edward was succeeded by Mary Tudor, who exiled Knox in 1554. He went to Frankfort, but was expelled from there on a complaint of treason against the emperor Charles V. He went to Geneva, and with Christopher Goodman he began there the Puritan tradition. In 1555, he returned to Scotland and preached there for some time. In 1559, although the English crown had set a price on his head, he continued preaching, and at Perth and St. Andrew's his sermons were followed by the destruction of the monastaries. Knox advocated a freedom-of-conscience solution. In 1560, Knox and three others presented a confession of their Protestant faith. In planning this work he seems to have used his acquaintance with the *Ordonnances* of the Genevan Church under Calvin and the *Forma* of the German Church in London under John Laski. Mary Queen of Scots and her Catholic Lords forbade Knox to preach while she was in Edinburgh (1566). He preached at Stirling after Mary's abdication in 1567 at the coronation of the infant king. He wrote:

The History of the Reformation in Scotland, in which he incorporated his *Confession of the Protestant Faith* and the *Book of Discipline.* This history has been called Knox's autobiography.

On Predestination: an Answer to an Anabaptist (London, 1591)

On Prayer (1554)

On Affliction (1556)

A Godly letter sent to the Faithful in London, Newcastle, and Berwick.

A Faithful Admonition to the Proffessors of God's Faith in England.

The First Blast of the Trumpet against the Monstrous Regiment of Women (1558).

An Answer to a Scottish Jesuit (1572).

PATRICK HAMILTON (1504-1528), born in Lanarkshire, Scotland, burned at the stake in St. Andrew's. He studied in Paris, and graduated from the University in 1520. In 1521, he went to Louvain, where he listened to Erasmus. In 1523, he became a member of the University of St. Andrew's, and in 1524 he was admitted to its faculty of arts. In 1527, he fled from Scotland and went to Germany, visiting Luther at Wittenberg, and afterwards enrolling himself as a student, under Franz Lambert of Avignon, in the new University of Marburg. Late in 1527, he returned to Scotland, and was allowed to preach for a short time, but was accused of heresy and subsequently was burned at the stake. He wrote:

Loci communes (known as *Patrick's Places*) in which was set forth the doctrine of justification by faith and the contrast between the gospel and the law in a series of clear-cut propositions, for which he was executed.

GEORGE BUCHANAN (1506-1582), born in Killearn, Scotland, he died in Westminster. Educated at St. Andrew's University and the University of Paris. Became a member of the reformed faith, and for a time accompanied Govea, the Portuguese jurist who taught (1554-1555) at the University of Valence, to the University of Coimbra. In his religious views he was Protestant and while at Coimbra he was interned for being a heretic. He had a metrical version of the Psalms which he worked out while at Coimbra. He wrote two satires on the Franciscans and:

History of Scotland, written in Latin.

De Iure Regni, in which he states that the kings existed by the will of the people.

ANDREW MELVILLE (1545-1622), born near Montrose, Scotland, died at Sedan in France. He studied at the University of St. Andrew's, and in 1564, at the University of Paris. At the latter school he studied under Peter Ramus, whose philosophical method and plan of teaching he afterwards introduced into Scotland. In 1566 he studied civil law at Poitiers, and was made a regent in the college of St. Marceon. In 1574, Melville returned to Scotland, and received the appointment of principal of Glascow University, where he remodeled the educational system after a plan of his own. In 1575 he assisted in the reconstruction of Aberdeen University. In 1582 he took part in the organization of the Church and the Presbyterian method. In 1584, he was forced to flee Scotland when he had to escape imprisonment and probably a death penalty for a charge of treason arising from his prosecution of Bishop Robert Montgomery. He protected the liberties of the Scottish Church against all encroachments of the government. He spent the last eleven years of his life as a professor in the University of Sedan.

XLVI. THOMIST COMMENTATORS

PETER NIGRI (Schwarz; ca. 1434-ca. 1483) O.P., born at Kaaden. In 1452 he joined the Dominican order at Würzburg, following his brothers—Johannes, prior of Regensburg, and professor of theology at Ingolstadt; George, the provincial in Bohemia; and Nicolaus, the prior of Landshut. He studied at Montpellier, Salamanca, Freiburg, and Ingolstadt. He was a professor at

Ingolstadt in 1473 and 1474. In the latter year at Regensburg he preached and taught against the Jews. In 1481, he became rector of the University of Budapest, and there wrote his chief Thomistic works. He wrote commentaries on Porphyry. Wrote also:

Tractatus contra Judaeos (Esslingen, 1475), his Regensburg sermons.

Stern des Messias (Esslingen, 1477), an enlargement of his *Tractatus.*

Clipeus Thomistarum (Venice, 1481), which is called by some 'the most important philosophico-historic work of the time.'

PAUL SONCINAS (Paulus Barbus, Lombardei; d. 1494), O.P., died at Cremona. He was a professor at Milan, Ferrara, and Bologna, and was on friendly terms with Pico della Mirandola. He became well known through his Aristotelian and Thomistic commentaries and his commentary on the *Isagoge* of Porphyry. Most of his works however have been lost. He wrote:

Quaestiones super divina sapientia Aristotelis

Epitoma quaestionum in 4 libris sententiarum a Joanno Capreolo disputatarum

Quaestiones metaphysicales

JOHANNES A LAPIDE (Johann von Stein, Johann Heynlin; ca. 1430-1496); born at Pforzheim, died at Basel. He studied in Leipzig from 1448 to 1452, Louvain in 1453, and Paris from 1454 to 1464. He received a master of arts degree in 1455, and a bachelor of theology degree in 1464 from the University of Paris mainly because of his realistic tendencies. In 1464, he was appointed a professor at the University of Basel against the wishes of the faculty, and there, because of his equal rights with the others, was able to profess his realism. In 1465, along with Peter von Andlaw, he composed new university statutes. In 1467 he returned to Paris where he taught theology. In 1468 and in 1470 he was a prior of Sorbonne, and in 1469 was a rector of the University. In 1472 he was named a Doctor of Theology. He was a person of high morals, profoundly religious in character, and an untiring fighter for reform in the spirit of the Church. He wrote a commentary on the *Organon* of Aristotle. Wrote also:

Resolutorium dubiorum circa celebrationem missarum occurentium

De exponibilibus

FRANCISCUS TAEGIUS. He wrote:

A commentary on St. Thomas's opusculum *De fallaciis.*

MICHAEL SAVARETIUS. He defended Thomism against Scotism. He wrote:

Quaestiones de analogia contra scotistas
Quaestiones de universalibus
De primis et secundis intentionibus

DOMINIC OF FLANDERS (d. 1500) O.P. He was a master of theology. Taught at Bologna ca. 1470, and from 1478 to 1480 he was head of theological study in Florence. He was a well-known Aristotelian commentator. Like Köllin and Crockart he was a rigorous Thomist, and combated the Nominalists and Scotists. He was acquainted with Antonius of Florence and Hervӓus Brito. He wrote commentaries on the *Metaphysics,* the *Posterior Analytics,* and the *De Anima* of Aristotle. Wrote also:

Summa divinae philosophiae, taking Thomas Aquinas as his guide.

MARTIN POLLICH (d. 1513). Taught at Wittenberg. He commented on Thomist logic.

ERASMUS WONSIDEL. Professor at the University of Leipzig. He commented on the Thomist logic as did Pollich.

BARTHOLOMAEUS MARZOLUS, O.P. He attacked the logic of Paulus Venetus with Thomist arguments. He wrote:

Dubium super logicam P. Veneti

CHRYSOSTOMUS JAVELLI (Chrysostomus of Casale; ca. 1470-ca. 1538) O.P., died at Bologna. He followed the Aristotelian and Thomistic interpretations of Cajetan and Capreolus. He wrote about the immortality of the soul, contrary to the opinions of Pomponatius, and he was against the exaggerated theory of predestination of Luther. He engaged in a long controversy with the Scotist Antonius Trombeta. He wrote:

Totius rationalis, naturalis, divinae ac moralis philosophiae compendium

THOMAS DE VIO CAJETAN (1469-1534), O.P., born at Gaeta in Naples. In 1485 he entered the Dominican order, and studied at the university of Padua from 1491 to 1494, and taught metaphysics at that university. He was at Brescia from 1497 to 1500. In 1508 he became general of his order, and in 1517 he was made cardinal of Palermo. In 1518 he went as a papal legate to Germany to quiet the revolt of Luther. He was considered as one of the foremost defenders of the Thomistic school. He is said to have retained the best elements of the humanist revival in harmony with the Catholic orthodoxy, enlightened by a revived appreciation of the Augustinian doctrine of justification. Cajetan taught that the harmony of free choice and divine providence seems inexplicable and unintelligible in this life. Cajetan and Sylvester Ferrarensis hold the same view as Suarez that the intelligible habits are real habits distinct from the intelligible species. He wrote a commentary on the *De anima* of Aristotle (Florence, 1509), in which he abandons the position of St. Thomas Aquinas and contends that Aristotle had not taught the individual immortality of the human soul; he says that the doctrine of individual immortality is philosophically erroneous. He wrote also commentaries on the *Categories* and the *Posterior analytics* of Aristotle; on the *De ente et essentia* of St. Thomas Aquinas, in which he opposed Averroism; and on the *Summa theologica* of St. Thomas Aquinas (Rome, 1507-1522), his chief work. He wrote also:

De analogia nominum

De sensu agente et sensibilibus

CONRAD KÖLLIN (Cölln; ca. 1476-1536), O.P., studied in Ulm and Heidelberg and joined the Dominicans in 1492. He was prior in Heidelberg (ca. 1507) and professor at the University (ca. 1507-1511). He was a professor at Cologne from 1511, and director of studies of his order from 1511 to 1536. He was one of seven Dominicans who distinguished themselves in the struggle against Luther in Cologne. (The others were Jacob von Hoogstraten, Johann Host, Bernard von Luxemburg, Johann Pesselius, Tillman Soneling and Johann Slotanus.) He wrote a commentary on the *Summa theologica*, I-II, of St. Thomas Aquinas (Cologne, 1512), which was the first commentary on the *Summa* printed. He wrote also:

Quodlibeta XXVII per modum dialogi (Cologne, 1523)

Eversio Lutherani Epithalamii (Cologne, 1527)

Adversus caninas Martini Lutheri nuptias (Tübingen, 1530)

PETER CROCKART OF BRUSSELS (d. 1514), O.P.; he studied in Paris at the College of Montaigu where he was a pupil of the Ockhamist, John Mayor. Became a professor of philosophy in Paris when many Flemish people came to Paris, and he reformed the cloister of St. Jacques. In 1503 he became a Dominican. He taught Francisco de Vittoria. He wrote commentaries on various works of Aristotle, a commentary on the *De ente et essentia* of St. Thomas, a commentary on the *Summa Theologica* of St. Thomas, which, in 1509, was one of the first explanations of the *Summa*. Wrote also:

Quodlibeta

FRANCISCUS SYLVESTER FERRARENSIS (Francesco Ferraris, Sylvester Francis; 1474-1528), O.P., born at Ferrara, died at Rennes. He joined the Dominican order in 1488, and in 1510 was made a master of theology. He was a prior both in Ferrara and Bologna. In 1519 he was appointed vicar-general of the Lombard congregation of his order. He was a regent of the college at Bologna. In 1525 he was made the master general of his order. He wrote a commentary on the *Summa contra gentiles* of St. Thomas Aquinas (Paris, 1522) and commentaries on various books of Aristotle. Wrote also:

Apologia de convenientia institutorum Romanae Ecclesiaecum evangelica libertate (Rome, 1525), in which he defended the primacy and the organization of the Church against Luther.

XLVII. WRITERS OF SUMMARIES OF ST. THOMAS

CLEMENS DE TERRA SALSA (fl. 1486), he wrote:
Conclusiones formales (Cologne, 1486), an abbreviation of St. Thomas' *Summa theologica.*

JEROME DUNGERSHEYM (1465-1540), born at Ochsenfurt, died at Leipzig. He entered the University of Leipzig in 1483, and received a master of arts degree in 1489. He began his theological studies in 1493, and became professor in the faculty of philosophy at Leipzig in 1499. From 1501 to 1504 he lectured in Zwickau. He then went to Italy and received degrees in theology and canon law at Bologna and Siena. In 1506 he was appointed professor of theology at Leipzig, and of canon law at Zeitz. He published various works on practical and speculative theology. He was one of the first opponents of the Lutheran reformation in Saxony. He published a book on methods of preaching and drew up the 'conclusions' of the *Summa*. He wrote:

Aliqua opuscula (1531), seven Latin and ten German selections against Martin Luther.

De modo discendi et docendi ad populum sacra seu de modo praedicandi (1513), in which he treats of his subject on three points, the preacher, the sermon and the listener. He lays stress on Scripture as the book of the preacher.

SYLVESTER MAZZOLINI (Prierias; 1460-1523), born at Priero, Piedmont, died at Rome. In 1475 he entered the Order of St. Dominic. He was a brilliant student of philosophy and theology, and taught the latter at Bologna, Pavia, and in Rome, being called to the latter place by Pope Julius II in 1511.

In 1515 he was appointed Master of the Sacred Palace, holding that office until his death. His numerous works include treatises on the planets, the power of the demons, history, homiletics, the works of St. Thomas Aquinas, the primacy of the popes. He is credited with being the first theologian who by his wrtinigs attacked the subversive errors of Martin Luther. A controversy arose, as a result of Mazzolini's stand, between himself and Luther. He wrote:

De juridica et irrefragabili veritate Romanae Ecclesiae Romanique Pontificis (Rome, 1520)

Epitoma responsionis ad Lutherum (Perugia, 1519)

Errata et argumenta M. Lutheri (Rome, 1520)

Summa Summarum, quae Sylvestrina dicitur (Rome, 1516)

Rosa aurea (Bologna, 1510), an exposition of the Gospels of the year.

In theoricas planetarum (Venice, 1513)

BERARD BONGEAN (d. 1574); made a summary of the works of St. Thomas.

LUKE CARBONI (d. 1597); he wrote:
Compendium absolutissimum (1587), on St. Thomas.

HUNNAEUS (d. 1578); he wrote:
S. Thomae totius summae conclusiones

JOHN OF OCHOA (d. post 1565), O.P., he wrote:
Primariae conclusiones, of the works of St. Thomas.

XLVIII. OCCUPANTS OF THE CATHEDRA DE PRIMA IN THE UNIVERSITY OF SALAMANCA

FRANCISCO DE VITTORIA (1483/6-1546), O.P. Born at Salamac, Vittoria, in Navarre. He was a Dominican priest, under whose leadership there was a renewal of interest in the writings of St. Thomas Aquinas. He taught at the University of Salamanca from 1526-1544. Vittoria was a forerunner of Grotius in the study of international law. As regards the law of nations, he maintained that the Pope's authority was limited to religious matters, that the right to life, liberty, and property could not be denied to the pagans beyond the Atlantic because of their unbelief, that the noncombatants: children, women, farmers, strangers, and clergy, should not be slaughtered in war, that slavery was not a legitimate consequence of war, that hostages could not rightfully be put to death on a breach of faith by an enemy, and that looting was unlawful. He had sympathies for Erasmus, though he exposed him. Among his disciples were Melchior Canus, Martin of Ledesmo and Andreas of Tudela.

Reflectiones XII theologicae
Summa sacramentorum ecclesiae
Instruction refugio del alma
Confesionario
Commentaria in universam Summam St. Thomae

MELCHIOR CANUS (1509-1560), O.P. The first professor at Alcala, followed his teacher Victoria in the *cathedra de prima* at Salamanca (1546-1552). Among his pupils were Bartholomew of Medina, Dominic Bañez, and Louis de Leon. He wrote a commentary on the *Summa theologica* of St. Thomas Aquinas, and
De locis theologicis, in which he gives a scheme for the reform of theology and philosophy.

DOMINIC DE SOTO (1494-1560), O.P.; taught philosophy and theology at Burgos until 1532. Then he taught with Francisco de Vittoria at Salamanca where he later (1552-1560) occupied the *cathedra de prima*. Thomism was the basis of his philosophy but he was also influenced by terminism which was taught by Paulus Pergulensis (d. 1451), Gabriel Biel (1425-1495), and John Major (1478-1540). He believed that the three schools of thought were about alike and differed in few respects. He taught that it did not really matter whether one holds or rejects the real distinction between essence and existence, as long as existence is held to be the essence of God and not of creatures. He was among the theologians who commented on the *Summa theologica* of St. Thomas Aquinas. Also commented on Aristotle's *Physics* and *Categories*.

PEDRO DE SOTOMAYOR (d. 1564), O.P. Occupied the *cathedra de prima* at Salamanca, 1560-1564.

JOANNES MANCIO DE CORPORE CHRISTI (1497-1576), O.P. Occupied the *cathedra de prima* at Salamanca, 1564-1576. Disciple of Francisco de Vittoria, and a contemporary of Melchior Canus. Wrote:
Cronica de San Mancio

BARTHOLOMEW OF MEDINA (Barthelemi; 1528-1581), O.P. Occupied the *cathedra de prima* at Salamanca, 1576-1580. He introduced the opinion concerning probability. Wrote commentaries on St. Thomas Aquinas, and: *Instructions on the Sacrament of Penance*

DOMINICUS BAÑEZ (1528-1604), O.P. Theologian born in the Spanish province of Biscaya and died at Medina del Campo. He made rapid progress in philosophy and theology at the University of Salamanca where he had as teachers the famous Melchior Canus and Peter and Dominic de Soto. In 1581 he was appointed to the *cathedra de prima* in this university, which was then dividing honors and prestige with the Sorbonne. He took a prominent part in the controversy on divine grace, predestination, etc., in which he opposed the theories of Molina. For several years he acted as confessor to Saint Theresa. He was recognized as one of the most acute interpreters of the *Summa theologica* of St. Thomas Aquinas, and his chief works were commentaries on the same.

XLIX. MATHEMATICIANS

TARTAGLIA (the Stammerer, Nicolo of Brescia; ca. 1499-1557). Born at Brescia, died at Venice. Being too poor to pay tuition he gained a knowledge of Latin, Greek, and mathematics by his own aggressiveness. Taught at Verona, 1521. The most comprehensive rules for duplicating a cube, trisecting an angle, and dividing a sphere in a given proportion by means of an intersecting plane are accredited to him. By the application of these rules he was the victor in a mathematical contest of methods with Antonio del Fiore. His methods were printed by Girolamo Cardan who learned them in confidence from Tartaglia, whom he betrayed. Many of Tartaglia's other writings deal with contemporary problems in commercial arithmetic. He was professor of Euclid at Brescia for eighteen years, after which time he returned to Venice. Wrote:

Nuova scienza, dealt with methods of gunnery (Venice, 1537).

Quiestiti ed invenzoni Diverse, included problems in balistics and fortifications (Venice, 1551).

Regola generale per solevare ogni affondata Nave, intitolata la Travagliata Invenzione (Venice, 1551)

Ragionamenti sopra la Travagliata Invenzione (Venice, 1551)

Trattato de arithmetica (Venice, 1556)

Trattato generale de numeri e misure (Venice, two parts in 1556, four parts in 1560)

Opera del famossissimo Nicolo Tartaglia (Venice, 1616)

FRIAR LUCA PACIOLI. The remarkable shortening of the solutions of algebraic problems made possible by the use of abbreviations for the unknown quantity and its powers and for the words plus, minus, etc., was exemplified in the works of Pacioli. Pacioli, however, did not reach the stage, represented by modern algebra, where symbolic statements take the place of ordinary prose sentences. Wrote:
Summa (1494)

MICHAEL STIFEL (1486-1567). Born in Esslingen and educated in the monastery there. Become a Lutheran clergyman. He revived the practice of denoting unknown quantities by arbitrary letters of the alphabet. He represented the unknown and its successive powers by the current symbols R for res or radix (x), Z for zensus (x^2), C for cubus (x^3), etc. Stifel also occasionally represented powers by repeating the unknown the requisite number of times, e.g., writing it twice for a square, three times for a cube, and so on —a practice revived by Harriot at the beginning of the seventeenth century. He also did some work with the mystic numbers, being attracted principally by the part they play in the *Apocalypse* and in *Daniel.* Wrote:
Arithmetica integra

GIROLAMO CARDAN OF MILAN (1501-1576). Contemporary and colleague of Tartaglia. It is said that he learned Tartaglia's methods of Cubes from him in confidence, and betrayed that confidence by making them public in 1545. Cardan's chief contributions to algebra were related to the theory of equations. He paid attention to negative and imaginary roots of equations. He also anticipated certain relations between the roots and the coefficients of equations more clearly formulated later, and he did some pioneer work on probability. He wrote:
Practica arithmeticae generalis
Artis magnae sive de reulis algebra liber unus, a comprehensive treatise on algebra which appeared at Nurenberg in 1545. It was in this work that he published the solution to cubic equations discovered by Tartaglia.
De vita propria, Cardan's autobiography.

ROBERT RECORDE (ca. 1510-1558). Welsh physician and mathematician. Studied at Oxford (1525-1531), and later medicine at Cambridge where he received his M.D. degree in 1545. The author of many works on mathematics notably:

The Whetstone of Witte (1557), which is the first English treatise on algebra.

CUTHBERT TONSTALL (1474-1559). He studied at Oxford, Cambridge, and Padua, and drew freely from the works of Pacioli and Regiomontanus. Reprints of his arithmetic appeared in England and France.

FRANCOIS VIETA (Franciscus Vieta, 1540-1603). A French mathematician. Was born in 1540 at Fontenay-le-Comte, in Poitou. Vieta was brought up as a Catholic and died at Catholic, but there is definite proof he belonged to the Huguenots for several years. On completion of his studies in law at Poitiers, Vieta began his career as an advocate in his native town. This he left in 1567, and somewhat later we find him at Rennes as a councillor of the parlement of Brittany. The relígious troubles drove him thence, and Rohan, the well-known chief of the Huguenots, took him under his special protection. He recommended him in 1580 as a master of requests; and Henry of Navarre, at the request of Rohan, wrote two letters to Henry III of France to have him restored to his former position, but without result. When Henry of Navarre ascended the throne, Vieta served as councillor of the parlement at Tours. He afterwards became a royal privy councillor and remained so till his death, which took place very suddenly in Paris. His fame, however, rests entirely upon his achievements in mathematics. Being a man of wealth, he printed at his own expense the numerous papers which he wrote on various branches of the science and communicated them to scholars in almost every country in Europe. He wrote:

Isagoge in artem analyticam (1591)

Recensio canonica effectionum geometricarum, which consists of what we now term algebraic geometry.

Apollonius Gallus (1600)

Opera mathematica, a collection of Vieta's works issued by F. van Schooten at Leiden in 1646.

CHRISTOPHORUS CLAVIUS (1538-1612), S.J. He was born at Bamburg in Bavaria, and died at Rome. Entered the Society of Jesus in 1555. While in school he showed great talent for mathematics at Coimbra. Became teacher of mathematics at the Roman College. Taught there till his death. He was the teacher of Grienberger and Blacanus. Was called the 'Euclid of the 16th century.' Scientific opponents, it was said, would rather be censored by

Clavius than praised by another man. Towards the end of his life he re-issued his writings at Mainz in five volumes under the title of:

Christophori Clavii e Societate Jesu opera mathematica, quinque tomis distributa
> Volume I: contains the *Euclidis Elementorum libri XV*, and the *Sphaericorum libri III* of Theodosius
> Volume II: the *Geometria practia* and the algebra
> Volume III: contains the *Commentorius in Sphaeram Joannis de Sacro Bosco* and a dissertation on the astrolabe.
> Volume IV: contains a detailed discussion on gnomonics, the art of constructing all possible sun-dials.
> Volume V: contains *Romani calendarii a Gregorio XIII restituti explicatio* (Rome, 1603); *Novi calendarii Romani apologia adversus M. Maestlinum in Tumbingensi Academia mathematicorum* (Rome, 1588).

L. ANIMAL BEHAVIOR

EDWARD WOTTON (1492-1555), born at Oxford. Studied medicine in Oxford, and developed a wide and distinguished practice. He formed a division of the animal kingdom that is Aristotelian in nature. He criticizes many of the animals that his classical predecessor invented, but he has nothing to say about the new animal forms which explorers of his century brought home with them. He contributed much information regarding the medicines which may be extracted from the various animal forms. As a profound exponent of Aristotle and representative of his ideas, Wotten was influential on his age. He wrote:
De differentiis animalium, in which he shows himself a faithful follower of Aristotle, whom he imitates both in his method of classification and in the field of anatomy.

GUILLAUME RONDELET (1507-1556), born in Montpellier and died in the same city. He studied first in his own district and then in Italy, where he became acquainted with Ulisse Aldrovandi. He established an anatomical theatre and acted as a teacher there until he died. He wrote:
De piscibus marinis, in which he gives a number of particulars which are sometimes at variance with Aristotle.

ANDREAS VESALIUS (b. 1514/15). He was born at Brussels and died some time after 1564 when he made a trip to the East from which he never returned. In 1532 he went to Paris to study medicine but left in three years and went to Italy. In Venice he increased both his learning and reputation, and at the age of twenty-two he was appointed professor at the University of Padua. He was a follower of Galen, but when he realized that Galen's doctrines were not entirely exact he performed experiments, and as a result, he formed the modern science of anatomy. The followers of Galen, and Vesalius' teacher, Sylvius, were enraged at his expressions. As a result of his turn from Galen, he also swerved from Aristotle. He wrote:

De humani corporis fabrica (Basel, 1543) and a compendium of the same, Epitome (Basel, 1543), in which he disputed Galen.

KONRAD GESNER (1516-1565), born and died at Zurich. He studied at Basel, Paris, and Montpellier, acquiring a knowledge of classical and oriental languages, natural science, and medicine. He was professor of Greek in Lausanne, and later was appointed first town-physician at Zurich. He wrote:

Historia animalium which includes an arrangement of animals according to the principles of Aristotle. Among these principles are found 'the qualities of the soul' and 'poetical and philosophical speculations about the animal, anecdotes and resemblances to be found in different authors.'

ULISSE ALDROVANDI (1522-1605), born and died at Bologna. He studied jurisprudence in Bologna and then philosophy and medicine at Padua and Rome. In 1560 he was made professor at Bologna, where he worked for forty years. He followed Gesner and Aristotle in his writings and teachings.

HIERONYMUS FABRICIUS (Geronimo Fabrizio; 1537-1619), born at Asquapendente, Italy, and died at Venice. He studied under Fallopio and succeeded him as professor in 1565. He employed a comparative method in the study of embryology and in other fields of anatomy. He also studied the noises of animals, which led him to make an interesting attempt at animal psychology.

BARTOLOMMEO EUSTACCHI (d. 1574). Little is known of his early life, but in the middle of the sixteenth century he was practicing as a physician in Rome and then as a professor at a papal medical academy. He made important investigations of the ear—the Eustachian tube still bears his name —and also studied blood circulation and dental development of the embryo. He wrote:

Anatomical Engravings, which was not printed until long after his death, and consequently of no use, but some say that if it had been printed when he was alive, anatomical research would be about two centuries ahead of what it now is.

Opuscula anatomica, which contains his investigation of the auditory organ.

CONSTANZO VAROLIO (1543-1575), born at Bologna. He carried out important investigations into the nervous system; the 'pons Varolii' in the brain is named after him.

MARC' AURELIO SEVERINO (1580-1656), born in south Italy. He came at an early age to Naples, where he studied the humanistic sciences and philosophy under Campanella. He soon devoted his time to the study of medicine and was appointed professor of anatomy and surgery at Naples. He had a keen dislike for Aristotle, a feeling which he got from his studies under Campanella. Although he refuted Aristotelian doctrine, he did not create a new conception of natural phenomena in place of that of Aristotle. He wrote:

Zootomia democritea, which testifies to Severino's antipathy to Aristotle.

LI.   ITALIAN NATURALISM

GIROLAMO FRACASTORO (Hieronymus Fracastorius; 1483-1553), born at Verona, died at Casi. He was Italian physician and poet and was skilled in most of the arts and sciences. He studied at Padua, and in 1502 became a professor of philosophy there. He was friendly with Cardinal Bembo, Julius Scaliger, Gianbattista Ramusio, and other famous men of the time. He took the same view as Leonardo da Vinci, concerning the possibility of fossils—that they were the remains of animals once living in the locality. He wrote:

Syphilidis, sive morbi Gallici, libri tres (Verona, 1530)

De vini temperatura (Venice, 1534)

Homocentricorum (Venice, 1535)

De sympathia et antipathia rerum (Venice, 1546)

De contagionibus (Venis, 1546)

JULIUS CAESAR SCALIGER (1484-1558), born at Verona, died at Agen. He preferred a soldier's life in his earlier days to the study of philosophy and art. He was tutored in the latter by Albrecht Dürer. In 1514 he entered the University of Bologna. He studied medicine and in 1525, he went to Agen as a physician. It cannot be contended that he anticipated in any manner the inductive philosophy. His botanical studies did not lead him to a natural system of classification, and he rejected the discoveries of Copernicus. He followed Aristotle in metaphysics and natural history, and Galen in medicine. He was considered by Leibnitz as the best modern exponent of the physics and metaphysics of Aristotle. He wrote commentaries on Theophrastus' *De causis plantarum* and Aristotle's *Historia animalium*. Wrote also:

Exercitationes exotericae ad Cardani libros XV de subtilitate (Basle, 1557), a refutation of the teachings of Cardan.

De causis linguae Latinae, a Latin grammar.

Poetice (1561)

GIROLAMO CARDAN (Hieronimo Cardano; 1501-1576), born at Pavia, died at Rome. He graduated in medicine from the University of Padua. After some discussion he was admitted into the College of Physicians at Milan in 1539. He corresponded with Nicolo Tartaglia, who discovered a solution of cubic equations, and in spite of his promise to Tartaglia, Cardan divulged the discovery in a treatise on algebra. He was a believer in astrology. In 1547 he was appointed professor of medicine at Pavia. In 1551 he served as the medical advisor of Archbishop Hamilton of St. Andrews, Scotland. He accepted a professorship at Bologna in 1562, but was soon arrested on the charge of heresy. He was released from prison under the influence of high church officials, and spent the rest of his years in Rome in receipt of a pension from the pope. He wrote:

Practica arithmeticae generalis

Artis magnae sive de regulis algebrae liber unus (Nüremberg, 1545), a comprehensive treatise on algebra in which the discovery of Tartaglia was disclosed.

De subtilitate rerum (1551) and *De Varietate Rerum* (1557), which are usually considered as one book. Much of these works is an explanation of ordinary natural phenomena, but the chief interests lie in the hints of principles beyond his comprehension, and which the world was then by no means able to attain.

De vita propria is his autobiography.

BERNARDINO TELESIO (1509-1588), born at Cosenza near Naples. He was educated at Milan, Rome, and Padua, studying the classics, science, and philosophy. He attacked Aristotelianism which was flourishing at that time in Padua and Bologna. He was the head of a great South Italian movement, protesting the authority of abstract reason. Instead of postulating matter and form, he bases existence on matter and force, the latter having two opposing elements: heat which expands, and cold, which contracts. He said that the soul is influenced by material conditions; consequently the soul must have a material existence. He held that knowledge is sensation, and that intelligence is a collection of isolated data, given by the senses. The whole system of Telesio shows breaks in argument and ignorance of essential facts, but at the same time it is a forerunner of empiricism, scientific and philosophical. He wrote:

De rerum natura (1563 or 1565)
De his quae in aere fiunt
De cometis et circulo lacteo

FRANCESCO PATRIZZI (Franciscus Patritius; 1529-1597), born at Clissa in Dalmatia, and died in Rome. He was appointed to the chair of philosophy at Ferrara, and was soon invited to Rome by Pope Clement VIII. He found time to make a study of contemporary science in spite of his Aristotelian controversies. In his philosophy he was mainly concerned to defend Plato against the followers of Aristotle. He wrote:

New geometry (1587), a treatise in 15 books.
Discussionum peripateticorum libri XV (Basel, 1571)
Nova de universis philosophia (Basel, 1591)

GIORDANO BRUNO (ca. 1548-1600), O.P., born near Nola, and burned at the stake for heresy at Rome. Became a Dominican at Naples in 1563. He left Italy and lectured on philosophy at Toulouse, and arrived at Paris in 1581. He wrote a number of logical treatises at Marburg and Wittenberg in 1586, and several important metaphysical works at Frankfurt. He rejected the Aristotelian astronomy for that of Copernicus, which allowed for the possibility of innumerable worlds. He said that amid all the varying phenomena of the universe there is something which gives coherence and intelligibility to them, and this something is God. Among his works the following might be mentioned:

De umbris idearum (1581)
Ars memoriae (1581)
De compendiosa architectura et complemento artis Lulii (1581)
Cantus Circaeus (1581)
Cena de la Ceneri (1583), a criticism of English social life and an exposition of the Copernican theory.
Universo e mondi (1583), metaphysical works.

Spaccio della Bestia Tronfante (1583), an allegory treating of moral philosophy and expressing his opposition to religion.

De triplici minimo et mensura (1590)

De monade, numero, et figura (1590)

De immenso et innumerabilibus (1590)

TOMMASO CAMPANELLA (1568-1639), O.P., born at Stilo in Calabria. Entered the Dominican order in 1583. He studied philosophy in the convent at Morgentia in Abruzzo, and theology at Cosenza. His first philosophical work was a defense of Telesio. In 1599 he was imprisoned, and remained there for twenty-seven years. He went to Paris in 1634, where he became acquainted with Cardinal Richelieu. He considered philosophy as based on perception. To him the all important fact of philosophy was the certainty of individual consciousness, to which he assigned power, will, and knowledge. In natural philosophy, Campanella advocates the experimental method, and lays down heat and cold as the fundamental principles. In political philosophy he expresses an ideal communism. He is one of the beginners of empirical science. He wrote:

Philosophia sensibus demonstrata (1591), the defense of Telesio.

Civitas solis, on political economy.

De monarchia Hispanica, an account of contemporary politics.

De sensu rerum et magia

Apologia pro Galileo

Universalis philosophia

LII. REFORMERS OF SWITZERLAND

ULRICH ZWINGLI (1484-1531). Swiss reformer born at Wildhaus in Tannenburg valley, in the canton of St. Gall. Went to Vienna to study philosophy in 1500. In 1502 studied at Basel, and in 1519 went to Zurich. Escaped the plague of 1519. Broke with the Church, 1522. Differed from Luther in that he believed in the salvation of infants and pious heathens. Guiding principle of his philosophy is the absolute and unlimited sovereignty of God. Denied man's free will. Did not view the sacrament of the Lord's Supper as a repetition of the sacrifice of Christ but as a faithful remembrance that the sacrifice had been made once and for all. Believed in self-government in both civil and ecclesiastical orders. To Zwingli the true source of learning lay in the Scriptures which had supreme authority. Denounced the worship of images and the Catholic doctrine of the Mass. Preached against fasting, celibacy, and the veneration of Saints. Wrote:

Von Erkiesen und Fryheit der Spysen (1522)

De canone missae epichiresis (1523)

Commentarius de vera et falsa religione (1525)

Vom Touf, vom Wiedertouf, und vom Kindertouf (1525)

Ein klare Unterrichtung vom Nachtmal Christi (1526)

De providentia Dei (1530)

Christianae fidei expositio (1531)

Sixty-Seven Articles of Zurich (1523), published by a number of his associates.

Ten Theses of Bern (1528)

JOHN CALVIN (1509-1564). Protestant reformer. Born at Noyan, France. Studied law but later became interested in theological studies. Fled France because of his views and settled in Switzerland in 1536. His dominant thought is the sovereignty of God. He maintains that while God is all good man is corrupt and evil, and every movement of man towards the good proceeds directly from God. Believed man to be essentially bad. The five points of Calvinism are: (1) election; (2) redemption; (3) bondage of will; (4) grace; (5) perseverance of the Saints. Wrote:

Christianae religionis institutio (1536)

Commentaires sur la concordance ou harmonie des Evangelistes

In novum Testamentum commentarii

In libros Psalmorum commentarii

In librum Geneseos

WOLFGANG CAPITO (Köpfel; Fabricius; 1478-1541). Born in Hagenau in Alsace. Entered the University of Ingolstadt in 1505. Became bachelor at Freiburg the same year, and master at Ingolstadt in 1506/07. Received his licentiate in theology at Ingolstadt in 1511 and his doctorate of canon law after 1520. Preacher in several places between 1511 and 1520. Professor of theology in Basle, 1520-1523. Took an ecclesiastical position in Strassburg, became associated with Martin Bucer and was soon a significant force in the reformation in Alsace and more especially in Switzerland. Died in Strassburg.

WILHELM FAREL (1489-1565). Born at Gap (Dauphiné). Became the pupil of Jacobus Faber in Meaux. Member of the circle of Guillaume Briconnet II, who was bishop of Meaux. Fled from France to Basle where he became associated with Johann Ökolampadius (1482-1531) and learned the teachings of Ulrich Zwingli. Entered into dispute with Erasmus of Rotterdam and then became a wandering preacher of the reformation in western Switzerland, settling finally in Neuchatel (Neuenburg) where he died. His correspondence constitutes his chief writing.

LIII. REFORMERS OF GERMANY

MARTIN LUTHER (1483-1546). Leader of the religious revolt in Germany. Luther attended a Latin school at Mansfield. At 14 years of age (1497) he attended a school at Magdeburg and the next year he went to Eisenach. In 1501 he entered the University of Erfurt where he received the degree of bachelor of philosophy. He studied philosophy under Jodocus Trutwetter von Eisenach and Bartholomaus Arnoldi von Usingen. Luther entered the Augustinian monastery at Erfurt in 1505, and was ordained in 1507. In 1508 he began teaching philosophy and dialectics at the University of Wittenberg. In 1510 he made a pilgrimage to Rome. In 1512 advanced to the doctorate and was admitted to the faculty of theology at the University of Wittenberg. In 1517 he nailed 95 theses on the church door. By 1520 he had made a distinct break with the church and when 41 sentences taken from his works were condemned as heretical the same year he burned the papal bull and other works in Wittenberg. He aligned himself with powerful nobles and in other ways spread his opposition to the Pope. Philosophically he was opposed to Aristotle. His attitude towards theology was as follows: The Bible is the only source of faith; human nature has been totally corrupted by original sin, and man accordingly, is deprived of free will. Whatever he does, be it good or bad, is not his own work, but God's. Faith alone can work justification and man is saved by confidently believing that God will pardon him. This faith not only includes a full pardon of sin, but also an unconditional release from its penalties. The hierarchy and priesthood are not divinely instituted or necessary. There is no visible church or one specifically established by God whereby men may work out their salvation. All sacraments with the exception of baptism, Holy Eucharist and penance are rejected. His numerous writings include the following:

An den Adel deutscher Nation von des christl. Standes Besserung (1520)
De captivitate Babylonica ecclesiae praeludium (1520)
Von der Freiheit eines Christen menschen (1520)

De servo arbitrio (1525), an answer to Desiderius Erasmus's *Diatribe de libero arbitrio* (1524)
Wider das Bapstum zu Rom vom Teufel gestifft (1545), concerning the convoking of the Council of Trent (1545-1563).

THOMAS MÜNZER (1489-1525); born in Stolberg (Harz). Studied in Leipzig and in Frankfurt a. O. Became acquainted with Luther in 1519. Influenced by Luther, Tauler, Hus, and Joachim of Fiora, he gave up his priestly work and became a Lutheran in 1520. He was very influential in preaching social changes. He hoped to construct a Christian Communism. Led a military group during the religious wars and was put to death.

JOHANN ÖKOLAMPAD (Ökolampadius, Husschyn, Heussgen; 1482-1531). Born in Weinsberg in Württemberg. Studied law at Bologna, and beginning in 1499 pursued humanist and theological studies at Heidelberg where he became bachelor of arts in 1503. Studied theology (1513-1515) in Stuttgart where he heard Reuchlin, and in Tübingen where he met Melancthon in 1513. At Heidelberg he studied Hebrew with a baptized Jew. In 1518 he became a doctor of theology in Basle. He was influenced by Capito and Melancthon; he took part in many of the religious disputes. His letters and sermons are important.

MARTIN BUCER (Butzer; 1491-1551). Educated in his native Schlettstadt in Alsace. In 1506 he entered the Order of St. Dominic. In 1517 he entered the University of Heidelberg. He met Martin Luther in Heidelberg and was won over to Luther's ideas. He left the Dominicans in 1521, married in 1522, and became one of the most influential reformers. He tried hard, but in vain, to keep the reformation from breaking into sects. In 1549 at the invitation of Archbishop Cranmer, he went to England, where he was made regius professor of divinity in the University of Cambridge.

ANDREAS OSIANDER I (Osanner, Hosiander; 1498-1552). Born in Gunzenhausen near Nürnberg. Ordained priest in 1520 in Eichstätt. Taught Hebrew to the Augustinians in Nürnberg. Became influenced by Luther. Took part in the reformation in Nürnberg. He taught theology in the University of Königsberg in 1551 where he died. He wrote:
De lege et evangelio, a disputation.

ANDREAS RUDOLF OF KARLSTADT (Bodenstein; ca. 1480-1541). Born in Karlstadt. He was first a friend, but later an opponent, of Luther. Taught at the University of Wittenberg in 1505. He became a doctor of theology in

1510 and a doctor of both laws in 1516. Through the influence of Luther he gave up his Thomism in 1517, and drew Luther's doctrines to their logical conclusions, thereby inviting the opposition of Luther. He fled, and was finally given asylum by Zwingli in 1531 in Switzerland. He died in Basle.

JOHANN BUGENHAGEN (Pomeranus; 1485-1558). Studied at Greifs-wald. In 1504 he became rector of the academy at Treptow. In 1509 he became a priest. His religious views were changed when he read writings of Luther's. Taught at the University of Wittenberg. After Melancthon, he was the most important man among Luther's associates. Sermons and letters constitute the greater part of his writing. He also wrote:
Interpretatio in librum Psalmorum (1523)

JUSTUS JONAS (Jodocus Koch; 1493-1555). Born in Nordhausen. Studied at Erfurt where he received his licentiate in the two laws in 1518 and became professor. Furthered humanist reform and the Lutheran movement. He became one of the principal associates of Luther and Melancthon. Had a controversy with Witzel. Translated many of the works of Luther and Melancthon.

MATTHIAS FLACIUS ILLYRICUS (Vlacich; 1520-1575). German Lutheran theologian and controversialist. Born in Albona. He studied at Venice under Baptista Egnatius. Went to Augsburg, Basle, Tübingen, and Wittenberg. In 1544 he was appointed to chair of Hebrew at Wittenberg. Opposed Melancthon. Was professor of the New Testament at the University of Jena, 1557-1561. Went to Regenburg, Strassburg, and Frankfurt a. M. Wrote over two hundred works, of which the following are most notable:
Clavis scripturae sacrae (1567)
Novum Testamentum . . . Glossa compendiaria (1570)
Catalogus testium veritatis
Ecclesiastica historia . . . secundum singulas centurias . . . per aliquot studiosos et pios viros in urbe Magdeburgica, 8 vols. covering thirteen centuries (1559-1574). Known simply as the *Centuries of Magdeburg.*

GEORG MAJOR (1502-1574). Born in Nürnberg. Studied in Wittenberg. Became alternately preacher and teacher in various places, notably in Wittenberg, Magdeberg, and Eisleben. Opposed in his theology by M. Flacius and N. Amsdorf in what is known as the 'Majoristenstreit.' Died in Wittenberg.

MARTIN CHEMNITZ (1522-1586). Born in Treunbrietzen. Studied in Magdeburg (1539-1542), Frankfurt a. Oder, and Wittenberg (1545). In

1547 he was a teacher, in 1550 librarian in Königsberg, and in 1544 a preacher in Braunschweig where he died. He aided in the establishment of the University of Helmstedt. Influenced by Melancthon. Wrote:

Examen Concilii Tridentini (1563-1573). Opposed by J. Rovesteyn of Louvain, Diego Andrade, Robert Bellarmine, Gregory of Valencia, and Franz Coster.

Theologiae Jesuitarum praecipua capita
Loci theologici

NICOLAUS TAURELLUS (1547-1606). Born at Mömpelgard. Studied theology at Tübingen and medicine at Basle, where he lectured on physical science. Later professor of medicine at Altdorf where he died. Opposed the doctrine of Ramus. Opponent of Andreas Caesalpinus. As a representative of the Protestant Church Taurellus combated not only the Averroistic Aristotelianism of Caesalpinus, but also Aristotelians in general, and all human authority in philosophy. He undertook to frame a new body of doctrines, in which there would be no conflict between philosophical and theological truths. He held that but for man's fall, philosophy would have sufficed, but in consequence of the fall, revelations became necessary. He wrote:

Philosophiae triumphus (1573), the triumph of philosophy emancipated from Aristotelianism and in harmony with theology is celebrated in this book.

Synopsis Metaphysicae Aristotelis (1596)
Caesae Alpes (1597)
De vita et morte libellus
Cosmologia
De rerum aeternitate (1604)

LIV. PHILIPP MELANCTHON AND HIS FOLLOWERS

PHILIPP MELANCTHON (1497-1565). Taught by Johannes Hungarus and Georg Simmler at the academy in Pfortzheim. Received his bachelor of arts degree from Heidelberg and master of arts from Tübingen. Upon graduation he became professor of Greek (1518) at Wittenberg where he tried to make Greek philosophy a source of advantage to Protestantism. He awakened the admiration of Luther and became associated with him in the revision of the translation of the Bible and the carrying on of the Reformation. He drafted most of the public documents of the Reformers, notably the 17 articles known as the *Augsburg Confession*. He taught a somewhat modified Aristotelianism.

To this he added certain principles borrowed from Cicero and Christian theology; namely that the sources and criteria of knowledge are, besides logical inference, universal experience, innate ideas, and the truth of Revelation. He presented the more rational side of Protestantism. He believed in natural light and the saying of the Apostle Paul that the law is written in the human heart. Underlying all argumentation, reckoning and computing, every assumption of first principles in science and every moral judgment, are certain ideas innate in every man, and without doubt implanted by God.

It has been maintained that except in natural and civil law Melancthon's philosophy was entirely borrowed and that by 'his substitution of the Bible for canon law' he helped to promote the evolution of the philosophy of law. Among his writings are:

Dialecticae Libri IV (1520)
De Anima (1520)
Initiae doctrinae physicae (1547)
Epitome philosophiae moralis (1538)
Ethicae doctrinae elementa (1550)
Declamationes (1544-1565)

JOACHIM CAMERARIUS (1500-1574). Professor at Nüremburg and Leipzig; wrote on classics and religion. He favored Aristotelianism and aided Melancthon in the drawing up of the 'Confessions of Augsburg.'

JACOB SCHEGK (1511-1587). Professor of natural philosophy at Tübingen.

DAVID CHYTRAEUS (1520-1600). A Lutheran theologian; studied at Tübingen and Wittenberg where he was a pupil of Melancthon. He was a professor of theology at Rostock. Employed by Maximilian II to arrange affairs of the Evangelical church in Austria. He was the principal author of the statutes of Helmstedt and one of the authors of the 'Formula of Concord.'

VIKTORIN STRIGEL (1524-1589). Studied at Wittenberg under Melancthon and became a professor at Jena in 1548. He was involved in the synergistic controversy and went to Leipzig in 1562, where he was charged with holding Calvinistic views; later (1567) he went to Heidelberg. He wrote:
Loci theologici (1581-1584)

PHILIP SCHERBIUS (d. 1605). Professor of logic and metaphysics at Altdorf, and pupil of Jacob Schegk.

CORNELIUS MARTINI (1568-1621). Professor at Helmstedt until 1621.

JAKOB MARTINI (1570-1649). Professor at Wittenberg.

LV. THEOLOGIANS OF THE COUNCIL OF TRENT (1545-1563)

FRIEDRICH NAUSEA (Grau; 1480-1552), bishop of Vienna, was born at Waischenfeld in Franconia in 1480. He received his early education at Bamberg. He pursued theological studies at Pavia, Padua and later at Siena and he taught at Nurenburg. He died at Trent. Works:

Catechismus catholicus

Pastoralium inquisitionum elenchi tres

Isagogicon de clericis ordinandis

GIROLAMO SERIPANDO (1493-1563). At the age of 14 he entered the Augustinian Order at Viterbo. In 1515 he was appointed lecturer at Siena. Professor of theology 1517 at Bologna, vicar general 1532. Appointed superior general in 1539 and made Cardinal 1561. Published works include:

Novae constitutiones ordinis S. Augustini (Venice, 1549)

Oratio in funere Caroli V. imperatoris (Naples, 1559)

Prediche sopra il simbolo degli Apostoli etc. (Venice, 1567)

Commentarius in D. Pauli epistolam ad Galatas (Venice, 1567)

Commentaria in D. Pauli epistolas ad Romanos et ad Galatos (Naples, 1601)

De arte orandi (Lyons, 1670)

JOHN GROPPER (1503-1555). Born at Soest in Westphalia. Entered the University of Cologne at 14 years receiving degree of doctor of civil law in 1525. The religious question of the day led him to study theology. He became known as 'os cleri Coloniensis.' He wrote much and was very forward in his opposition to the reformers. So much so that his zeal sometimes led him to sacrifice Catholic principles. However when the Council of Trent established the doctrine of justification he accepted at once its decision. In several of his writings he defends the Catholic faith, refuting the errors of the reformers. He died in Rome. Among his writings:

Institutio compendiaria doctrinae christianae (Cologne, 1538)

Enchiridion (Paris, 1541)

Antididagma seu christianae et catholicae religionis propugnatio (Cologne, 1544)

De appellationum abusu (Cologne, 1552)

Formula examinandi designatos seu praesentatos ad ecclesias parochiales (Cologne, 1552)

[89]

Vonn warer, Wesenlicher vnd Pleibender Gegenwertigkeit des Leybs und Bluts Christi nach beschener Consecration (Cologne, 1548)

CARDINAL ERCOLE GONZAGO (1505-1563). He was born at Mantua, November 23, 1505. He studied philosophy at Bologna under Pomponazzi, and later took up theology. He died at Trent. Work:
Vitae Christianae institutio

STANISLAUS HOSIUS (Hosz; 1504-1579). Attended University of Cracow. Received his B.A. in 1520 and later attended the University of Padua and Bologna. Among his professors at Padua was the famous humanist, Lazaro Buonamico. He pursued the humanities under Romulo Amasio. In 1543 he was ordained a priest and in 1550 he was consecrated bishop at Cracow. Among his writings are:
Confessio fidei catholicae christianae (1553)
Verae, christianae catholicaeque doctrinae solida propugnatio una cum illustri confutatione prolegomenorum, quae primum Jo. Brentius adversus Petrum a Soto theologum scripsit, deinde vero Petrus Pauls Vergerius apud Polonos temere defendenda, suscepit (Cologne, 1558)
Dialogus de communione s. eucharistia sub utraque specie; de conjugio sacerdotum et de sacro in vulgari lingua celebrando (1558)
De expresso verbo Dei (1558)
De oppresso verbo Dei (1559)
Judicium et censura de judicio et censura Heidelbergensium Tigurinorumque ministrorum de dogmate contra adorandam Trinitatem in Polonia nuper sparso (1564)
De loco et authoritate Romani Pontificis
Palinodiae Quadrantini (1567)

LUIGI SIMONETTA. Nephew of Giacomo Simonetta. Was Bishop of Pesaro, 1537-1561. He attended the Council of Trent in 1546-1547. He was made Cardinal in 1561 and legate and advisor of Pope Pius IV at the Council of Trent.

DIEGO ANDRODA DE PAYVA (1528-1575). Portugese theologian, born at Coimbra, son of the grand treasurer of John III. He earned distinction in 1562 at the council of Trent, as envoy to King Sebastian. Between 1562 and 1567 he published many controversial tracts, especially against the Lutheran, Martin Chemnitz. He was known for his fine work in theology and was known as an apologist of some note. His works include:

De Societatis Jesu origine, which led to his being erroneously thought a Jesuit.
De conciliorum auctoritate, welcomed in Rome as exalting the Papal authority.

Defensio tridentina fidei catholicae (1578), remarkable for its learned statements on the Immaculate Conception.

Orthodoxae questiones adversus haereticos

Theologiae Jesuitarum praecipua capita. Decem libri orthodoxarum explicationum

ALPHONSUS SALMERON (1515-1585). Jesuit Biblical scholar born at Toledo and died at Naples. He studied literature and philosophy at Alcala and later went to Paris for theology. Here he met Ignatius Loyola, through Lainez. In 1541 he enlisted as one of the first followers of Ignatius Loyola, as a professed member of the Jesuit society. In 1541 he was sent by Pope Paul III as apostolic nuncio to Ireland. In 1546 he went with Lainez to the Council of Trent as theologian to Paul III. At the council he was prominent in the dogma of justification. In 1549 Salmeron and his companions Le Jay and Canisius took their doctorate at the University of Bologna. In 1551 he was sent back to the council as theologian. In 1551 he was chosen with Lainez to go back to the Council of Trent as theologian to Pope Julius III, and in 1562 as theologian to Pope Pius IV. From 1564-82 he was engaged in preaching and writing. His chief writings are sixteen volumes of scriptural commentaries, eleven of which are on the Gospels, one on the Acts, and four on the Pauline Epistles. The Gospel volumes and that on the Acts are entitled *Alfonsi Salmeronis Toletani e societate Jesu theologi, commentarii in Evangelicam historiam et in Acta Apostolorum, in duodecim tomos distributi* (Madrid, 1598-1601).

JAMES LAINEZ (1512-1565). Went to the University of Alcala, 1531, and won his licentiate in philosophy, 1532. At the University of Paris he met Ignatius Loyola, falling under his influence in 1533. In 1534 he became a Jesuit. He was sent to the Council of Trent by Pope Paul III. At Trent he bore the brunt of the battle for Catholic truth in the matter of justification. His chief published works include:

Disputationes Tridentinae

JOHANN HEINRICH HESSELS (1522-1566). He was a distinguished theologian of Louvain. He taught for eight years at Parc, the Dominican house near Louvain. He was appointed professor of theology at the university in

1559. He drew his philosophy from the fathers, especially Augustine, rather than from the schoolmen. At the council of Trent he prepared the decree, 'De invocatione et reliquiis sanctorum et sacris imaginibus.' At Trent the scholastic party found fault with his departure from the beaten tracts of learning. Hessels upheld the doctrine of the Immaculate Conception. He was a protagonist of papal infallibility in his *De perpetuitate Cathedrae Petri et ejus indefectibilitate*, which is an appendix to his polemical work *Confutatio novitiae fidei quam specialem vocant adv. Johannem Monhemium* (Louvain, 1565). He also wrote:

De invocatione sanctorum . . . censura (1568)

Probatio corporalis praesentiae corporis et sanguinis dominici in Eucharistia (Cologne, 1563)

Confutatio confessionis haereticae, teutonice emissae, qua ostenditur Christum esse sacrificium propitiatorium (Louvain, 1565)

De passione Domini (Louvain, 1568)

LVI. OTHER OPPONENTS OF THE REFORMATION

JOHANNES FABRI (Faber; 1478-1541). Roman Catholic bishop called the 'Hammer of Heretics.' Family name Heigerlin. Born at Leutkirch, near Lake Constance in 1478. Studied theology and canon law in Tübingen, and in Freiburg in Breisgau where he became doctor of the two laws. In 1518 became vicar general of the diocese of Constance. Friendship with Erasmus, Melancthon and Zwingli, but in 1522 issued a work against Luther, and was one of the most indefatigable and formidable opponents of the movement. He took a leading part in the disputation in Zurich, Jan. 1523, and the diets of Nuremberg, 1523. In 1529 he was at Speir and in 1530 at Augsburg. In 1531 he was bishop of Vienna. He died at Baden, near Vienna. Wrote:

Malleus in haeresim Lutheranam (Cologne, 1524)

Opuscula quaedam J. Fabri episcopi Viennensis (Leipzig, 1539), among which are his polemical writings.

JOHANN COCHLAEUS (Dobeneck; 1479-1552). Surnamed Cochlaeus (from 'cochlea,' a snail shell) after his birthplace, Mendelstein, near Schwalbach. In 1500 made his humanistic studies under Grienniger at Nuremberg; 1504 studied at Cologne; 1510 in Nuremberg where he became an intimate friend of Pirkheimer. Made further humanistic and legal studies at Bologna; received doctorate in theology in 1517. Came under the influence of the

Oratorio del Divino Amore at Rome; ordained at Rome. Went to Frankfurt and became an active opponent of the Lutheran movement. In 1525 the Lutheran movement drove him to Cologne. In 1526 he was at the Diet of Speyer. In 1520 he labored strenuously to refute the Augsburg confession. In 1535 he obtained the canonry in Meissen; later obtained canonry in Breslau and Eichstatt. Published many pamphlets against Luther, Melancthon, Zwingli, Butzer, Bullinger Cordatus, and Ossiander. Wrote also:

De utroque sacerdotio (1520)

De gratia Sacramentorum (1522)

De baptismo parvulorum (1523)

Philippicae, against Melanchthon.

Commentaria de actis et scriptis M. Luther, one of the greatest works against Luther.

MICHAEL SERVETUS (Michael Served y Reves; 1511-1553). Born at Tudela. Studied law at Toulouse, medicine at Paris and Montpellier, and theology at Louvain. Wrote:

De Trinitatis erroribus (1531)

Christianismi restitutio (1535). Servetus was burned at the stake October 26, 1553 for publishing this work and because of John Calvin's enmity.

LVII. THE DIVINE RIGHT OF KINGS CONTROVERSY

JAMES I (1566-1625). Tutored by George Buchanan. Received a sound training in languages. In 1583 began to govern. He suppressed the nobles, quelled the attempts of Protestants to found a 'Presbyterian Hildebrandism,' and enforced the superiority of state over church. Upheld the doctrine of the divine right of kings. Wrote:

The True Law of Free Monarchies

An Apology for the Oath of Allegiance (Triplici nodo triplex cuneus) which was answered by Bellarmine in *Responsio Matthaei Torti presbyteri, et theologi, papiensis, ad librum inscriptum: Triplici nodo triplex cuneus.* Which in turn was answered by Lancelot Andrewes, in the king's name, in *Tortura Torti, sive ad Matthaei Torti librum responsio.*

Declaration du Roy Jacques I . . . pour le droit des Rois which was answered by Du Perron in *Replique à la résponse du Roy de la Grande-Bretagne.*

JACQUES DAVY DU PERRON (1556-1618). Born at St. Lô in Normandy. Received education at Bern in Switzerland. Was appointed reader to the king.

Created bishop of Evreux by Henry IV. His zeal and eloquence was largely instrumental in withstanding the progress of Calvinism. In 1604 was sent to Rome as charge d'affaires de France. He was made a cardinal, and became in 1606 archbishop of Sens. After the death of Henry IV he took an active part in the states-general of 1614, in which he upheld the ultramontane doctrines against the Third Estate. He opposed King James I of England, who answered with his *A defense of the Right of Kings, against Cardinal Du Perron.* Wrote:

Traité du sacrament de l'Eucharistie written against Duplessis-Mornay in 1600 at Fontainebleau. In it is a comparison of the Eucharist and the other sacraments of the New Law and with those of the Old Law; the tradition of the Fathers; the practice of the Church concerning the adoration of the Eucharist.

Replique à la Response du Roy de la Grande-Bretagne
Treatise on vocation
Acts of the Fontainebleau Conference
Refutation of the work of Tilenus on Apostolic traditions

GEORGE BLACKWELL (ca. 1545-1613). Born in Middlesex. Admitted to Trinity College, Oxford, 1562; received the degree of bachelor of arts in 1563 and his master's degree in 1567. Admitted to the English College at Douai in 1574, and ordained priest in 1575. Returned to England in 1576, was imprisoned, but released. After the death of Cardinal Allen, he was appointed arch-priest over the secular clergy by Pope Clement VIII in 1598. In 1606 he urged his clergy to take the oath of allegiance, and in 1607 he himself did so, thereby causing a storm of controversial letters many of which are listed by Thompson Cooper in his article on Blackwell in the *Dictionary of National Biography, V* (1886), 144-146. Cardinal Robert Bellarmine wrote him several letters on the subject. He died still insisting upon his right to take the oath.

ROBERT BELLARMINE (1542-1621). Attended Jesuit College and was good student in Latin, Rhetoric, and the humanities. In 1600 received into Society of Jesus in Rome. Studied at Roman College under Peter Parra. In 1563 began teaching at Padua. In 1570 went to Louvain where he studied theology. He was the first Jesuit allowed the honor of teaching at the University of Louvain. While there he made a very elaborate commentary on the *Summa theologica* of St. Thomas Aquinas. He held the chair of controversies at the Roman College, 1576-1595. He was a personal friend of Galileo, who dedicated one of his works to him. As the most learned and important member of the Sacred College, he was compelled to warn Galileo against unwarranted theological interpretation of the new Copernican theory. Bellarmine did not personally reject the theory, but he maintained that it should be received only as a theory until the scientific proof was complete and final. He wrote an autobiography and many other books, notably:

Disputationes de controversiis christianae fidei adversus hujus temporis hereticos. This work contains his lectures delivered in the Roman College.

Christianae doctrinae applicatio

De potestate summi Pontificis in rebus temporalibus, which was directed against the work of William Barclay (father of John Barclay) who denied the temporal power of the pope.

Responsio Matthaei Torti presbyteri et theologi, papiensis, ad librum inscriptum: Triplici nodo triplex cuneas. (Cologne, 1608). Which was an answer to *An Apology for the Oath of Allegiance of James* I. It was answered by Lancelot Andrewes in the king's name in *Tortura Torti, sive ad Mathhaei Torti librum responsio.*

De translatione imperii Romani a Graecis ad Francos, adversus Flaccium Illyricum

Apologia Roberti S. R. E. Cardinalis Bellarmini, pro responsione sua ad librum Jacobi, Magnae Britanniae regis, cujus titulus est: Triplici nodo triplex cuneus: in qua apologia refellitur praefatio monitoria regis ejusdem (Rome, 1609), to which Lancelot Andrewes answered with his *Responsio ad Apologiam Cardinalis Bellarmini* (London, 1610).

De scriptoribus ecclesiasticis (Rome and Cologne, 1613).

In omnes Psalmos dilucida explanatio (Rome, 1611).

De ascensione mentis in Deum per scalas rerum creatarum (Antwerp and Rome, 1615)

De aeterna felicitate sanctorum (Antwerp and Rome, 1616).

De gemitu columbae, sive de bono lacrymarum (Antwerp and Cologne, 1617).

De arte bene moriendi (Antwerp and Rome, 1620).

De officio principis christiani (Antwerp and Rome, 1619)

De cognitione Dei

Exhortationes domesticae

LANCELOT ANDREWES (1555-1626). English divine, born in London. Received education at Cambridge where he received his bachelor of arts degree in 1575, his master's degree in 1578. He took orders in 1580. Gained reputation as lecturer and casuist. He became chaplain of Queen Elizabeth. July 4, 1601 he became dean of Westminster. Took part in 1604 in the Hampton Court conference. Became bishop of Chichester in 1605. In 1618 he became bishop of Winchester. Wrote sermons and:

Tortura Torti, sive ad Matthaei Torti librum responsio which was an answer, written in the name of James I, to Bellarmine's *Responsio Matthaei Torti presbyteri, et theologi, papiensis, ad librum inscriptum: Triplici nodo triplex cuneus.*

Responsio ad Apologiam Cardinalis Bellarmini (London, 1610)

First Answer to Cardinal du Perron who had challenged James I's use of the title 'catholic.'

JOHN BARCLAY (1582-1621). He was born in Lorraine. Received education at the Jesuit College. Became a bitter foe of the Jesuits because of whom he fled to England where he received the favor of James I. Wrote:

Euphormionis Satyricon which was a political satirical romance against the Jesuits (1607).

Apologia (1611)

Icon Ammorum (1614)

Paraenesis ad sectarios, an attack on the position of Protestantism.

FRANCISCO SUAREZ (1548-1617), S.J. Born in Granada; entered Society of Jesus at Salamanca in 1564. Studied philosophy and theology (1565-1570); ordained in 1572. Taught philosophy at Avila and Segovia (1571), and later, theology at Avila and Segovia (1575), Valladolid (1576), Rome (1580-1585), Alcala (1585-1592), Salamanca (1582-1597) and Coimbra (1597-1616). In regard to universals he chose a middle course between the realism of Duns Scotus and the nominalism of William of Ockham. In theology he followed the doctrines of Luis Molina. In Scholasticism he founded 'Suarism,' of which the chief principles are: (a) the principle of individuation by the proper concrete entity of beings, (b) the pure potentiality of matter, (c) the singular as the object of direct intellectual cognition, (d) a conceptual distinction between the essence and the existence of created things, (e) possibility of holding one and the same truth by both science and faith, (f) belief in Divine authority contained in an act of faith. Wrote commentaries on St. Thomas's *Summa theologica*. Also many other works among which are:

De Deo Incarnato (Alcala, 1590)

Disputationes metaphysicae (1597)

Tractatus de legibus ac deo legislatore. He says that all authority in the state, as well as parental authority, is derived from God, and that the authority of every law resolves itself into His. He rejects the patriarchal theory of government and the divine right of kings.

Defensio catholicae fidei contra anglicanae sectae errores, written against the *Oath of Allegiance* of James I, at the request of Pope Paul V.

LVIII. ENGLISH COLLEGE AT DOUAI

WILLIAM CARDINAL ALLEN (1532-1594). Studied at Oxford. On accession of Elizabeth, and re-establishment of Protestantism, Allen was one of those who remained loyal to the Catholic faith and it is due to his labors in large measure that the Catholic religion was not stamped out in England. To train clergy and controversialists ready to return to England at the propitious time, he labored to found the College of Douai. He was created Cardinal in 1587 at the request of Philip of Spain. He wrote:

Certain Brief Reasons Concerning the Catholick Faith (Douai, 1564)

A Defense and Declaration of the Catholike Churches Doctrine touching Purgatory and Prayers of the Soules Departed (Antwerp, 1565)

Treatise Made in Defense of the Lawful Power and Authoritie of the Preesthoode to remitte sinnes (1567)

De Sacramentis (Antwerp, 1565; Douai, 1603)

An Apology for the English Seminaries (1581)

Apologia Martyrum (1583)

Martyrium R. P. Edmundi Campiani, S.J. (1583)

An Answer to the Libel of English Justice (1584)

The Copie of a Letter written by Doctor Allen concerning yielding up of the Citie of Daventree unto His Catholike Majestie, by Sir. Wm. Knight (Antwerp, 1587)

An Admonition to the Nobility and People of England and Ireland, concerning the present Warres made for Execution of His Holines Sentence, by the highe and mighty kinge Catholike of Spain, by the Cardinal of Englande (1588)

Declaration of the Sentence and Deposition of Elizabeth the usurper and pretended Queene of England (1588)

RICHARD BRISTOW (1538-1581). Studied at Oxford. Eloquent orator; disputed before Queen Elizabeth. Changing his religious opinions, he went to Louvain and became righthand man of Cardinal Allen at Douai. Became one of the revisers of the Douai Bible. Douai records speak of him as rivalling Allen in prudence, Stapleton in acumen, Campion in eloquence, Wright in theology, and Martin in languages. Wrote:

A Briefe Treatise of diverse and sure wayes to finde out the truthe in this doubtful and dangerous time of Heresie; conteyning sundry worthy motives unto the Catholic faith, or considerations to move a man to believe the Catholikes and not the Heretikes.

Tabula in Summam Theologicam S. Thomae Aquinatis

A Reply to William Fulke

Demandes to be proposed of Catholikes to the Heretikes

A Defence of the Bull of Pope Pius V

Annotations on the Rheims translations of the New Testament

Carmina Diversa

Motiva omnibus catholicae doctrinae orthodixis cultoribus per necessaria

THOMAS STAPLETON (1539-1598). Studied at Oxford. Retired to Louvain upon accession of Elizabeth. In 1568 joined Allen at Douai and took an active part in founding the English College there. Professor of Scripture at Louvain, 1590. Translated Ven. Bede's *History of the Church in England* and Hasius's *The Expresse Word of God.* Wrote:

A Fortress of Faith

A Return of Untruths (Antwerp, 1566)

A Counterblast to M. Horne's vain blast (Louvain, 1567)

Orations funebres (Antwerp, 1577)

Principiorum fidei doctrinalium demonstratio (Paris, 1578)

Speculum pravitatis haereticae (Douai, 1580)

De universa justificationis doctrina (Paris, 1582)

Tres Thomae (Douai, 1588)

Promptuarium morale, 2 parts (Antwerp, 1591-2)

Promptuarium Catholicum in Evangelia Dominicalia (Cologne, 1592)

Promptuarium Catholicum in Evangelia Ferialia (Cologne, 1594)

Promptuarium Catholicum in Evangelia Festorum (Cologne, 1592)

Relectio scholastica (Antwerp, 1592)

Authoritatis ecclesiasticae circa S. Scriptuarum approbationem defensio (Antwerp, 1592)

Apologia pro rege Philippo II (Constance, 1592) under pen name of Didy-
mus Veridicus Henfilandus.
Antidota Apostolica contra nostri temporis haereses (Antwerp, 1595)
Antidota Evangelica (Antwerp, 1595)
Antidota Apostolica in Epistolam Pauli ad Romanos (Antwerp, 1595)
Triplicatio inchoata (Antwerp, 1596)
Antidota Apostolica in duas Epistolas ad Corinthios (Antwerp, 1598)
Vere admiranda, seu de magnitudine Romanae Ecclesiae (Antwerp, 1599)
Orationes academicae miscellanae (Antwerp, 1602)
Oratio academica (Mainz, 1608)

EDMUND CAMPION (1540-1581). Received early education at Christ's
Hospital. Became fellow of St. John's College, Oxford, in 1557. Won regard
of Queen Mary. Took deacon's orders in English church although he held
Catholic doctrines. Under suspicion of papistry, he eluded arrest and escaped
to Douai. Became a Jesuit in 1573. Returned to England in 1580 with the
Jesuit mission. Imprisoned and put to death in 1581. Beatified in 1886.
Wrote:
Decem Rationes, against the Anglican church.

GREGORY MARTIN (d. 1582). Born at Sussex. Entered Oxford in 1557,
where he was a close friend of Campion. Left England in 1570 and became
candidate for priesthood under Dr. Allen at Douai. Ordained in 1573. Helped
to found the English College at Douai. Took the most active part in translation of Bible into English; collaborators were Worthington, Bristow, Reynolds and Allen. Works:
Treatise of Schisme (Douai, 1578)
*Discovery of the Manifold Corruptions of the Holy Scriptures by the Here-
tikes of our Daies* (Reims, 1582)
Reims Testament and Douay Bible (The Rheims New Testament appeared in
1582).
Treatise of Christian Peregrination (Reims, 1583)
Of the Love of the Soul (St. Omer, 1603)
*Gregorius Martinus ad Adolphum McKerchum pro veteri et vera Graecarum
literarum pronuntiatione*

FRANZ SYLVIUS (1581-1649). Thomist commentator who died at Douai.

DR. RICHARD SMITH. First chancellor of University of Douai; formerly
regius professor of divinity at Oxford.

DR. OWEN LEWIS. Regius professor of Canon Law at Douai.

RICHARD WHITE. First principal of Marchiennes College.

DR. RICHARD BARRETT. Successor of Allen as guiding light of English establishment.

DR. REYNOLDS. Aided in translating the Bible at Douai.

DR. WORTHINGTON. Third president.

DR. KELLISON. Fourth president, 1631-1641.

DR. HYDE. President, 1646-51.

DR. GEORGE LEYBRUN. President, 1652-70.

LIX.   SPANISH ADVOCATES OF A NEW PHILOSOPHY OF TASTE

FRANCISCUS SANCTUS BROCENSIS (El Brocense). Professor of rhetoric at the academy in Salamanca. Wrote:
De arte dicendi (1556)
Organum dialecticum et rhetoricum (first edition, Salamanca, 1573)

ALFONSO GARCIA MATAMOROS

SEBASTIAN FOX MORCILLO. Wrote:
De imitatione seu informandi styli ratione (1554), a primer of the art of style.

MIGUEL SAURA. Wrote:
Instituciones oratorias (1588)

JERÓNIMO COSTA

BARTOLOMÉ BANIENTOS. Wrote:
De periodorum sive ambitium distinctionibus

FRANCISCO GALLÉS. Wrote:
Epitome troporum et schematum (1553)

LX.   JESUIT OPPONENTS OF THE SCHOOL OF BROCENSIS AND VIVES

BALTHAZAR ALVAREZ (1534-1580). Born in Cervera in Old Castile. Entered the Society of Jesus in 1555. Spiritual adviser of St. Teresa of Avila. Wrote:

De institutione grammatica (first published, 1593)
Tractatus de anima separata, the last of the *Commentarii collegii conimbricenses.*

PEDRO JUAN PERPIÑAN (1530-1566); became professor of rhetoric at the Roman College in 1561. He was one of the best readers of Latin in his time. He wrote:
Orationes, delivered in 1561, published in 1587 at Rome.
De vita et moribus B. Elizebethae Lusit. reginae

JEAN DE SANTIAGO (1532-1604); born at Toledo; died at Marchena. He became professor of eloquence at Seville, where he entered the Society of Jesus in 1565.

BARTOLOMÉ BRAVO (1564-1607); born at Martin-Miñoz, diocese of Avila. He was admitted into the University of Salamanca in 1572 at the age of 18, and occupied the chair of humanities at the age of 27. He died at Medina del Campo. Among his works are:
De arte rhetorica
De syntaxi
De prosodia progymnasmata

RODRIGO DE ARRIAGA (1592-1667); born at Longrono; died at Prague. He became a Jesuit about 1606. He studied philosophy at Salamanca. He wrote:
Disputationes theologicae

BALTHAZAR GRACIAN (1601-1658); born at Belmonte; died at Tarazona. He was a vigorous opponent of individualism. Schopenhauer admired Gracian and translated his works which he fitted to his own philosophy. He wrote:
El Héroe (1637)
El criticon
Agudeza y arte di ingenio
El discreto (1646)
Oráculo manual (1647)

LXI. THE ROMAN COLLEGE

JAMES LEDESMA (1519-1575), S.J. Born at Coullar in France. He studied at Alcala, Paris, and Louvain. In 1557, when already professor of theology, he joined the Society of Jesus and taught theology at the Roman College

until his death. He was thought highly of by James Lainez. He did consider-
able preliminary work on the *Ratio studiorum.* Wrote:
De divinis scriptionis quavis passim lingua non legendis (1570)
Doctrina christiana

PETER PARRA, S.J. He taught at the Roman College from 1560 to about
1585. Was a teacher of Robert Bellarmine, 1560-1563. Defended a rigid
Thomism.

FRANCISCO TOLETUS (1536-1596), S.J. Born at Cordova. Studied philos-
phy at Valencia, and theology under Domingo de Soto at Salamanca. In 1555,
he became doctor of theology and teacher of philosophy at Salamanca. He
entered the Society of Jesus in 1558, and later became professor of philosophy
and theology, and prefect of studies at the Roman College. Wrote:
Introductio in dialecticam Aristotelis (Rome, 1561)
In universam Aristotelis logicam (Rome, 1572)
In I Posteriorum
De inventoribus philosophiae
In libros de phys. auscultatione (Venice, 1573)
In libros de anima (Venice, 1574)
De instructione sacerdotum libri septem
Summa casuum (Lyons, 1599)

JUAN DE MARIANA (1537-1624), S.J. Spanish historian born at Talavera.
Studied at the University of Alcala, and admitted at the age of seventeen into
the Society of Jesus. Taught theology in Rome in 1561, where Robert Bellarmine was a student. Became a cardinal. Travelled in Sicily and in 1569 was
sent to Paris, where his expositions on the writings of St. Thomas Aquinas
attracted large audiences. In 1574, he returned to Spain, and later died at
Madrid. Wrote:
Historiae de rebus Hispaniae (Toledo, 1592)
De rege et regis institutione (Toledo, 1598), in the sixth chapter of which
  he decides that it is lawful to overthrow a tyrant. This caused some hatred
  against the Jesuits, especially after the assassination of Henry IV of France,
  in 1610.
Tractatus VII theologici et historici (Cologne, 1609). This work contained
  two tracts, *De morte et immortalitate,* and *De mutatione monetae,* which
  caused Mariana to be imprisoned by the Inquisition.

[102]

Discursus de erroribus qui in forma gubernationis societatis Jesu occurrunt (Bordeaux, 1625), which is a criticism of the Jesuits.

MANOEL DE SA (Emmanuel Sa; 1530-1596), S.J. Portuguese theologian born at Villa do Conde (Province of Entre-Minhoe-Douro). Distinguished himself as a student at the University of Coimbra. Joined Society of Jesus at the age of fifteen. Taught philosophy first at Coimbra, and next at Gandia, where he was tutor to St. Francis Borgia. In 1557, he became professor at the Roman College. Founded several houses of his order in upper Italy. Wrote an unpublished life of John of Texeda, the Capuchin confessor of St. Francis Borgia. Wrote also:

Scholia in quatuor Evangelia (Antwerp, 1596)

Notationes in totam Scripturam Sacram (Antwerp, 1598), in which he sets forth the literal sense of the Holy Writ.

Aphorismi confessariorum ex doctorum sententiis collecti (Venice, 1595), which was censured in 1603, because the Master of the Sacred Palace held that some of its maxims were contrary to opinions commonly received among theologians, but it was later corrected and removed from the Roman Index (1900).

BENEDICT PEREIRA (Perara, Pererius; 1535-1610), S.J. Born at Ruzafa, near Valencia, in Spain. Entered Society of Jesus in 1552, and taught successively literature, philosophy, theology, and Sacred Scripture in Rome. He published eight works and left a large amount of manuscripts. Wrote 137 dissertations on *Exodus* (Ingolstadt, 1601), 188 dissertations on the *Epistle to the Romans* (Ingolstadt, 1603), 183 dissertations on the *Apocalypse* (Lyons, 1605), and 358 dissertations on the *Gospel of St. John* (Lyons, 1608). Wrote also:

Commentariorum in Danielem prophetam libri sexdecim (Rome, 1857)

GABRIEL VAZQUEZ (c. 1549-1604), S.J. Born at Villaescusa de Haro, near Belmonte, Cuenca. Made his grammar studies at Belmonte. Went to Alcala for philosophy. Entered Society of Jesus in 1569. Studied at University of Alcala. Taught theology at College of Ocana, Madrid and Alcala, and later at the Roman college. Noted for his exact knowledge of the opinions and theories of the different schools and authors. He was a rival of Suarez in the Roman college. Wrote:

De cultu adorationis libri tres et disputationes duae contra errores Felicis et Elipandi (Alcala, 1598)

Commentariorum ac disputationum in (partes) S. Thomae (Alcala, 1598)

Paraphrases et compendiaria explicatio ad nonnullas Pauli Epistolas (Alcala, 1612)

Metaphysicae disputationes (Madrid, 1617), which comprises the philosophical questions dispersed throughout his works.

BENEDETTO JUSTINIANI (ca. 1550-1622), S.J. Theological and Biblical writer born at Genoa. Entered Society of Jesus at Rome in 1579. Taught rhetoric in the Roman college, and theology at Toulouse, Messina, and Rome. Head of the Roman college and 'regens' of the Sacred Poenitentiara for twenty years. Also became chief preacher to the pope. Clement VIII appointed him as theologian to Cardinal Cajetan, during the latter's legation in Poland. Wrote:

In omnes B. Pauli Epistolas explanationes (Lyons, 1512; 1613)

In omnes Catholicas Epistolas explanationes (Lyons, 1621)

Apologia pro libertate ecclesiastica ad Gallo-Francos

De gratia

De natura brevis disputatio

De Sacramentis

De poenitentia

De confessario

De legitima Romani Pontificis electione libri sex

LXII. THE RATIO STUDIORUM

CLAUDIO AQUAVIVA (1543-1615), S.J. Joined the Jesuit order in 1581. Noted for his attempt to increase the importance and effectiveness of the order through the enforcement of a rigid and uniform system. He did considerable work upon the *Ratio Studiorum*, which was formally issued to the Society in 1599 by him as general. The *Ratio* was an organized formulation of the curriculum and of the appropriate method of teaching. In 1584 Father Aquaviva had called to Rome six experienced schoolmen to consider the matter of preparing a plan of studies. This eventually became the *Ratio*. Wrote:

Directorium Exercitiorum Spiritualium

JAMES LAINEZ (Diego Laynez; 1512-1565), S.J., Loyola's pupil and successor. Delivered theological lectures in a university in Rome (Sapienza). His theory concerning the power of the sovereign was that it was delegated to him

by the people, and that the sovereign was accordingly responsible to the people for ensuring a just rule. Wrote:
Disputationes Tridentinae

HIERONYMUS NADAL (Natalis; 1507-1580), S.J. Nadal was born in Palma on the Island of Mallorca. He met St. Ignatius in Rome but did not join the Society of Jesus until 1545 when he had finished his studies and had completed seven years in the sacred ministry in his native city. From 1548 to 1552 he was provincial and first rector of the Jesuit College in Messina. He travelled in Spain and Portugal. From 1564 to 1566 he was rector of the Roman college. He held in the next fifteen years many important offices in the Society of Jesus and did much to lay the plan for the *Ratio Studiorum*. His letters were especially significant in that connection. He wrote also:
Adnotationes et meditationes in Evangelia, quae in ss. missae sacrificio leguntur
Scholia in Constitutiones et Declarationes Sancti Ignatii

LXIII.   CONIMBRICENSES

PEDRO DA FONSECA (1528-1597), S.J., a Portuguese philosopher and theologian born in Cortizada. Entered Society of Jesus in Coimbra in 1548; studied at the University of Evora; taught philosophy at Coimbra. Has been called the 'Portuguese Aristotle.' Many institutions in Lisbon, notably the Irish college, owe their existence to his zeal and piety. He also aided in the drawing up of the Jesuit *Ratio Studiorum*. Fonseca shares the fame of the *Conimbricenses*, as it was during his office as provincial, and through his initiative that this work was undertaken by the Jesuit professors of Coimbra. The work itself was published at the direction of the general of the order, Claudius Aquaviva. It consisted of commentaries on Aristotle, published under the title of *Commentarii colegii conimbricensis Societatis Jesus*, sometimes called *Cursus conimbricensium* or *Collegium conimbricense*. Fonseca set the fashion for this series by publishing in 1577 the first volume of his commentary on Aristotle's *Metaphysics* under the title of *Commentarii in libros metaphysicorum Aristotelis Stagyritae* (Rome, 1577). In his writings he attempted to reconcile the clash between grace and free will, by the use of a 'scientia media' in God. Wrote:
Institutionum dialecticarum libri octo (Lisbon, 1564)
Isagoge philosophica (Lisbon, 1591)

COSMOS MAGGALLIANO (Magalhaens; 1553-1624), S.J. Edited the commentary of Emmanuel de Goës on the *De anima* of Aristotle to which the *Tractatus De anima separata* of Balthazar Alvarez was added. Wrote:

Tractatio aliquot problematum ad quinque sensus spectantium, which, together with Alvarez's *Tractatus de anima separata*, and Maggalliano's edition of De Goës' commentary on the *De anima*, constituted volume seven of the *Commentarii colegii conimbricensis Societatis Jesus*.

EMANUEL DE GOËS (1560-1597), S.J. Wrote volumes of the *Conimbricenses*, which are the commentaries on Aristotle, under the title of:

Vol. I: *Commentarii colegii conimbricensis Societatis Jesu in octo libros physicorum Aristotelis Stagyritae* (Coimbra, 1591)

Vol. II: *Commentarii colegii conimbricensis Societatis Jesu in quattuor libros Aristotelis de coelo* (Coimbra, 1592)

Vol. III: *Commentarii colegii conimbricensis Societis Jesu in libros meteorum Aristotelis Stagyritae* (Coimbra, 1592)

Vol. IV: *Commentarii colegii conimbricensis Societatis Jesu in libros Aristotelis qui parva naturalia appellantur* (Coimbra, 1592)

Vol. V: *Commentarii colegii conimbricensis Societatis Jesu in libros ethicorum Aristotelis ad Nichomachum aliquot cursus conimbricensis disputationes in quibus praecipua quadam ethicae disciplinae capita continentur* (Coimbra, 1595)

Vol. VI: *Commentarii colegii conimbricensis Societatis Jesu in duos libros Aristotelis de generatione et corruptione* (Coimbra, 1595)

SEBASTIAO DO COUTO (ca. 1567-1639), S.J. Edited Fonseca's commentary on the logic of Aristotle which constituted volume eight of the series, called,

Commentarii colegii conimbricensis Societatis Jesu in universam dialecticam Aristotelis nunc primum editum (Venice, 1606)

BALTHAZAR ALVAREZ (1561-1630), S.J. A Spanish mystic born at Cervera; studied philosophy and theology at the University of Alcala, and later at Avila; entered Society of Jesus at Alcala in 1555. Became a priest in 1558. The continued interruptions of his studies impeded his progress in scholastic theology, but he compensated for it by the eminence he achieved through prayer, which fitted him for the office he subsequently held as confessor, master of novices, rector, provincial, and director of persons. He was the spiritual director of St. Teresa and defended her against critics. In 1574, he was made rector of Salamanca. Wrote:

Tractatus de anima separata, a treatise which was appended to Emanuel de Goës's commentary (edited by Cosmos Maggalliano) on Aristotle's *De anima*. These two, together with the *Tractatio aliquot problematum ad quinque sensus spectantium* of Maggalliano, constituted volume seven of the *Commentarii colegii conimbricensis Societatis Jesus*, entitled, *Commentarii colegii conimbricensis Societatis Jesu in tres libros Aristotelis de anima* (Coimbra, 1595)

LXIV.   OTHER JESUITS

JOHANNES MALDONATUS (1534-1583). Born at Casas de Reina. At age of fifteen went to University of Salamanca to study Latin, Greek, philosophy, and theology. Later taught same subjects at Salamanca. Was disciple of Francis de Vittoria and a personal friend and fellow student of Bellarmine. Became a Jesuit in 1563. In 1563 he was sent to teach at College de Clermont at Paris. Was assigned by the pope to teach theology at Toulouse. Calvinists prevented his reaching his destination. In 1564 commenced lecturing on Aristotle's *De anima*. He was a man of eminent virtue, of subtle intellect, excellent memory, immense reading and erudition. Has been accused of certain rash utterances and of inordinate attachment to his own opinions. Works:

Commentarii in quatuor Evangelistas

Disputationum ac controversiarum decisarum et circa septem Ecclesiae Romanae Sacramenta

De fide

De caeremoniis tractatus

LUIS DE MOLINA (1535-1600). Born at Cuenca. Was student of Fonseca. He became a Jesuit at Alcala at the age of eighteen. He studied theology and philosophy at Coimbra; afterwards becoming a professor in the university of Evora, Portugal. After twenty years was called to the chair of moral theology in Madrid, where he died. Enormously concerned with opposing the Protestant Reformation or with asserting and reasserting the theology of the Council of Trent. Maintains man is free to perform or not perform any act he so desires. These circumstances render the grace of God neither unnecessary nor impossible. Not impossible, for God never fails to bestow grace upon those who ask it with sincerity; and not unnecessary, for grace, although not an efficient cause, is a sufficient cause of salvation. His doctrines showed the marked opposition to the teachings of Luther and Calvin. The Dominicans claimed that Molina placed too much stress on liberty. The controversy which arose was finally ended by order of the Pope. Wrote:

De justitia et jure. To this work is attributed his great fame.

Librii arbitrii cum pratiae donis, divina praescientia, providentia, praedestinatione et reprobatione, concordia (1588)

Commentaria in primam partem D. Thomae, 2 vols. (Cuenca, 1592)

GREGORY OF VALENCIA (1550-1603). Entered Society of Jesus in 1565 and began studying philosophy and jurisprudence at the University of Salamanca. Ordained while teaching philosophy at Rome. Appointed to chair of theology at Dilligen and after two years transferred to a similar position at Ingolstadt where he was a professor for seventeen years. Taught theology at Rome for a number of years and held the position of prefect of studies in the Roman college. Wrote:

Commentariorum theologicorum tomi quatuor

De rebus fidei hoc tempore controversis

Commentarii theologici

Apologeticus de idololatria

COSMUS ALAMANNI (1559-1634). Born in Milan. Became a Jesuit in 1575. Taught philosophy and dogmatic theology from a Thomist point of view. He studied under both Vazquez and Suarez at Roman college, 1584-1588. Wrote:

Summa totius philosophiae e divi Thomae Aquinatis doctrina (Pavia, 1618-1623). This work follows the form of the *Summa theologica* of St. Thomas Aquinas and, so far as possible, the very words of the Saint.

PETER ARRUBAL (1559-1608), a Spanish Jesuit. Taught theology at Alcala, Rome, and Salamanca. Took a leading part in the controversy between the Dominicans and the Jesuits (1599-1600). He refuted the *Apologia* of the Dominicans, composed by them against the teaching of Molina. Wrote:

De auxiliis gratiae divinae

In primam partem Summae theol. S. Thomae

ST. PETER CLAVER (1581-1653). Born at Verdu in Catalonia. Joined Jesuits in Tarragona in 1602. Studied philosophy in Mallorca where he came under the influence of the Jesuit lay-brother Saint Alphonsus Rodriquez, who urged him to go as missionary to the Spanish possessions in the New World.

Studied theology in Barcelona for two years, and in 1610 set sail for South America. In Santa Fe de Bogotá he completed his theological studies and was ordained priest in Cartagena (Colombia, South America). By its position on the Caribbean Sea, Cartagena became the chief slave-mart of the New World. For forty years St. Peter Claver worked there trying in every way possible to alleviate the suffering of the slaves and to curb the brutality of their oppressors. His recommendations to the ecclesiastical and civil authorities constitute a notable achievement in this division of international law and of morals.

JOHN DE LUGO (1583-1660). One of the most eminent theologians of modern times. Born at Madrid. At the age of three he could read books. At ten he received the tonsure; at fourteen he defended a public thesis in logic; and about the same time he was appointed by Phillip II to an ecclesiastical benefice which he retained until his solemn profession in 1618. He went to the University of Salamanca to study .He entered the Society of Jesus in 1603. After completing his studies he was appointed professor of philosophy at Medina del Campo in 1611, and later professor of theology at Valladolid where he taught for five years. His fame as professor of theology attracted the attention of the general of the Jesuits, Mutius Vitelleschi, who summoned de Lugo to Rome in June 1621. Here he was ordered to print his books. In the years 1633, 1636, and 1638 he published three volumes. When the fourth was ready for publication his superiors thought it would be well for him to dedicate it to Pope Urban VIII and as a result, he had to present himself to the Pope. Urban VIII became interested in his works and frequently consulted him. In 1643 he created him cardinal. He died at the age of seventy-seven. Wrote:

De Incarnatione Domini
De Sacramentis in genere
De justitia et jure
De venerabili Eucharistiae Sacramento et de sacrosancto Missae Sacrificio
De virtute et Sacramento poenitentiae, de suffragiis et indulgentiis

SYLVESTER MAURUS (1619-1687). Born at Spoleto. Died in Rome. He entered the Society of Jesus in 1636. Studied at College of Macerata. Taught humanities and philosophy for three years at same place and then in Rome for several years. He was then promoted to the chair of theology at the Roman college; was also rector of Roman college. His doctrine was noted for its soundness and solidity. He constantly put into practice St. Paul's principle, 'not to be more wise than it behoveth to be wise, but to be wise unto sobriety.' Wrote:

Quaestionum philosophicarum Sylvestri Mauri, Soc. Jesu, in Collegio Romano philosophiae professoris

Aristotelis opera quae extant omnia, brevi paraphrasi, ac litterae perpetuo inhaerente explanatione illustrata

Bibliotheca theologiae et philosophiae scholasticae

Quaestionum theologicarum libri sex

Opus theologicum

LXV. JESUITS AT LOUVAIN

LEONARD LESSIUS (Le Porc; 1554-1623). Born at Brecht near Antwerp. He finished the village school at thirteen. Won the Brecht scholarship to the University of Louvain where he studied the classics and philosophy. He became a doctor of philosophy at seventeen. He was admitted to the Jesuit seminary community in 1572, and after two years was sent to teach at Douai in the Jesuit college. While teaching there he made his own theological studies and was ordained. Then he studied under Bellarmine and Suarez. His works:

De jure et justitia

De gratia efficaci, decretis divinis, libertate arbitrii, et praescientia Dei condicionata disputatio apologetica (Antwerp, 1610), an exhortation to temperance in eating and drinking; written partly from the moral and partly from the medical point of view.

Defensio summi pontificis (1610)

De summo bono

De perfectionibus moribusque divinis

De L. nominibus Dei, an ascetical work on the purgative, illuminative and unitive ways.

CORNELIUS A LAPIDE (Van den Steen; 1562-1637). A widely known commentator on Scripture. Lectured on Scripture at Louvain and in Rome. Pupil of Lessius. His fame rests upon his commentary on all the Bible except Job and the Psalms; the first complete edition was published in 10 volumes, folio (Antwerp, 1681).

RENAISSANCE PHILOSOPHERS

GILES DE CONINCK (Regino; 1571-1633). At 21 he entered the Jesuit community. Had Lessius as his teacher. Succeeded Lessius to the chair of scholastic theology, which he held for 18 years. Wrote:

Commentariorum ac disputationum in universam doctrinam D. Thomae, his most important work (Antwerp, 1616)

De moralitate, natura et effectibus actuum supernaturalium (Antwerp, 1623)

Responsio ad dissertationem impugnantem absolutionem moribundi sensibus destituti (Antwerp, 1625)

Disputationes theologicae (Antwerp, 1645).

LXVI. PETRUS RAMUS AND HIS SCHOOL

PETRUS RAMUS (1515-1572), a French humanist, was born at the village of Cuth in Picardy. Received a degree from the college of Navarre, and chose as his graduating thesis, 'Everything that Aristotle taught is false.' Pupil of Johannes Sturm. After his graduation he gave a lecture course, and was accused of undermining the foundations of philosophy and theology. Ramus was found guilty of having 'acted rashly, arrogantly, and impudently. His lectures were interdicted in 1544. He left soon afterward, but returned when the decree against him was repealed by the influence of the Cardinal of Lorraine. In 1551 he was appointed professor of philosophy and eloquence at the College de France by Henry II. The anti-scholastic work continued. Ramus finally adopted Protestantism. The opposition against him rose to new heights and his library at Fontainebleau was burned in 1561. He himself fell victim to a massacre at St. Bartholomew in 1572. The logic of Ramus is his main reason for fame, his text books appear in Scottish universities. Ramus's logical works do not however mark an epoch in the history of logic. Logic falls, according to Ramus, into two parts: invention, treating of the notion and definition; and judgment, comprising the judgment proper, syllogism and method. Ramus also set forth the modern fashion of deducing the figures from the position of the middle term in the premises, instead of basing them, as Aristotle does on the different relation of the middle to the so-called major and minor terms. Wrote:

Dialecticae partitiones (1543). Later published under the title of *Institutionum dialecticarum libri III* (1553) and *Aristotelicae animadversiones* (1543)

Somnium Scipionis explicatum (1546)

Dialectique (1555). Also published under the title of *Dialecticae libri II* (1555)

Scholarum physicarum libri octo, in totidem acroamaticos libros Aristotelis (1565)

Scholarum metaphysicarum libri XIV (1566)

Scholae in liberales artes (1569)

Defensio pro Aristotele adv. Jac. Schecium (1571)

Commentaria de religione Christiana, edited by Ramus's friend Banos (Frankfort a. M., 1576)

AUDOMAR TALAEUS (d. 1562). He was the first pupil of Peter Ramus in Germany.

WILHELM AD. SCRIBONIUS IN CORBACH

THOMAS FREIGIUS. A professor at Altdorf (1543-1583). He wrote:
Quaestiones logicae et ethicae (Basel, 1576)
Logicae Rameae triumphus (Basel, 1583)

FRANZ FABRICIUS (1527-1573). Rector of the Düsseldorfer Gymnasium.

ARNAUD D'OSSAT (1537-1604). French cardinal, diplomat, and writer born at Larroque-Magnoac (Gascony). Studied at college of Auch and Paris, where he became the pupil and friend of the famous Ramus, whom he defended in two pamphlets against Charpentier, rector of the university. He also studied law at Bourges. His outstanding achievement was the negotiation of the reconciliation of Henry IV with the Pope. He was appointed Bishop of Rennes (1596), and cardinal (1589) and finally Bishop of Bayeux. Wrote:
Arnaldi Ossati in disputationem Jacobi Carpentarii de methodo (Paris, 1564)
Arnaldi Ossati additio ad expositionem de methodo (Paris, 1564)

KASPAR PFAFFRAD (d. 1622) in Helmstedt.

RUDOLF SNELLIUS VAN ROYEN (1546-1613). A mathematician born at Oudewater; lived in Leiden; professor at Marburg. He undertook the education of Jacobus Arminius for a short time during his boyhood. Wrote:
De ratione discendi et exercendi logicam per analysin et genesin facili et perspicua (Herborn: C. Corvini, 1599)
Commentarius doctissimus in dialecticam P. Rami (Herborn, 1587)

WILLIAM TEMPLE (1553-1623) at Cambridge.

J. COMBACHIUS (1585-1657). Professor at Marburg. Wrote:
Metaphysicorum liber singularis (Marburg, 1613)

LXVII. OPPONENTS OF RAMUS

JACOB SCHEGK (1511-1587). Teacher in Tübingen.

PHILIPP SCHERBIUS (d. 1605). Professor in Altdorf.

JACQUES CHARPENTIER (Jacobus Carpentarius; 1524-1574). A theologian born in Clermont in the department of Oise. In 1550 he was rector of the University of Paris and later professor of medicine. In 1564 he was also professor of mathematics. He defended the philosophy of Aristotle against the views of Peter Ramus and his followers. He is said to have been a chief opponent of Ramus and to have bribed assassins to kill Ramus in the Bartholomew massacre of 1572. Wrote:
Animadversiones in libros III dialecticarum institutionum Petri Rami (Paris, 1555)
Artis analyticae sive judicandi descriptio (1561)
Universae naturae brevis descriptio ex Aristotele (1560)
Platonis cum Aristotele comparatio (1573)

CAYET (Pierre Victor Palma; 1525-1610). Born in Montrishard. Pupil of Ramus and his friend. Won over to Calvinism by Ramus. Studied theology and Hebrew in Genf. Taught Henry of Navarre in 1562. In 1593 he went to Paris where he was converted by Cardinal Duperron. In 1600 he became a priest. He wrote numerous works, many of which are polemical. A list of these is given by E. Mangenot in an article in the *Dictionnaire de théologie catholique*, II (1923), 2046-2048.

F. BEURHUSIUS (1536-1609). Translated the *Dialecticae* of Peter Ramus into German (Erfurt, 1587).

NICODEMUS PHILIPP FRISCHLIN (1547-1590). Best known German dramatic poet of the latter half of the sixteenth century. Born at Balingen in Württemberg. Educated at the University of Tübingen, where he taught history and poetry in 1568. Received the poet laureateship from Emperor Maximilian II. Also taught in the Brunswick gymnasium. He was later imprisoned for writing libellous letters. He wrote versions of Callimachus and Aristophanes and commentaries on Persius and Virgil. Wrote also:
Hebraeis (1590), a Latin epic based on the Scripture history of the Jews.
Dialogus logicus contra P. Rami sophisticam (Frankfort a. M., 1590)

CORNELIUS MARTINI (1568-1621). Professor of philosophy at Helmstedt.

LXVIII. COMMENTATORS ON ARISTOTLE'S LOGIC

CHARLES DUMOULIN (Molinaeus; 1500-1566). A French jurist born at Paris; a relative of Anne Boleyn. Became a doctor of law and lectured at Orleans in 1521. Later became an advocate of the Parlement of Paris. In 1542 he became a Calvinist and later became a Lutheran. In 1553 he lectured on law at Tübingen. He became reconciled to the Catholic Church on his death bed. Wrote:

Commentarius ad edictum Henrici II, contra parvas datas et abusus curiae Romanae (1552)

Conseil sur le fait du Concile de Trente, reception ou rejet d'icelui (1564), which caused him to be cast into prison.

Consilium super commodis et incommodis novae sectae Jesuitarum (1604)

PETRUS A MATRE DEI (Abraham Bertius; 1610-1683). Born in Leyden. In 1627 he became a Carmelite in Charenton in France. In about 1650 he returned to Leyden at the request of the Pope to work among the Walloons. Wrote:

Modus convertendi haereticos (Paris, 1650)

Clara demonstratio articulorum religionis catholicae (Antwerp, 1671)

Brevis catechismus (1671)

Clara relatio missionis Holland. et proviniciarum confoederatarum (1658)

AGUSTINUS HUNNAEUS, listed by Burgersdijk.

FORTUNATUS CRELLIUS, listed by Burgersdijk.

LXIX. LATER LOGICIANS OF ENGLAND

THOMAS WILSON (ca. 1525-1581). Educated at Eton. Studied at King's College, Cambridge. Received degree of bachelor of arts in 1545 and master of arts in 1549. Wrote:

The Arte of Rhetorique (1553)

The Rule of Reason conteinyng the arte of Logike (London, 1567)

Oratio de clementia

A Discourse uppon Usurye by Waye of Dialogue and Oracions

RALPH LEVER (Leaver; d. 1585). Native of Lancashire. Educated in St. John's College, Cambridge. Received degree of bachelor of arts in 1547-8 and master of arts in 1551. Wrote:

The Assertion of Ralph Lever touching the Canon Law, the English Papists, and the Ecclesiastical Offices of this Realm, with his most humble Petition to Her Majesty for Redress
The Philosophers Game
The Arte of Reason

JOHN CASE (d. 1600). Educated at Oxford. Elected to fellowship at St. John's College, which he had to resign because of his Roman Catholic sympathies. Opened school of philosophy in Oxford. Wrote commentaries on Aristotle, notably on the *Organon, Ethics, Politics* and *Physics*. Wrote also:

Summa veterum interpretum in universam dialecticam Aristotelis (1584)
Speculum moralium quaestionum in universam ethicen Aristotelis (1585)
Sphaera civitatis (1588)
Reflexus speculi moralis (1596)
Thesaurus economiae (1597)
Lapis philosophicus (1599)
Ancilla philosophiae (1599)
Apologia musices, tam vocalis quam instrumentalis et mixtae (1588)
The praise of musicke

DUDLEY FENNER (1558-1587). Puritan divine. Born in Kent. Matriculated as a fellowcommoner of Peterhouse in 1575. Considered among the ablest exponents of Puritan views. Wrote:

A Brief Treatise upon the First Table of the Lawe
An Answer unto the Confutation of John Nichols his Recantation
A Counter Poyson
The Artes of Logike and Rethorike (1584)
Sacra theologia sive veritas quae est secundum pietatem ad unicae et verae methodi leges discripta
The Song of Songs, a translation from Hebrew into English.
A Short and Profitable Treatise of Lawful and Unlawful Recreation
Dudley Fenner his Catechisme
The Whole Doctrine of the Sacraments
Certain Godly and Learned Treatises
A Parte of a Register

EDWARD BREREWOOD (Bryerwood; ca. 1565-1613). Born and educated in Chester. Attended Brasenose College, Oxford. Received degree of bachelor of arts, 1586-7, and master of arts, 1590. Wrote:

Enquiries touching the Diversities of Language and Religions through the chief parts of the world, 1614-1647

Elementa Logicae, in gratiam studiosae juventutis in Academia Oxoniensi (1614-1615)

Tractatus quidam logici de praedicabilibus et praedicamentis (1628)

Tractatus duo; quorum primus est de meteoris, secundus de oculo (1631)

A Treatise of the Sabbath (1630)

Commentarii in Ethica Aristotelis (1640)

A Declaration of the Patriarchal Government of the Antient Church (1641)

RICHARD CRAKANTHORPE (1567-1624). Born near Strickland in Westmoreland. Became fellow of Queen's College, Oxford, in 1598. Received degree of doctor of divinity in 1612. Ambassador to Germany under James I. Wrote:

Introductio in Metaphysicam (1619)

Defence of Constantine, with a Treatise of the Pope's Temporal Monarchy (1621)

Logicae libri quinque de praedicabilibus praedicamentes (1622)

Tractatus de providentia Dei (1622)

Defensio Ecclesiae Anglicanae (1625)

THOMAS BLUNDEVILLE (fl. 1561). Probably studied at Cambridge. Wrote books on horsemanship and:

Three Moral Treatises

The Art of Logic (London, 1617)

The Theories of the Planets

A Treatise on how many Counsels and what manner of Counselers a Prince that will govern ought to have

ABRAHAM FRAUNCE (fl. 1587-1633). Native of Shropshire and educated at Shrewsbury School and John's College, Cambridge. Received degrees of bachelor of arts in 1579-80 and master of arts in 1583. Friend of Edmund Spenser. Wrote:

The Lawiers Logike, exemplifying the praecepts of Logike by the practise of the common Lawe (1588)

Arcadian Rhetorike

Abrahami Fransi Insignium Armorum . . . explicatio

NATHANAEL CARPENTER (1588/9-ca. 1628). Born in Northleigh, Devonshire. Matriculated at St. Edmund Hall, Oxford, in 1605. Was elected a fellow of Exeter in 1607. Died in Dublin. Wrote:

Philosophia libera triplici exercitationum decade proposita, an attack on Aristotelianism.

Achitophel or The Picture of a Wicked Politician, three sermons.

Chorazin and Bethsaida's Woe, a sermon.

Encomia varia, a manuscript which now belongs to Trinity College, Dublin.

ROBERT SANDERSON (1587-1663). Born in Yorkshire. Educated at Lincoln College, Oxford. Took orders in 1611. Favorite of the king who made him regius professor of divinity at Oxford until 1646. Promoted to the bishopric of Lincoln in 1661. Wrote:

Cases of Conscience

Logicae artis compendium (Oxford, 1640)

SAMUEL SMITH (1587-1620). Born in Lincolnshire. Entered as a commoner at Magdalen Hall, Oxford, in 1604 and became a fellow of Magdalen College in 1608. Received degree of bachelor of arts in 1608-9, master of arts in 1612 and bachelor of medicine in 1620. Wrote:

Aditus ad Logicam, in usum eorum qui primo Academiam salutant, an elementary manual of logic. (Oxford, 1613)

JOHN SANDERSON. Native of Lancashire. Matriculated as a sizar of Trinity College, Cambridge, in 1554. Received degree of bachelor of arts in 1557 and in 1561 commenced work toward his master's degree. Expelled from his fellowship for suspicious doctrines. Went to Rome, France, and Flanders, and in 1570 was enrolled among the students of the English College at Douay. In 1580 became divinity professor in the English College at Rheims. Appointed canon of the cathedral church at Cambray where he died. Wrote:

Institutionum dialecticarum libri quattuor

Tabulae vel schema catechisticum de tota theologia morali

De omnibus S. Scripturae locis inter pontificios et haereticos controversis

THOMAS GRANGER. Wrote:

Syntagma logicum or the divine logike (London, 1620)

ALEXANDER RICHARDSON. Wrote:

The logician's school-master (London, 1657)

LXX. LOGICIANS WHO COMBINE ARISTOTLE WITH RAMUS (SEMI-RAMISTS)

RUDOLPH GOCLENIUS (1547-1628). He was well known around Marburg, lecturing to large audiences. He compiled numerous works of logic following both Ramus and Aristotle, and because of this he was called a semi-Ramist. He wrote:

Isagoge in organon Aristotelis (Frankfort, 1598)

Lexicon philosophicum, quo tanquam clave philosophiae fores aperiuntur (Frankfort, 1613)

Isagoge in peripateticorum et scholasticorum primam philosophiam, quae dici consuevit metaphysica (Frankfurt, 1598)

CLEMENS TIMPLER (ca. 1600), a pupil of Goclenius, and later a professor in a grammar school in Steinfurt. He wrote:

Metaphysicae systema methodicum (Steinfurt, 1604)

F. BEURHUSIUS (1536-1609), translated the *Dialectics* of Ramus into German. This is the oldest book of Logic in the German language, and was published in Erfurt in 1587.

BARTHOLOMEW KECKERMANN (1571-1609). He composed many works on metaphysics, logic, physics, astronomy, politics, and ethics. He wrote:

Systema ethicae, which was against the *Ethice christiana* of Lambert Danaeus, and in which he asked for an ethics with a philosophical background and a theological ethics about which nothing could be generally stated.

Metaphysicae brevissima synopsis et compendium

JOHANNES HEINRICH ALSTED (1588-1638), a student of Keckermann, and later a professor in Herborn. He wrote:

Panacea philosophica (Herborn, 1610)

Metaphysica (Herborn, 1613)

Theologia scholastica (1618)

Cursus philosophici encyclopaedia (Herborn, 1620)

Compendium philosophicum (1626)

Encyclopaedia septem tomis distincta (Herborn, 1630)

[118]

JOHANNES COMBACHIUS (1585-1638), professor in Marburg. He wrote:
Metaphysicorum liber singularis (Marburg, 1613)

LXXI. GERMAN LOGICIANS

JAKOB MARTINI (1570-1649). Professor at Wittenberg. Wrote:
Disputationes domesticae, universam Aristotelis logicam breviter continentes
(3rd edition; Wittenberg: P. Helvvigij, 1617)

JOACHIM STERCK VON RINGELBERGH (ca. 1499-ca. 1536). Wrote:
Dialectica et rhetorica (Paris, ca. 1534)

MARCIN SMIGLECKI. Wrote:
Logica (Oxonii: H. Crypps, 1634)

JOHAN STIER (d. 1648). Wrote:
Praecepta doctrinae: logicae, etc. (London: R. Danielis, 1652)

JOHANNES CAESARIUS (ca. 1468-ca. 1550). Wrote:
*Dialectica accessit huc Joan. Murmellii Isagoge in decem Aristotelis praedica-
menta* (Lugduni: A. Vincentium, 1545)

CARL BUMANN. Wrote:
*Hypomnemata logica, ex summis philosophis, graecis et latinis, maxime vero
Platone, et Aristotele, Cicerone, et Quintiliano, Scaligero et aliis deducta*
(Frankfurt a. M.: A. Wecheli heredes, 1597)

LXXII. LATER AVERROISTS

ANDREAS CAESALPINUS (1519-1603). Born in Tuscany. Studied anatomy
and medicine at Pisa. In 1555 became professor of materia medica and di-
rector of the botanical garden. In 1592 he was appointed physician to Pope
Clement VIII and moved to Rome where he died. Was an eminent botanist
and physiologist. Wrote:
Daemonum investigatio peripatetica (1580)
Quaestionum medicarum libri II (1593)
De metallicis (1596)
Quaestionum peripateticarum libri V (1571)

FRANCISCO PICCOLOMINI (1520-1604). Died in Padua. Was a follower
of Zimara. Wrote
Universa philosophia de moribus, in which he opposed the logical theory of

Zabarella, to which Zabarella answered with his *Apologia de doctrinae ordine*.

Comes politicus, in answer to Zabarella's *Apologia*.

SEPULVEDA (d. 1572). A Spanish philosopher; pupil of Petrus Pomponatius. He was inclined to an Alexandrian interpretation of Aristotle.

JACOB ZABARELLA (1532-1589). Especially influential through his logical writings which were widely spread in text books. He is sometimes classified among the Averroist and sometimes among the Alexandrian interpreters of Aristotle. In his commentaries on Aristotle he sometimes presents opinions which are not reconcilable with Christianity. Wrote:

Apologia de doctrinae ordine, written in answer to Francisco Piccolomini's *Universa philosophia de moribus*. Piccolomini countered with his *Comes politicus*.

Liber de quarta syllogismorum figura

De rebus naturalibus liber (Padua, 1589)

Physica (Padua, 1601)

In liber Aristotelis de anima

CESARE CREMONINUS (Cremonini; 1550-1631). Professor of philosophy at Padua where from 1590 on he was a follower of Zabarella whose theories he taught. He thought highly of Aristotle and took a middle position in the Alexandrian-Averroist controversy. He thought of God as possessing the highest intelligence but not as the creator of the world. Although he was a friend of Gailleo, he opposed the Corpernican theory. Wrote:

Aristoteles redivivus

LUCILIO VANINI (Giulio Cesare; 1585-1619). Born near Naples. Studied philosophy and theology at Rome. Led the attack on scholasticism and helped lay the foundation of modern philosophy. Studied law at Padua and was ordained a priest. Led a roving life in France, Switzerland and the low countries. Arrested and put to death for being an atheist. Wrote:

Amphitheatrum aeternae providentiae divino-magicum (1615), which he wrote against the atheists to clear himself of the suspicion of being one.

De admirandis naturae reginae deaeque mortalium arcanis (1616)

LXXIII. SCEPTICS OF FRANCE

DE LA BOÉTIE (d. 1563). An intimate friend of Montaigne. He was an exponent of republican aspirations and his free opinions in politics were precisely similar in principle to the liberty which Montaigne advocated in philosophy and religion. Wrote:
Contre Un

MICHEL DE MONTAIGNE (1533-1592). Born in Bordeaux. Educated at College of Guinne till he was 13. Then he entered course of legal training at Toulouse or Paris. He was a member of court of Aides in Pengord and later *Conseiller* of the Parliament of Bordeaux. At 37 he retired from public functions determining to spend the rest of his life in studious seclusion. However in 1581 he was elected mayor of Bordeaux at a time when France was in the midst of religious wars. He died in 1592. Montaigne believed that our senses lead us to erroneous and uncertain conclusions. He also urged the weakness of reason and the untrustworthiness of experience. He considered enquiry better than acquisition, and search preferable to discovery. He held that truth does not exist for them, and man should not wish to possess it. Wrote:
Essais 3 volumes (Paris, 1582-1588)

PIERRE CHARRON (1541-1603). A French theologian and philosopher. He was originally a lawyer but became a famous preacher. He was a pupil of Montaigne. He held that all our knowledge commences with sense, that none of our faculties enable us to distinguish truth from error, and that reason is the ultimate criterion. He believed that man should be good for purely natural reasons and not because he feared damnation. He wrote:
De la sagesse (Bordeaux, 1601) in defence of the Catholic faith against Protestantism, in which he says that human nature is the foundation of ethics and discussed the relation of religion to morality. He further states that goodness must not be made dependent upon religion.

FRANCISCO SANCHEZ (1552-1632). A Portuguese physician and professor at Toulouse, a humanist and an empiricist; sometimes classed as a sceptic. He held that man can know nothing, since things are infinite in number; and even if they were numerically finite, their connections are infinite. Through the senses we learn only the accidents of things and not their essences. Reflections can give only confused and uncertain results. Our only recourse is Christian faith. Wrote:

De divinatione per somnum ad Aristotelem

Tractatus de multum nobili et prima universali scientia quod nihil scitur (Lyons, 1581), referred to simply as *Quod nihil scitur*, a treatise on the 'noble and high science of nescience.'

LXXIV. SCEPTICS OF ITALY

ADRIANO DE CORNETO (A. Castellesi; 1458/9-1521). Born in Corneto. Entrusted with ecclesiastical offices in Scotland and England from 1488, notably the reform of the English clergy by order of Pope Alexander VI. Made bishop of Hereford, 1502, and cardinal in 1503. Wrote:

De vera philosophia ex quattuor doctoribus ecclesiae (Bologna, 1507) in which he shows that whatever truth the heathens had is rightly the property of the Christians. He holds that Holy Scripture alone contains true knowledge and that philosophy cannot teach it.

De sermone latino et modo latine loquendi (Basle, 1513)

MARIUS NIZOLIUS OF MODENA (1488/98-1566/76). Born in Brescella (Modena). Taught in Parma and Sabbioneta. Influenced by the nominalism of Ockham. He opposed scholasticism. Substituted the science of words for the science of being. He denied the real value of the universe and maintained that only individual things are real substances, that species in general are only subjective concepts. He held that all knowledge must come from sensations which are the only source of immediate certainty. Wrote:

Thesaurus Ciceronianus

Antibarbarus philosophicus sive de veris principiis et vera ratione philosophandi contra Pseudophilosophos (1553). In this work he advocated the substitution of rhetoric for logic and metaphysics.

LXXV. SATIRISTS

SEBASTIAN BRANT (1457-1521). Born in Strassburg. Studied in Basel where he became doctor of both laws in 1489. He is one of the most famous political, religious, and humanistic writers before the Reformation. He is noted as a defender of the Immaculate Conception. Though he wrote much, he is remembered almost exclusively for:

Das Narrenschiff (1494), a didactic, satirical poem which sincerely and forcefully tells the faults of the times.

HERMANN VON DEM BUSCHE (H. Buschius, Pasiphilus; 1468-1534). Born in Sassenberg. Was a pupil of Rudolph of Langein in Münster, and of Hegius in Deventer in 1484, in Heidelberg, and then in Tübingen. From 1486 to 1491 he travelled in France and Italy. He taught in Cologne in 1494, in Wittenberg in 1502, and in Leipzig from 1503 to 1507. In 1508 he returned to Cologne. In the Reuchlin controversy he declared himself first to be against Reuchlin and then for him. He thought highly of Aristotle and taught Aristotelianism. In 1514 he joined the younger humanists under Hutten. Among his writings are:

Epigramme (1504)

Spicilegium philosophia (1511-1513)

Vallum humanitatis (1518)

JOHANN CROTUS (Johannes Jäger, Venatoris, Crotus Rubianus; ca. 1480- ca. 1539). Born in Dornheim, Thuringia; went to the University of Erfurt. His friendship with Conrad Mutianus and Ulrich von Hutten led him from being an upholder of scholasticism to becoming a partisan of humanism and opponent of the older learning. In about 1510 he became associated with Reuchlin and his supporters at Cologne. While in Bologna he had become acquainted with Luther's writings and approved of them. Later he became disgusted with the public disturbances resulting from the Lutheran movement and returned to Catholicism. Among his works are:

Epistolae obscurorum virorum, a larger part of which he wrote, and in which scholasticism and monasticism are criticized.

Apologia (1531), in which he showed that the Reformation had resulted in the sanctioning of all kinds of immorality and blasphemy.

Christliche Vermahnung (1526), directed against the new master of the Teutonic Order.

ULRICH VON HUTTEN (1488-1523). A German poet, humanist and reformer. He was destined for the cloister but his thirst for knowledge drew him away from the monastic ilfe. He wandered from Griefswald and Rostock to Wittenberg, Leipzig, and Vienna. The murder of a relative by the Duke of Wittenberg led him to employ satire in his desire for vengeance. At this time he openly espoused the cause of Luther and attacked the papal claims over Germany. His arrest was ordered by Pope Leo X. With the downfall of the knightly order to which Hutten had attached himself came his downfall also. He was refused refuge by Erasmus, but found it later with Zwingli on a little isle on a Zurich lake where he died. He wrote:

Ars versificandi (1511)

Nemo (1518)

Vadiamus, written in his controversy with Erasmus.

Morbus Gallicus (1519)

Epistolae obscurorum virorum, the greater part of which was written by Johann Crotus.

ROBERT BURTON (1577-1640). Born at Leicestershire. Attended Brasen-ose and Christ College, Oxford. His religious theories contained many satirical references to Scholasticism. He wrote:

Anatomy of Melancholy (1521), in which he remarks on the prevalence of madness and gives a wealth of material on the life, thought and conflicts of the time.

LXXVI. POLITICAL THEORISTS

JEAN BODIN (1530-1596), a French political philosopher, born at Angers. He believed in conformity between religion and politics. He defines the state as a collection of families united by common interests living under a sovereign who was supreme and also absolute and subject to no law. He believed that a universal religion was to be found in all men whatever their conception of the Deity. Sovereign power he thought to be subordinate to natural and moral laws. The family was the cornerstone of the state. Climatic conditions were emphasized in his studies of the determination of types of humanity. His works include:

Colloquium Heptaptomeres

Six liveres dela republique

Methodus ad facilem historiarum cognitionem, this may be classed as his chief philosophical work.

Responsio ad Paradoxa Malestretti

ALBERICO GENTILI (1552-1608), an Italian-English jurist. Attended the University of Perugia. His Protestant views caused his flight to England. He believed man to be naturally a social being, and that right existed only between individuals. War was justifiable only for the purpose of peace. Gentili was greatly interested in the philosophy of war and Law. Among his works are:

De legationibus (1585)
De jure belli (1598)
Hispanicae advocationis libri duo

RICHARD HOOKER (1553-1600), an English philosopher and theologian, graduated from Oxford and took Holy Orders in 1582. He held that there is one and only one being which is law unto itself, all others act according to a law, not of themselves, but of being, God is the author. The law of God's activity is reason or rational will. The most important of his works is the *Laws of Ecclesiastical Polity.*

JOHANNES ALTHUSIUS (1557-1638), a German professor of law and ethics at Herbon; he is believed to have influenced Rousseau. He was a zealous Calvinist. He claimed there could be only one sovereignty and that indivisible. The sovereignty could reside in only one place and could neither be transferred nor alienated. He is the author of several texts on political theory, the most important being:
Politica methodice digesta, one of the first German works on politics.

HUGO GROTIUS (Huig de Groot; 1583-1645), a Dutch jurist and theologian, considered to be the first authority on international law. Because of his political and theological disputes he was sentenced to life imprisonment but escaped. The state for him existed only by and for the individual. He distinguishes between civil right and social; for while man has a tendency towards life in society he has actually assumed social obligations and privileges by a sort of free compact. He says that the origin of social authority is the social contract, of the free volition of individuals who for the sole end of better safeguarding their rights live in common. His works include:
De jure belli et pacis, on international law.
Annotationes in Vetus Testamentum
De veritate religionis Christianae

CHRISTOPHER BESOLD (1557-1638), a German political scientist. Taught at Tübingen and Ingolstadt. Was familiar with history, law, philosophy, and many languages. His political views showed a trend toward Bodin and opposition to Machiavelli. He insisted on the maintenance of a public treasure and suggested the use of a public pawnshop. Wrote:
Collegium politicum (1614)
Politicorum libri duo (1620)
Discursus politici (1623)

[125]

OLIVER CROMWELL (1599-1658). 'Lord Protector of England.' He was educated at the free school of Huntingdon under Dr. Thomas Beard. In 1616, entered Sidney Sussex College at Cambridge, for just a short time. Studied law at Lincoln's Inn. His active public career began in 1640. He was very much interested in constitutional reforms and also in ecclesiastical matters. He caused the overthrow of the monarchy by means of his armed forces, and the execution of King Charles I. Cromwell's religious policy included the maintenance of a national church, a policy acceptable to the army, that wanted the state to control the church. His foreign policy was to support and extend the Protestant faith, and to promote English trade. His colonial policy aimed at the recognition and extension of the British empire. As a statesman Cromwell has been charged with substituting military tyranny, instead of law and liberty, in place of the abolished absolutism. His writings consist mainly of letters and speeches.

HUBERT LANGUET (1518-1581). Huguenot Statesman, born at Vitteaux near Autun. Studied in Poitiers, Padua and Bologna. In 1549 he went to Melancthon at Wittenberg. He travelled widely and held several political positions. Died in Antwerp. His correspondence has been published. He is sometimes mistaken as the author of the *Vindiciae contra tyrannos* written by Philipp Du Plessis-Mornay.

PHILIPP DU PLESSIS-MORNAY (1549-1623). Born in Castle Buhy, Normandy. Educated as a Calvinist; became later a very prominent Huguenot. Opponent of Duperron who worsted him in a disputation before King Henry IV at Fontainebleau. He wrote:
Mysterium iniquitatis s. historia papatus (1611), in which he opposed Baronius and Bellarmine.
De l'institution de l'Eucharistie (1598)
Traité de la vérité de la religion chrétienne (1581)
Vindiciae contra tyrannos (1579), written under the pseudonym of Stephanus Junius; often attributed to Hubert Languet.

JOHN VALENTINE ANDREAS (1586-1654). Nephew of the Lutheran theologian Jakob Andrea (1528-1590). Attended the University of Tübingen until 1607. Held ecclesiastical positions in Calw, Stuttgart, and Adelberg. Wrote more than one hundred, mostly small works, among which is the following:
Reipublicae christianopolitanae descriptio (1619)

ALESSANDRO TURAMINI (ca. 1556-1605)

JOHN OLDENDORP (d. 1651), attacked the philosophy of Philip Melancthon.

BENEDICT WINKLER (d. 1648)

FRANÇOIS HOTMAN

LXXVII. SPANISH MYSTICAL WRITERS AT ALCALA

ST. IGNATIUS OF LOYOLA (1491-1556). The founder of the Society of Jesus in 1540. Born in the Basque country; baptized Inigo; converted in Pamplona during a French attack on the city; studied at Universities of Alcala and Paris; his entire life was one of intense devotion to God. Wrote:

Ejercitatorie de la vida espiritual. This work deals with the art of contemplation. The aim of the exercises is to train the soul in meditation and to guide her in making an election and resolutions as to a state of life. These exercises are part of the standing orders of the Society of Jesus and have governed its organization and contributed to its success.

JUAN DE LOS ANGELES (ca. 1536-1609). Born near Orospesa in the diocese of Avilla; contemporary and friend of Francis Borgia; belonged to Franciscan Order; became Provincial of San Jose in 1601; also became Provincial of the Franciscan Order; founded the nunnery of barefooted Franciscans at Madrid. Wrote:

Lucha (1589). In this work he explains the uniqueness of the love of God and the sublime mystery of the transformation when He is beloved.

Conquista (1595). This is written in the form of a series of dialogues between a religious named Deseoso and his spiritual instructor. The aim is to give knowledge of the Kingdom of God and teach the order to be observed to enjoy it.

Spiritual and Amorous Strife between God and the Soul (1600). This treats of the action of God upon the soul. There are three steps of love: the wounds of love, the chains of love, and the sickness of love.

Spiritual Treatise of the Divine Sacrifice of the Mass (1604)

Treatise on the Presence of God (1604). This work is concerned with contemplation.

Manual of the Perfect Life (1608)

Spiritual Considerations upon the Book of the Song of Songs of Solomon
(1607). This work deals with the stages of the mystic way, the purgative
way, and the illuminative way.

Spiritual Garden of the Religious Soul (1610). This deals with the Passion
of Christ, and the obligation of Christians.

JERONIMO GRACIAN (1545-1614). In religion known as Jeronimo de la
Madre de Dio; born at Valladolid on June 6; educated at Valladolid, Toledo
and the University of Alcala; joined Discalced Carmelites at Pastrana in 1572;
friend of St. Teresa; became provincial of Discalced province. Called before
the 'Consulta' in 1592 and expelled from the Order; captured by Turks; re
instated in Carmelite Order in 1596. Wrote:

The Pilgrimage of Anastasius (1613). This describes the miseries he suffered
while in captivity in Tunis.

Lampara encandida (1586). This explains how the soul should act toward
God, his neighbor and himself, and also explains the vows of obedience,
chastity, and poverty.

Flores Carmeli (not printed)

Cerco espiritual de la conciendia tentada

Jubilee of the Holy Year (1599). This is a brief summary of confession and
communion written in Italian.

Josephina (1602). This is on the life of the Patriarch Saint Joseph.

Suffrage of the Souls in Purgatory. This is written in Italian.

Dilucidario (1704). This work expounds the doctrine of the books of the
Mother Teresa de Jesus.

The Heavenly Road (1601). This is a text book on mystical theology.

Book of the Rule and Discipline (1611)

Life of the Soul (1609). This attacks those who set perfection in total an-
nihilation.

The Catholic Soldier (1611). Consists of conversations between a Protestant
and two Catholic soldiers.

The Ten Lamentations on the Miserable Estate of Atheists in Our Times
(1611)

Virtues and Foundations of the Holy Mother Teresa de Jesus (1611)

Discourses on the Mysterious Name of Mary (1612)

Leviathan (1614)

Art of Holy Dying (1614)

Arbor Salutis. This is a manual of confession.

Seven Treasures of Perfection

TOMAS DE JESUS (Diego Sanchez Davilla, 1564/68-1627) Founder of the Desierto; born in Baeza; studied at the college in Baeza which was founded by Juan de Avilla; studied law and theology at the University of Salamanca; took the habit of the Discalced at Valladolid; became lector in theology at colleges of Alcala and Seville; became prior of convent at Zaragoza; became provincial of Old Castile from 1597 to 1600; became definitor general of the Spanish Congregation in 1600; founded convent of Discalced Carmelites in Brussels and Louvain. He is important with regard to his position on the subject of acquired contemplation. Wrote:

Order of Our Lady of Carmel. This traces the history of the Order.

Summary and Compendium of the Degrees of Prayer (1610). The aim of this work is to reduce the doctrine of St. Teresa to a brief summary in the matter of prayer and things of the spirit.

Stimulus missionum (1610)

De procuranda salute omnium gentium. Also known as *Thesaurus sapientiae divinae in gentium omnium salute procuranda.* Sections one through five deal with the necessity and utility of missions. Sections six through twelve deal with the evangelization of various classes of unbelievers.

Commentaria de statu monachorum (1617)

The Practice of the Living Faith (1617). This is a constructive account of the Catholic faith.

Rules for Examining and Discerning a Soul's Interior Progress (1620). In this work, the aim is not to help those led by the higher road of supernatural prayer, but those who are living at lower levels.

Divinae orationes sive a Deo infusae methodus, natura et gradus (1623). This book treats of supernatural prayer.

De regularium visitatione liber (1625). This is a textbook for conventual visitors.

LXXVIII. SPANISH MYSTICAL WRITERS AT SALAMANCA

GARCIA DE CISNEROS (1455-1510). A Benedictine monk of Montserrat; born at Cisneros in the province of Leon; believed to have been educated at Salamanca; entered monastery of St. Benedict in 1475; prior of Monserrat monastery in 1493; abbot in 1499; Spanish ambassador to France in 1497; influenced St. Ignatius of Loyola. Wrote:

Ejercitatoris de la vida espiritual (1500). This book was written primarily for monks. Sections 1, 2 and 3 lay down exercises connected with the purgative, illuminative and unitive way. Section 4 deals with contemplation.

Directorio de las horas coanonicas (1500). This book gives clear instructions on preparation for the Divine Offices.

ST. THOMAS OF VILLANOVA (1488-1555). Known as preacher who brought mysticism into the pulpit. Born at Fuentellana, near Cuidad Real; studied at the University of Alcala; lectured in philosophy; friend of Domingo de Soto; called to chair of moral philosophy at Salamanca in 1516; Augustinian priest; became prior of Salamancan monastary in 1519; became prior at Burgos in 1522 and prior at Valladolid later; became provincial of Andalusia in 1527 and archbishop of Valencia in 1545; known as father of the poor; canonized in 1658. Wrote:

Concines sacrae (published 1581). This consists of about 350 Latin sermons.

FRANCISCO DE OSUNA (1497-1542). Born in Osuna; entered Franciscan Order when very young; studied at the University of Salamanca; travelled in France; elected Franciscan commisary general to the Indies in 1530, but refused commission either because of ill health or because he felt his vocation lay in his writing. Wrote:

Alphabets (1525-1554). This book is in six treatises. The first treats of the circumstances of the Sacred Passion of the Son of God. The second is planned as a manual for persons of active life with little time for devotional chapters, discussing themes of love, the mutability of temporal things, preparation for the Mass, etc. The fourth treatise is called 'Law of Love' and treats of the mysteries, questions, and exercises of love and the theology which pertains to the understanding and the will. The fifth treatise deals with poverty and the right use of riches. The sixth is a consideration of the wounds of Jesus Christ for the exercise of all devout persons. The purpose of the third spiritual alphabet was to show to all how they may serve the Universal Lord.

ST. PETER OF ALCANTARA (San Pedro De Alcantara; 1499-1562). Born in Alcantara in the province of Estremadura; studied at Salamanca; entered Franciscan convent of Manjurez in 1515; ordained in 1524; became superior of Franciscan Order at Badajoz; provincial of his order in Estremadura in

1538; founded Order of Barefooted Franciscan friars; his reform influenced St. Teresa; died at convent of Mount Areno; canonized in 1669. Author of a number of books which are all lost but one, and there is controversy as to whether this book was written by him or by Luis de Granada:

Tratado de la Oracion y Mediacion. This book is called the Golden Treatise and is chiefly concerned with the lower stages of the mystical life, on meditation and contemplation.

ALONZO DE OROZCO (1500-1591). Augustinians claim he is the most eminent figure among our mystical and ascetic writers; Platonist; born in Oropesa; studied at Cathedral of Toledo and then at the University of Salamanca; Augustinian priest; prior of Augustinian houses at Soria, Medina del Campo and Valladolid. Wrote:

Confessiones. This book deals with his life.

Garden of Prayer (1544). This book is a devotional guide.

Mount of Contemplation (1544). A dialogue between two characters which describes the four stages of the journey which the would-be contemplative must take.

Chronicle of the Order of St. Augustine (1551)

Examination of the Conscience (1551)

Government of the Soul

Memorial of Holy Love (1554). Aims at awakening the memory of the holy love of God.

Seven Words of the Virgin (1556)

History of the Queen of Sheba (1565). Shows how every Christian should serve and adore Jesus Christ.

De la Suavidad de Dios. Written to console those who cannot feel in prayer, contemplation, and the use of the sacraments the sweetness and favour which the Lord gives when He pleases.

DIEGO DE ESTELLA (1523-1578). Family name, Diego de San Christabal. Born in Estella south west of Pamplona; studied at French University of Toulouse and University of Salamanca; preacher. Wrote:

Life of St. John the Evangelist (1554)

Book of the Vanity of the World (1562)

Modus concionandi et explanatio in Psalmum. This treatise is on preaching and also includes a series of 6 sermons on the psalm, 'Super flumina Babylonis.'

Meditaciones devotisimas del amor de Dios (1576). In this work he states
that contemplation must be pursued with the view, not to knowledge, but
to love; not for its own sake, but for the sake of its object, God.

Enarrationes in sacrosanctum evangelium secundum Lucam. In this work he
says that silence and solitude are the walls of devotion, and in God is
man's satisfaction. It is divided into three parts. The first is on vanity, the
second on perverse deceptions of the world, and the third part discusses
the all-sufficiency of God.

PEDRO MALON DE CHAIDE (ante 1550-1589). Platonist; born at Cas-
cante; entered Augustinian Order at Salamanca in 1557; studied at the University of Salamanca under Luis de Leon; prior at convent of Zaragoza in
1575; believed to have held teaching posts at the Universities of Huesca and
Zaragoza; became master of his order in 1582. Wrote:

Conversion de la Magdalena. Part I describes Magdalen in her sins; part II
describes her in her penitence, and part III in her state of grace. He says
the purpose of the book is to enkindle the will to desire God and prepare
it to enjoy Him.

LUIS DE LA PUENTE (1554-1624). Born at Valladolid; studied theology
at Dominican college of St. Gregory and at the Jesuit College of St. Ambrose;
admitted to Society of Jesus in 1574; taught in Jesuit colleges of Leon and
Salamanca; became rector of St. Ambrose from 1594 to 1596, and from 1601
to 1602. Wrote:

*Meditaciones de los misterios de nuestra santa Fe, con la practica de la oracion
mental sobre ellos.*

*De la Perfeccion del Cristiano en los estados y oficios de las tres republicos,
seglar, eclesiastica y religiosa Exposito Moralis et Mystica in Canticum
Caticorum.* This is a commentary on the *Song of Songs* in ten books.

Spiritual Guide. This, the best known of his works, deals with prayer, meditation, contemplation, Divine visits, extraordinary graces of mortification,
and heroic acts.

Spiritual Maxims and Sentiments (1671). This consists of meditations of a
personal and informal kind, interspersed with records of experience.

JUAN FALCONI (1596-1638). Born at Finana in Province of Granada;
took the habit of the Order of Our Lady of Mercy in 1611 at Mercedarian
convent at Madrid; studied at University of Salamanca; lectured in theology
at Valladolid and the College of Conception at Alcala de Henares; consid-

ered the father of quietism. His works were published after his death as follows:

A Primer Whereby We may Learn to Read in Christ the Book of Eternal Life (1637). In this he states that the book is for all, since none may excuse himself from prayer.

The Incomprehensible and Divine Life of God (1660). This is a series of meditations on Divine attributes.

Treasury of the Mercies of God (1660). This consists of a series of prayers to God for the sinner, concerned with sin and forgiveness.

Our Daily Bread (1660)

Letter to a Spiritual Daughter (dated 1628; published 1657).

Letter to a Religious (dated 1629; published 1657).

A Straight Road to Heaven (1783). This treats of mental and spiritual prayer.

Brief Compendium of Most Eminent Christian Perfection (1783). In this he states that the perfection is founded upon two principles. The first is a disregard or contempt for all created things and particularly for oneself, and the second is a most lofty conception of God, coming by readiness of will, humility of heart, and self-surrender.

LXXIX. THE SPIRITUAL FAMILY OF JUAN DE AVILA

JUAN DE AVILA (1500-1569). Called the Apostle of Andalusia; born at Almadovar del Camp in the diocese of Toledo; studied law at Salamanca; studied theology at the University of Alcala under Domingo de Soto; entered Holy Orders; missionary in Andalusia. Juan de Dios, Francis Borgia, Teresa de Avila, and Luis de Granada all regarded him as their spiritual father; imprisoned several months at Seville in 1534 by the Inquisition; founded Jesuit College of Cordoba; died at Montilla; beatified in 1894. Wrote:

Audi, Filia (also known as *Libro Espiritual*; 1530). A treatise on the Ten Commandments. It treats of the evil conversations of the world, the flesh and the devil and the remedies against them, of faith and self-knowledge, penitence, prayer, meditation, the Passion of our Lord Jesus Christ, and the love of one's neighbor.

Platicas para sacerdotes (1563)

Epistolario Espiritual (1578). Book I is addressed to the clergy and religious, Book II to the nuns, Book III to the ladies of the world, and Book IV to the men of the world.

Book of the Most Holy Sacrament of the Eucharist, of the Holy Spirit and of Our Lady the Virgin Saint Mary

LUIS DE GRANADA (1504-1588). The first mystic to make the Castilian language his medium; born in Granada; Dominican priest at the convent of the Holy Cross (Santa Cruz) ; received fellowship at College of St. Gregory in Valladolid; appointed Prior of the convent of Escal Coelo, near Cordoba; confessor of Queen Catherine of Portugal; became Dominican Provincial of Portugal in 1556; refused archbishopric of Braga; retired to St. Dominic convent in Lisbon in 1560. Wrote:

Contemptus mundi (1536)

Libro de la Oracion y Meditacion (1554). The first part consists of 14 meditations concerned with the Passion, Death, and Resurrection of Jesus, and chapters on method of prayer in meditation. The second part deals with devotion in general.

Libro llamado Guia de Pecadores (1556). This work treats of the practice of virtue and the service of God. It also deals with counsels against the 7 deadly sins and certain venial sins, and the steps man must take to lead a life of virtue.

A Manual of Divers Prayers and Spiritual Exercises. In this work, he says that prayer is the business of all times and the companion of life.

Compendio de Doctrina Christiana (1559)

Vita Christi (1561)

Translation of Scala Paradisi of St. John Climacus (1562)

Memoriae de la Vida Christiana (1565). The first part contains 7 considerations to have sorrow for our sins, 7 counsels on confession, and 3 methods of making satisfaction. The second part is made up of prayers.

The Additions (1574). This is in two volumes. The first part begins with a treatise on the love of God, and the second part is composed of meditations on the life of Christ.

Introduccion del Simbolo de la Fe (1585). This is an apologia for the religion of the creed. The first part sets forth the benefits to be derived from the consideration of the works of nature. The second part shows the necessity of faith. The third part deals with the subject of original sin. The fourth part enlarges on Redemption, and the fifth part is an independent work with a treatise on presenting the Christian doctrine to the newly converted.

ST. TERESA (1515-1582). Known as Carmelite foundress; profoundly influenced by Asuna's Third Alphabet; born in Avilla; entered Carmelite Convent of Incannation at Avilla in 1535; established the first Reformed Foundations for men with the help of St. John of the Cross; canonized in 1622. Wrote:

Letters. This is a collection of letters writen in her life which throw light on her personality.

Libro de su Vida (1562-1565). This is an account of the spiritual progress in her life, describing the degrees of prayer.

Constitutions (1564)

Camino de Perfeccion (1565). This work is for general devotional reading.

Conceptions of the Love of God (1567)

Fundaciones. This work is concerned with the foundations of reform.

Exclamaciones (1569)

Moradas (1577). In this work, she describes the Mystic Way. She thinks of the soul as a castle formed of transparent crystal, in which there are many rooms or mansions, and in the midst of them all is the chief one where secret things pass between God and the soul.

Relaciones (1560-79). This consists of reports sent to her directors of her spiritual life.

LUIS DE LEON (Luis Ponce de Leon; 1527 or 1528-1591). Born in Belmonte, in the province of Cuenca; studied at the University of Salamanca; entered Augustinian Order when 15 years old; elected professor of theology at Salamanca (chair of St. Thomas Aquinas) which excited enmity against him especially from the rival order of St. Dominic; imprisoned for 5 years by the Inquisition; appointed to chair of Sacred Literature in 1572; a disciple of Luis Granada; described as best Hebrew critic and poet of mysticism. Wrote three prose masterpieces:

Song of Songs (1561). (Translated from Hebrew into Spanish).

La Perfect Casada (1583). This book is an exposition of the final chapter of the Book of Proverbs, which describes the virtuous woman.

Numbres de Cristo (1583). A series of commentaries upon the appelations given to Jesus in the Scriptures, as King, Son of God, Shepherd, Beloved etc. The book is cast in the form of conversations between three friends, Juliano, Sabino, and Marcelo.

Exposition of the Book of Job. This work was written for the Venerable Anne of Jesus.

ST. JOHN OF THE CROSS (Juan de Yepes; 1542-1591). Born at Honti-
veros, near Avilla; attended school at Medina in 1551; entered Order of
Carmel in 1563; studied at the University of Salamanca; founded reformed
Carmel house for men at Duruelo in 1658 with the help of St. Teresa; imprisoned for nine months in 1577 since his holy self-denying life was a re-
proach to unreformed friars; founded and governed a reformed house in
Baeza in 1579, and later that of Segovia; became prior of Granada in 1581;
became vicar provincial of Andalusia in 1585. In 1591, having opposed some
harsh measures of the Chapter, he was treated with great cruelty and banished
to the solitary convent of Pegnela in Sierra Morena. Wrote:

Subida del Monte Carmelo (1583)

Noche oscura del sentido. This work describes the spiritual desolation through
which he had passed, and the spiritual awakening when the grace of God
regenerates the soul.

Cantico espiritual (1584). In this work he describes the illuminative life,
saying that it is a high estate and union of love, known as the spiritual
betrothal with the Word, the Son of God.

Llama de Amor Viva (1584). This is a poem of the life of transformation
in Union. The soul, in union with God is described as transformed in the
fire of Love.

Colloquies Between Christ and the Spouse and His Bride the Soul. This is a
brief treatise of the dark knowledge of God, and also contains spiritual
sentences and maxims.

LXXX.   MISCELLANEOUS SPANISH MYSTICAL WRITERS

BERNARDINO DE LAREDO (1482-1540). Born at Seville; received doctorate of medicine at the University of Seville; became a lay brother in the
Franciscan convent of San Francisco del Monte, near Seville in 1510; his
works influenced St. Teresa. Wrote:

Metafora medicinae (1522)

Modus faciendi cum medicandi (ca. 1527). In both these works he considers
religion and medicine as complementary means of healing.

Subida del Monte Sion (1529). This work is in three volumes. Book I is on
self-knowledge and the purgative way; book II is a meditation on the
life of Christ; book III contains essays on contemplation and quiet.

CRISTOBAL DE FONSECA (1550-1621). Born in Sant Ollala (50 miles from Madrid) in diocese of Toledo; entered Augustinian monastery in Toledo; became prior of Augustinian monastery of Segovia in 1591. Wrote:
Treatise on the Love of God (1592). This work, according to the author's words, is on love in general and the love of all things in particular.
First Part of the Life of Christ Our Lord (1596). This work is in five parts. Part I relates events of Christ's earthly life; parts II and III deal with His miracles and parables; parts IV and V are homiletic.
Fifth Part of the Life of Christ Our Lord (1614). This work consists of sermons for Lent.

LXXXI. THE CAMBRIDGE PLATONISTS

EVERARD DIGBY (1550-1592). Attacked Ramism; strongly influenced by Reuchlin; scholastic tendency; favored Alexandrian-Cabalistic eclectism. Wrote:
Theoria Analytica
De Duplici Methodo

MARTIN FOTHERBY (1559-1616)

JOHN DAVIES OF HEREFORD (1565-1618)

SIR JOHN DAVIES (1569-1626). Baptized at Tisbury, Wiltshire; educated at Winchester College; an English philosophical poet; chief aim was to establish Protestant religion in Ireland. Wrote:
Nosce teipsum (1599), a philosophical poem on the nature and immortality of the soul.

THOMAS WHITE (Vitus, Anglus, ex Albis; 1582-1676)

FRANCIS GLISSON (1597-1677). Educated at Oxford and Cambridge; became Professor of Physics at Cambridge; appears to have had some influence on Leibnitz. Wrote:
De Natura Substantia Energitica, in which he conceives substances as forces.

KENELM DIGBY (1603-1665). Grandson of Everard Digby.

THOMAS BROWNE (1605-1682). An English physician and antiquary whose favorite theme was the mystery of death and what lies beyond the grave. He wrote:
Religio Medici, in which he says, 'Persecution is a bad and indirect way to plant religion. It hath been the unhappy method of angry devotion.'

ROBERT GREVILLE (Lord Brooke; 1608-1643).

BENJAMIN WHICHCOTE (1609-1683). Born in Shropshire; attended Cambridge from 1626 to 1633; was tutor and fellow of Emanuel College, Cambridge from 1633 to 1643; was a successful preacher in Trinity church from 1644 to 1660; became provost of King's College in 1644 and vice-chancellor of the University in 1650; extremely devoted to Scriptural study. He said that the greatest concern of man is religion, which begins with reason. Also believed in religious tolerance. Said that the essential principles of the moral law are written within man, that moral goodness is the best and highest thing in life.

PETER STERRY (d. 1672). Born in Surrey; entered Emanuel College, Cambridge in 1629; received B. A. in 1633; elected Fellow in 1636; received M. A. in 1637; was nominated as one of the divines for the Westminster Assembly in 1643; influenced by Henry More; combined mysticism with Platonism; was an intense Calvinist, believing in religious tolerance and desiring to reconcile the waning Christian forces. Wrote:
A Discourse of the Freedom of the Will (published 1675).
The Race and Royalty of the Kingdom of God in the Soul of Man (published 1683). This consists of sermons.
Sermons (published 1710).

HENRY MORE (1614-1687). Born at Grantham, Lincolnshire; at Eton from 14 to 17 years of age; student and Fellow of Christ's College, Cambridge from 1631 to 1639; entered Holy Orders, yet signed the 'Covenant' and the 'engagement'; was opposed to Descartes and Hobbes; strove to establish the rights of reason and nationality in religion. Wrote:
Antidote Against Atheism
Immortality of the Soul
Grand Mystery of Godliness (1660). In this book he refutes Familism and Quakerism.
Mystery of Iniquity
Divine Dialogues (1667). In this work he defends the Quakers.
Philosophical Poems (1647)
Enchiridion metaphysicum (1671)

JOHN SMITH (1616-1652). Born in Achurch on the Nene, one of the smallest villages of Northamptonshire; probably educated at Oundle grammar school; attended Emanuel College, Cambridge in 1636; became friend of his tutor, Benjamin Whichcote; received M. A. in 1644; became a Fellow of Queen's College in 1644; delivered the Discourses in Queen's College chapel; in general agreement with Whichcote. Wrote:

Select Discourses (published 1660). There are ten discourses in number, the first one entitled 'Concerning the True Way or Method of attaining Divine Knowledge,' and another is on 'The Excellency and Nobleness of True Religion.' On immortality, he says you must do and be in order to know; to act as if there were a God and the highest dictates of reason were the dictates of His will, as if the obedience of these were the business of life, and as if your purest thoughts were in correspondence with Divine grace and truth, and thus you learn the excellency of true religion.

RALPH CUDWORTH (1617-1685). Born at Aller in Somerset near Langport; attended Cambridge in 1632; became Fellow and tutor in 1639; became Regius Professor of Hebrew in 1645; succeeded Whichcote as Rector of North Cadbury in 1650; became Master of Christ's College in 1654; rejected Calvinism early in life; presented an Arminianistic sermon before House of Commons in 1647; opposed to Hobbes and Descartes; particularly familiar with the neo-Platonic Jewish school of thought. Wrote:

The True Intellectual System of the Universe (1678). In this work he tried to establish by rational proof the existence of God, the truth of moral conceptions and the freedom of the will.

Treatise on the Immutable Morality (published 1731). Mind in God and mind in man are the same. The rational, therefore, is the real and immutable, whether it appear under the aspect of intellectual or moral truth.

NATHANIEL CULVERWEL (ca. 1618-1651). Probably born in London; entered Cambridge in 1633; received B. A. in 1636 and M. A. in 1640; elected a Fellow in 1642; was a strict Calvinist. Wrote:

Spiritual Opticks (published 1652). This is composed of eight sermons.

Discourse of the Light of Nature (published 1857). In this work he opposes the doctrine of innate ideas and the preexistence of the soul. He says that all knowledge originates primarily through the senses. The eternal law, discerned by reason, is God himself, who embraces in a single great order both matter and spirit. Law originates in reason and is for reason and is essentially moral in character.

THOMAS STANLEY (1625-1678). Wrote a history of philosophy in English, in four volumes (1655-1662).

JOHN NORRIS OF BEMERTON (1657-1711). Attended Oxford University; became a High Churchman; belonged to Tory party; influenced by Henry More; also a disciple of Malebranche (1638-1713); considered a moralist and metaphysician. Wrote:

Theory of the Ideal and Intelligible World. This work is an answer to Locke's theories on the existence of God and the immortality of the soul.

LXXXII. OPPONENTS OF PHILOSOPHY

DANIEL HOFMANN (ca. 1540-1611). Wrote:

Disputatio pro duplici veritate Lutheri a philosophia impugnata et ad pudendorum locum ablegata (Magdeburg, 1600)

WENZEL SCHILLING. Pupil of Daniel Hofmann, and continuer of his opposition to philosophy.

J. ANDR. WERDENHAGEN. Pupil of Daniel Hofmann and continuer of his opposition to philosophy.

LXXXIII. STOICISM

DIRK VOLCKERTSZOON COORNHERT (Cornhert; 1522-1590). A Dutch scholar, politician and theologian born in Amsterdam. Active as a champion of political and religious liberty. He incurred the disapproval of the Spanish government and was imprisoned at the Hague in 1567, but escaped to Cleves. In 1572 he was recalled and made Secretary to the State of Holland. He was apparently influenced by the writings of Sebastian Franck. Arminius, employed to refute the teachings of Coornhert, was won over by his arguments. Coornhert stood for toleration and against capital punishment for heretics. He was opposed to the orthodox Protestant party and disapproved of Calvin's doctrine. He was convinced of man's freedom of will. He held that, though man had been marred by the 'fall' from his highest possibilities, he still possessed native gifts and graces, and bore deep within himself an unlost central being, which joined him indissolubly to God. He believed that religion is an inward experience of the Word of God, and grows and deepens in man's own heart. Coornhert started a Dutch version of the New Testament, following the Latin of Erasmus, but it was never completed. Also wrote:

Abraham uytgang (1630). This is a poetical work.

Comedie van de blinde van Jericho (1630). This is a poetical work also.

Zedekunst dat is wellevens kunst (1630). This is a prose work on ethics.

JUSTUS LIPSIUS (Joest Lips; 1547-1606). A Belgian scholar born at Ober-
rysscha or Overyssche, a small village in Brabant, near Brussels. He was a
philologian and humanist, and he wrote in defense of Roman Stoicism. He
studied law and humanism at the Jesuit College in Cologne and at the University of Louvain. He became a Lutheran and taught history at the University
of Jena. In 1579, he became professor of history at Leyden, embracing the
Calvinistic faith. In 1590 he was reconciled with the Catholic church and
received the chair of Latin at Louvain. His contemporaries, H. Stephanus,
Joseph Scaliger and Sagittarius, all assailed and belittled him. Wrote:

De Constantia (1584). Here he attempts to define the right attitude of a
thoughtful man towards public evils. The book consists of a dialogue
between Lipsius himself and Langius of Liege. The author says that travel
does not avail to cure the weariness and despondency which such evils
induce. It is the mind itself which must be changed, and made constant;
and a true constancy is founded on the judgments of right reason. The
nature and origin of public evils form the four main propositions of the
book. They are: (1) that public evils are sent by the Providence of God,
(2) that they are necessary and derived from Fate, (3) that they are ad-
vantageous in several ways and (4) that they are neither intolerable nor
novel.

Politicorum, sive civilis doctrinae libri sex (1589). In this work he seems to
exhibit a return to Catholicism.

Philosophia et physiologica Stoica (1604). This book has one interlocutor, a
youth. In part one, Lipsius divides philosophy into contemplative and
active, or, as Seneca, into moral, natural and rational. By studying philosophy and having in mind the stoic decrees or axioms we arm ourselves
against the anxieties of life. The axioms are: (1) the recognition of the
object or end, (2) the understanding of the nature of the good, and
(3 paradoxes. In part two, Lipsius takes up physiologica or physics, corporeal or principia, and incorporeal or elementa. He also discusses external and internal evils, man's nature and the mind, and the divisions of
the soul.

JAMES ARMINIUS (1560-1609). Born in Oudewater, near Utrecht in
southern Holland. Family name was Herman or Harman. Studied at Uni-

versity of Leyden for six years; then studied at the University of Geneva, being attracted there by the celebrated Beza. He then transferred to the University of Basle, because he had given offense at Geneva by defending Ramus in opposition to Aristotle. At Basle he heard Gyrnaeus, and also delivered theological lectures. He returned to the University of Geneva to study divinity. In 1588, he became pastor of the Dutch Reformed Church in Amsterdam. In 1603 he became professor of divinity at the University of Leyden. As a result of investigation of Coornhert's criticism of Calvin's views, Arminius organized his doctrinal views which compose the Arminian theology. One of his followers was Episcapus. Arminius discarded all five points of Calvinism. He was opposed to absolute predestination and particular redemption. He believed that some place must be found for the human will in salvation, that atonement was full and complete, whereas election was conditional. Wrote:

Declaration of Sentiments (1608). This was delivered before the States in a full assembly at the Hague.

Apology Against 31 Articles (1609)

Orations. This is a collection of sermons.

THOMAS GATAKER (1574-1654). Puritan clergyman, critic and author, born in London. Studied at St. John's College, Cambridge. In 1596 was one of the earliest fellows of Sidney Sussex College. Became rector of Rotherhithe (Surrey) in 1611 and appointed member of the Westminster Assembly of Divines in 1643. Wrote:

Of the Nature and Use of Lots (1627). In this work he defended the use of lots, but not for divination. His opinions here brought him into disrepute with some.

A Collection of Sermons (1637)

Annotations (1645 and 1651). This works consists of commentaries on Isaiah, Jeremiah and Lamentations.

KASPER SCHOPPE (Kasper Scioppius; 1576-1649). A classical scholar and controversialist, born at Neumarket in the Palatinate. Studied at Heidelberg, Altdorf, and Ingolstadt. In 1591 he became a Roman Catholic and shortly thereafter made a series of attacks on Protestantism. He assailed Joseph Justus Scaliger, and in 1611 attacked King James of England in libelous pamphlets. Wrote:

De arte critica (1597)

Symbola critica in Apuleii Opera (1605)
De rhetoricarum exercitationum generibus (1628)
Grammatica philosophica, sive institutiones grammaticae Latinae (1628)
Rudimenta grammaticae philosophicae (1629)
De studiorum ratione (1636)

DAVID HEINSIUS (1580-1655). A Dutch scholar of distinction and a pupil of Scaliger, born in Ghent. Considered a leading figure of the Dutch Renaissance. Became professor of Greek at Leyden. Wrote poetry in Latin. He edited Theocritus, Bion, Maschus, Horace, Aristotle, Seneca, Terence and Livy. Wrote:
Orationes (1609 and 1621)
The Massacre of the Innocents (1613). This is a Dutch tragedy.

LXXXIV.   JACOB BÖHME AND HIS FOLLOWERS

JACOB BÖHME (1575-1624). A naturalistic theosophist. He divided speculation into three branches: philosophy, treating of God and the origin of the heavens and the elements; astrology, treating of the origin of all mundane things, from the stars and the elements; and theology, which treats of the Kingdom of Christ. He believed that all things have their source in God and conversely all things are, without giving up their being, contained in God; the distinction between God and nature (including man) is one that is in some way eternally in God himself, for only so is God all in all. He endeavors simultaneously to apprehend God as the fundamental source of all existence, and at the same time not to deny the enormous power of the devil. He says, 'It is not the head, but the heart that finds God. God is felt, not known in the sense of being grasped and defined by reason. . . . With the resignation of the human will to the divine, comes an inner understanding of the very heart of God.' Among his works are:
Aurora
Signatura rerum
Threefold Life of Man
Mysterium magnum

ANGELIUS SILESIUS (Johannes Scheffler; 1624-1677). Follower of Böhme. Defended mysticism.

SIGMUND VON SCHWEINITZ. Follower of Böhme.

ABRAHAM VON FRANKENBURG. Friend and biographer (1637) of Böhme.

CHARLES I OF ENGLAND (reg. 1625-1649). Follower of Böhme.

LXXXV. ENGLISH ATOMISTS

WILLIAM GILBERT (Gylberde; 1544-1603); born at Colchester, and died either in London or Colchester. Entered St. John's College, Cambridge, in 1558, and graduated with an M.D. degree in 1569. He was admitted to the College of Physicians about 1576, and in 1599 was appointed president of the College. He was the physician of Queen Elizabeth. He conducted numerous experiments on magnets and magnetical bodies and on electrical attractions. Moreover, his great conception that the earth is nothing but a large magnet, and that it is this which explains, not only the direction of the magnetic needle north and south, but also the variation and dipping or inclination of the needle is important. He is not only the first, but the most important man contributing to the sciences of electricity and magnetism. He wrote:

De magnete, magneticisque corporibus, et de magno magnete tellure (London, 1600), a treatise on magnetism.

ROBERT FLUDD (Flud or Robertus de Fluctibus; 1574-1637), born at Milgate, Kent. English physician and mystical philosopher; studied at St. John's College, Oxford. He became acquainted with writings of Paracelsus, and attempted to form a system of philosophy founded on the identity of physical and spiritual truth. His system is described as a materialistic pantheism. His opinions have been refuted by Kepler, Gassendi, and Mersenne.

HERBERT OF CHERBURY (Edward Herbert; 1583-1648); born at Eyton-on-Severn, died in London. He entered University College, Oxford, in 1596. He was appointed by Buckingham as ambassador to Paris in 1619. In 1647 he became acquainted with Gassendi at Paris. He wrote:

De causis errorum, an unfinished work on logical fallacies.

De veritate prout distinguitur a revelatione, a versimili, a possibili, et a falso (1624), a combination of a theory of knowledge with a partial psychology, a methodology for the investigation of truth, and a scheme of natural religion. Contains the five notes of natural religion, which led some to term him the 'first deist.'

De religione gentilium

NICHOLAS HILL (1570-1610); propounded an Epicurean philosophy in Paris in 1601.

LXXXVI. FRANCIS BACON

FRANCIS BACON (1561-1626). English philosopher, statesman and essayist. Born in York Place, in the Strand; his father was the famous counsellor to Queen Elizabeth. Entered Trinity College in Cambridge in 1573 under Doctor John White-gift; began to oppose the current Aristotelian philosophy; entered *de societate magistrorum* at Gray's Inn in 1576; sent abroad with English ambassador at Paris; selected law as his profession; became confidential advisor to the Earl of Essex in 1591; became member of Middlesex Parliament in 1593; finally became Lord Chancellor of England under James I. Aimed to reform human knowledge completely. Wrote:

Abcedarium naturae, a lost metaphysical work.

Historia ventorum (1622)

Historia vitae et mortis (1622-1623)

Historia densi et rari

Historia gravis et levis

De augmentis scientiarum (1623)

The New Atlantis (1624)

Instauratio magna (1625). This work was to be in six parts of which only the first two were written. The six parts are: *The Divisions of Sciences; the Novum organum*, or *Directions concerning the Interpretation of Nature; The Phenomena of the Universe*, or *A Natural and Experimental History for the Foundation of Philosophy; The Ladder of the Intellect; The Forerunners*, or *Anticipations of the New Philosophy; The New Philosophy or Active Science*. Part one gives a general description of the knowledge which the human race at present possesses. The second part concerns the better and more perfect use of human reason, a logical method by which rash generalization is rejected. The third part was to embrace the phenomena of the universe, and such natural history as may serve for the foundation to build philosophy upon. The fourth part was to apply the work of the second in detail. The fifth part intended to anticipate the new philosophy, and the sixth part was to set forth his philosophy. In the work, Bacon aimed to reform all human knowledge completely, intending to illustrate the inaccuracy of the traditional scholastic mode of thought. The work is a strong criticism of Aristotelian philosophy.

LXXXVII. ATOMISTS ON THE CONTINENT

EILHARD LUBLIN (1565-1631). He was the first to present an atomistic theory on universal, philosophic grounds.

DANIEL SENNERT (1572-1637), professor in Wittenberg, who postulated the corpuscular theory on chemical and physical grounds. He wrote:

Epitome scientiae naturalis (1618), which does not contain the corpuscular notions which appeared in his later writings.

De chymicorum (1619), the first of his works to contain his corpuscular notions.

Physica hypomnemata (1636), in which he distinguishes between the corpuscular atoms which are as greatly divided as nature permits and from which bodies are constructed, and the elemental atoms of which there are four kinds.

CLAUDE GILLERMET DE BÉRIGARD (1578-1663), studied in Paris, and in 1628 he was called to Pisa, and to Padua in 1640. He wrote:

Circulus pisanus (1643), his chief work in the form of a dialogue in which he propounds an atomism based upon Anaxagoras. He holds that there is an infinite number of simple yet different self-moving substances, subject neither to generation nor corruption, called atoms.

JOACHIM JUNGIUS (1587-1657), mathematician, naturalist, and botanist. Influenced by Daniel Sennert. He looked upon physics as the proper foundation of all philosophy. He was interested more in actual relationships than in the cause-effect. He developed his own corpuscular terminology. Taking nominalism as his point of departure, he tried in his corpuscular theory to emphasize the many individuating differences of bodies. He opposed the alchemists' notions of three basic substances. He wrote:

Auctarium epitomes physicae clarissimi atque experientissimi viri Dr. D. Sennerti et aliis ejusdem libris excerptum (Hamburg, 1635)

Logica Hamburgensis (Hamburg, 1638)

Doxoscopiae physicae minores (Hamburg, 1662)

Isagoge phytoxopica (Hamburg, 1678)

DAVID VAN GOORLE (Gorlaeus), from Utrecht. He also starts with nominalist foundation which is an outgrowth of his critical attitude toward the peripatetic doctrine of nature and the elements. He asserts that universals have no reality, that the individual alone exists, that beings are not to be multiplied without necessity, that whatever is really divisible must consist of real parts, that parts which are themselves not divisible are atoms, that the elements cannot change from one kind to another, and that God made the atoms out of nothing. He wrote:

Exercitationes philosophicae quibus universa fere discititur philosophia theologica. Et plurima ac praecipua Peripateticorum dogmata evertuntur. Post mortem auctoris editae (Leyden, 1620)

Idea physicae (Ultrajecti, 1651)

JOANNES CHRYSOSTOMUS MAGNENUS, born in Luxeuil, quite probably studied medicine at the University of Dole. Beginning in 1646 he was professor of medicine in Pavia. Influenced by Sennert and Basso. He wrote:

Democritus reviviscens (Pavia, 1646), written according to a mathematical method. The atomism of Democritus is taken as the basis for understanding the continuum which he considers a central problem of the philosophy of nature. He holds that the continuum is not constituted of mathematical parts, but rather of corpuscles which differ from one another and occupy a certain limited space because of their smallness. The corpuscles are invisible, but capable of change. There are three kinds of substantial atoms: those of fire, water, and earth.

MAIGNAN, not to be confused with Magnenus. He wrote:

Cursus philosophicus (Toulouse, 1652), based upon the philosophy of Empedocles.

SEBASTIAN BASSO, quite probably influenced by Giordano Bruno. Basso's atomism utilizes the stoic concept of a besouled world aether, and the constitution of matter out of unchangeable atoms. The world aether is a corporeal, but very fine medium which fills up all of the space between the atoms. The atoms are very small and of several kinds. The unity of nature acts upon the universal world aether.

PIERRE GASSENDI (1592-1655). French philosopher, scientist and mathematician. He was born of poor parents at Champtercier. At an early age he showed remarkable mental powers and was sent to the college at Digne. He showed particular qualities in language and mathematics. Soon afterwards he entered the university of Aix, to study philosophy under P. Fesaye. In 1612 he was called to the college of Digne to lecture on theology. Four years later he received the degree of doctor of theology at Avignon, and in 1617 he took holy orders. The same year he was called to the chair of philosophy at Aix, and seems to have withdrawn from theology. He lectured principally on Aristotelian philosophy, conforming to the orthodox methods. He followed the work of Galileo and Kepler. He showed in the revolt against the Aristotelian philosophy his objections, which were not published. In 1624 he left Aix for a canonry at Grenoble. After 1628 he travelled in Flanders and Holland. In 1631 he returned to France and became provost of cathedral church at Digne. Later he again travelled through the province. In 1642 he was engaged by Mersenne in controversy with Descartes. His objections to the fundamental propositions of Descartes were published in 1642. In these writings his tendency toward the empirical school of speculation appears more pronounced than in any of his writings. In 1645 he accepted the chair of mathematics at the College Royal at Paris. In 1648 ill-health compelled him to give up his lectures at the College Royal and to go to southern France. In 1653 he returned to Paris where he died. Wrote:

Exercitationum paradoxicarum adversus Aristoteleos libri septem, in quibus praecipua totius peripateticae doctrinae atque dialecticae fundamenta excutiuntur, opiniones vero aut novae aut ex vetustioribus obsoletae stabiliuntur (Grenoble, 1624)

Epistola exercitatio in qua praecipua principia philosophiae Roberti Fluddi deteguntur et ad recentes illius libros adversus Patrem M. Mersennum scriptos respondetur (Paris, 1630)

Disquisitio metaphysica, seu dubitationes et instantiae adversus Renati Cartesii metaphysicam et responsa (Paris, 1644)

Institutio astronomica juxta hypotheses Copernici, Tychonis-Brahaei et Ptolemaei (Paris, 1647)

De vita, moribus et doctrina Epicuri libri octo (1647)

Commentarius de vita, moribus et placitis Epicuri, seu Animadversiones in libros X Diogenis Laertii (Lyons, 1649)

Syntagma philosophiae Epicuri (Hague, 1659)

Tychonis-Brahaie, N. Copernici, G. Peurbachii et J. Regiomontanis vitae (Paris, 1654)

Syntagma philosophicum (1658)

Notitia ecclesiae Diniensis

Commentarii de rebus celestibus

FRANÇOIS BERNIER (died 1688). Native of Angers. He was a doctor of medicine living in France for twelve years and going to Germany in 1685;

died in Paris in 1688. He was a follower of Gassendi, and an opponent of the Cartesians and the Jesuits. He wrote:

Abrégé de la philosophie de Gassendi, in seven volumes.

Voyages, published in Amsterdam in 1699.

Traité du libre et du volontaire (Amsterdam, 1685)

CYRANO DE BERGERAC (Savinien; 1619-1655), an auditor of Gassendi's private lectures together with Bernier, Mollier, Chapelle, and others. Influenced not only by Gassendi, but also by Campanella and Descartes. He spoke of a step-by-step evolution of matter in which was evident the tendency of nature toward the more perfect. He opposed Aristotle and all other authority, saying that reason alone was his ruler. Wrote:

L'histoire comique des états et empires de la lune (ca. 1656)

L'histoire comique des états et empires du solei (1662)

ÉTIENNE DE CLAVE, atomist who was forbidden by the Parlament in 1624 from holding a disputation on the subject. Wrote:

Paradoxes ou traittez philosophiques, contre l'opinion vulgaire auquels sont demontrez la materiere, la cause efficiente externe, la semence, la generation, la definition et la nutrition d'icelles (Paris, 1635)

Nouvelle lumiere philosophique des vrais principes et elemens de nature et qualité d'iceux. Contre l'opinion commune (Paris, 1641)

LXXXVIII. OPPONENTS OF GASSENDI

MARIN MERSENNE (pseudonym, Sieur de Sermes; 1588-1648). Born in Oizé and died in Paris. Educated at the Jesuit College of La Flèche, where he was a fellow pupil of Descartes. Joined the Minim friars in 1611. Opposed the atomism of Gassendi and others. Defended Descartes against clerical critics. In later life he turned to scientific research, especially in mathematics, physics and astronomy. He was head of a large group of intellectuals in Paris. Wrote:

Questiones celeberrimae in Genesim (1623)

L'impiété des déistes (1624)

La vérité de sciences (1624)

Questions théologiques, physiques, morales et mathématiques

Harmonie universelle (1636), which deals with the theory of music and musical instruments.

JEAN B. MORIN (1591-1659). Opponent of the atomism of Gassendi and of Descartes. Wrote:

Aleae telluris fractae (1643)

De atomis et vacuo contra Petri Gassendi philosophiam Epicuream (1650)

Astronomia Gallica (1661)

H. A. ENGELCKE OF ROSTOCK. Defended Aristotle against Gassendi. Wrote:

Philosophus defensus (Rostock, 1698)

LXXXIX.   THE HELIOCENTRIC UNIVERSE

JOHANNES KEPLER (1571-1630). Born in Weil der Stadt in Württemberg. He attended the protestant 'Klosterschule' at Adelberg after 1584, studied in Maulbronn in 1586 and at Tübingen in 1589 where he was introduced into the Copernican system through the efforts of Mästlin. In 1594, after Kepler had finished his theological studies, he was proposed by his teacher as a professor of mathematics at the provincial 'Stiftsschule' in Graz. In 1600 he went to Prague owing to the religious decree banishing Tycho Brahe; in 1601 he was appointed as the chief astronomer of the king; and in 1612 he went to the provincial school near Linz where he acted as a lecturer. In 1613, at the request of the king, he went before the Reichstag at Regensburg in defense of the reform of the Gregorian calendar. Kepler acquired his undying name through the establishment of three rules, named after him, concerning the movements of the planets, and as the formulater of the so-called 'mechanics' of the heavens. His numerous works dealt mainly with astronomical questions, but they have a theological interest in that they deal with the arguments for calendar reform, the chronology of the life of Christ, and of the dogmatic questions connected with the Copernican doctrine in dispute at Kepler's time. Kepler followed the philosophy of Plato and of Nicolaus Cusanus. He wrote:

Prodromus dissertationum cosmographicarum seu mysterium cosmographicum (Tübingen, 1596), by which he gained the friendship of Tycho Brahe and Galileo.

De fundamentis astrologiae certioribus (Prague, 1602), in which he declared his purpose of preserving and purifying the grain of truth which he believed astronomy contained.

Judicum de trigono igneo (1603)

Astronomiae pars optica (1604), containing important discoveries in the theory of vision, and a notable approximation towards the true law of refraction.

De stella nova in pede Serpentarii (Prague, 1606)

Astronomia nova aitiologetos, seu Physica coelestis tradita commentariis de motibus stellae Martis (Prague, 1609), which included two cardinal laws of modern astronomy: the laws of elliptical orbits and of equal areas.

Dissertatio cum Nuncio Sidereo, in which he welcomed Galileo's first announcement of celestial novelties.

Dioptrice (Augsburg, 1611), in which Kepler expounded the theory of refraction by lenses, and suggested the principle of the 'astronomical' or inverting telescope.

Nova stereometria doliorum (Linz, 1615) in which he contributed to the discovery of infinitesimal calculus.

De cometis (Augsburg, 1619), observations on the three comets.

De harmonice mundi (Augsburg, 1619), in which was announced the third law—that of the sesquiplicate ratio between the planetary periods and distances.

Epitome astronomiae copernicanae (Linz and Frankfort, 1618-1621), a textbook of Copernican science, remarkable for the prominence given to physical astronomy as well as for the extension to the Jovian system of the laws recently discovered to regulate the motions of the planets.

Chilias logarithmorum (1624)

Rudolphine Tables (Ulm, 1627), which included tables of logarithms and of refraction, together with Tycho's catalogue of 777 stars, enlarged by Kepler to 1005.

Notice to the Curious in Things Celestial (Sagen, in Silesia, 1629), which warned astronomers of the approaching transit.

GALILEO GALILEI (1564-1642). Born in Pisa, died at Arcetri near Florence. Through his early use of the Dutch invented telescope, he gained a knowledge of the stars, and by the discoveries of the law of falling bodies and of the law of the pendulum, he laid a groundwork for his studies of physics. As a student at Pisa and Florence, and as a teacher of mathematics in Pisa from 1589 to 1592, he formed opinions contrary to the Aristotelian natural philosophy, which at that time was the basis of the new natural science. Because of his opposition he had to leave Pisa, and from 1592 to

1609 he carried on his activities farther away at Padua, where the judgment of the fallacy of the geocentric view of life grew in his mind. In 1610 he returned to Pisa, and in 1611 he was appointed to the office of mathematics and astronomy of the grand-ducal house of Florence. In 1612 he studied the effects of the solar spots after the Copernican system, which he followed faithfully. By Galileo's discussion of the solar spots, a controversy which had long been dormant sprung up. Some well-meaning persons had suspected a discrepancy between the new view of the solar system and certain passages of Scripture—a suspicion strengthened by the anti-Christian inferences drawn from it by Giordano Bruno. Included in this dispute was a Benedictine monk, Benedetto Castelli, at that time professor of mathematics at the university of Pisa, who carried on a correspondence with Galileo. The theological issue of Galileo's study of the sun spots formed a decidedly controversial question in the court of the Pope. As a result, he was called before his friend, Cardinal Bellarmine, and told that since his doctrine of the heliocentric universe was in doubt he was forbidden to teach it (1616). Galileo was a warm friend of Pope Urban VIII (Maffeo Barberini) who wrote an enthusiastic letter to the grand-duke praising the astronomer's ability. In 1633, Galileo was again on trial and imprisoned in the court of the Inquisition on the charge that he had written in contravention of the decree of 1616, and in defiance of the command of the Holy Office communicated to him by Cardinal Bellarmine. His defence consisted mainly in a disavowal of his opinions, and an appeal to his good intentions. He was subsequently released and in 1634 he departed for Siena, and stayed in the house of his friend the archbishop, Ascanio Piccolomini, though still under sentence of imprisonment. In 1637 he became blind. He spent his later years, still under sentence, in his own villa at Arcetri near Florence, where he died a Catholic in 1642, the year in which Isaac Newton was born. His name is justly associated with that vast extension of the bounds of the visible universe which has rendered modern astronomy the most sublime of sciences, and his telescopic observations are a standing monument to his sagacity and acumen. He made great strides in physics, as well as in the astronomical field. Galileo formulated many ideas in natural philosophy, chiefly in the method he used in the exposition of fallacies. He took a middle course between the 'a priori' and the empirical systems, and exemplified with brilliant success the method by which experimental science has wrested from nature so many of her secrets. He wrote *Sermones de motu gravium* (Pisa, 1589-1591), commentaries on the *Orlando Furioso* and on the *Gerusalemme liberata,* and also:

Discorso intorno alle cose che stanno su l'acqua (1612), in which he used the principle of virtual velocities to demonstrate the more important theorems of hydrostatics.

Saggiatore (Rome, 1623), a polemical treatise written in reply to the *Libra astronomica* of Padre Grassi (under the pseudonym of Lotaria Sarsi), the Jesuit astronomer of the Collegio Romano.

Dialogo dei due massimi sistemi del mondo (Florence, 1632), which brought about Galileo's imprisonment by the Inquisition, because of its flaunting of the edict of 1616.

Dialoghi delle nuove scienze (Leiden, 1638)

Della scienza meccanica

MARCI VON KRONLAND (1595-1667). He was a professor of medicine at the University of Prague, and he studied the spectrum under the name of 'Iris trigonia.' He wrote:

Thaumantias (1648), an anticipation of Newton's observation that a second refraction did not change the colors.

XC. LATER THOMISTS

ANTONIUS SENENSIS (Antonio de Sena, Lusitanus; d. 1584), O.P., born in Guimarães near Braga. Taught philosophy at Lisbon and later (1564-1575) theology at Louvain. Was exiled by Philipp II because of his political views. Travelled much through France, Italy and England. Is noted for his editions of the *Summa theologica* (Antwerp, 1569), *Catena aurea* (Antwerp, 1571) and *Quaestiones disputatae* (Antwerp, 1573) of St. Thomas Aquinas. Wrote also:

Chronicon

Bibliotheca ordinis fratrum Praedicatorum (Paris, 1585)

ZANARDI (died 1642), an Italian Thomist.

JEROME MEDICES (died 1622). Wrote:

Formalis explicate S. Theol. S. Thomae

JOHN OF ST. THOMAS (John Poinsot; 1589-1644), theologian, born at Lisbon; died at Fraga, Spain. Studied at the Universities of Coimbra and Louvain. Joined the Dominicans at Madrid in 1612 or 1613. Professor of philosophy and theology in a monastery at Alcala. In 1630 and 1640 in charge of chair of theology in University of Alcala. His renown drew the largest number of scholars that had ever attended its theological faculties. In 1634 became the Royal Confessor of Philipp IV. His writings are considered the best expositions of St. Thomas's doctrine, of which he is acknowledged to be one of the foremost interpreters. Wrote:

Cursus philosophicus ad exactam veram et genuinam Aristotelis et Doctoris Angelici mentem. This work comprises logic, and general and special physics, including psychology.

Cursus theologicus. This is a commentary on the *Summa theologica* of St. Thomas.

Tractatus de approbatione auctoritate, et puritate doctinae D. Thomae Aquinatis

Compendium of Christian Doctrine, in Spanish.

Treatise on a Happy Death, written in Spanish at the command of Philipp IV.

XCI.   LATER SCOTISTS

JOHANNES DE COLONIA (d. 1572), O.P. died a martyr with eighteen other secular and religious priests during the religious wars in the capture of the city of Gorkum in South Holland.

HUGO CAVELLUS (Hugh Cavell; d. 1626), edited (Antwerp, 1620) those Oxford Commentaries on Duns Scotus which were printed after 1474.

ANTONIUS HIQUAEUS (d. 1641).

LUCAS WADDING (1588-1657), O.F.M.; born in Waterford, Ireland; died in Rome. Entered the religious life in 1604 at Matozinhos near Oporto, Portugal. Studied at Lisbon and Coimbra. Ordained in 1613. Studied further in Salamanca. Theologian of the Spanish group who in 1618 went to Rome to advocate that there be a dogmatic declaration of the Immaculate Conception. On this account pursued further studies at Rome and Naples. Founded in 1625 a Scotist college at Rome. Since the general chapter held at Toledo in 1633 had imposed the doctrines of Duns Scotus upon the Franciscan order, Wadding undertook, in company with John Ponce and others, the publication of all the works of Duns Scotus (published in 16 volumes, Lyons, 1639). In this edition the works of Mauritius a Portu, Franciscus Lychetus and Hugo Cavellus were utilized. Wadding is responsible also for the valuable collection of *Annales Minorum seu Trium Ordinum S. Francisci* (1208-1540) and the *Scriptores Ordinis Minorum*.

MERINERO (d. 1663). Professor of philosophy at Alcala. Author of a complete and precise course of Scotist philosophy, published in Madrid in 1663.

JOHN PONCE (Poncius; 1603-1672/3), O.F.M.; born in Cork, Ireland. Studied at Cologne, Louvain and from 1625 in the Roman Franciscan College established by Wadding. Was professor at the latter place and also (1630) at the College Ludovisi. He taught later at Lyons and Paris. Wrote:
Cursus philosophiae (3 vols. Rome, 1643)
Appendix apologetica (Rome, 1645)
Cursus theologicus (Paris, 1652)
Commentarii theologici in IV libros Sententiarum (4 vols. Paris, 1661)

XCII. SCHOLA AEGIDIANA

RAFFAELLO BONHERBA (died 1681). Followed opinions accepted in the Augustinian Order. Wrote:
Disputationes totius philosophiae . . . in quibus omnes philosophicae inter D. Thomam et Scotum controversiae principaliter cum doctrina nostri Aegidii Columnae illustrantur (Palermo, 1645-1671)

FEDERICO NICOLO GAVARDI (died 1715). The most important interpretor of Aegidius Colonna; belongs to later Augustinian school of theology. Wrote:
Theologia exantiquata iuxta orthodoxam S. P. Augustini doctrinam ab Aegidio Columna doctore fundatissimo expositam (6 vols. in folio; Naples and Rome, 1683-1696)

XCIII. LATER SCEPTICS OF FRANCE

FRANÇOIS DE LA MOTHE-LE-VAYER (1588-1672). He was influenced by Pierre Charron. Wrote:
Instruction of the Dauphin (1640)
Dialogues of Orasius Tubero (1633), his most significant work.
Sceptical Discourse on Music, in which he attempts to introduce doubt and uncertainty into the principles and functions of music.

SAMUEL SORBIÈRE (1615-1670), a pupil of François de la Moth-le-Vayer; translator of the *Hypotyposes Pyrrhoneae* of Sextus Empiricus.

SIMON FOUCHER (1644-1696), a canon of Dijon. Praised the scepticism
of the Academy in his writings which included:
Histoire des Académiciens (Paris, 1690)
De philosophia Academica (Paris, 1692)

XCIV. ITALIAN RHETORICIANS

CARMILLO PELLEGRINI, wrote:
Del concetto poetico, in which dialectic is made subservient to rhetoric.

MATTEO PELLEGRINI (Peregrini), wrote:
Delle acutezze, che altrimenti spiriti, vivezze e concetti, volgarmente si appellano (Genoa, 1639)
I fonti dell' ingegno (Bologna, 1650)

EMANUELE TESAURO, wrote:
Il carnocchiale Arestotelico (Turin, 1654)

XCV. LATER LUTHERAN PHILOSOPHERS

OTTO CASMANN (1562-1607). Rector in Stade. Influenced by Rudolf
Goclenius. Wrote numerous philosophical and scientific works, among them:
Psychologia anthropologica (Hanau, 1594)
Anthropologiae pars II (Hanau, 1596)
Philosophiae et Christianae et verae assertio (Frankfurt, 1600)
Nucleus mysteriorum naturae (Hamburg, 1605)

JOHN BARCLAY (1582-1621). Born at Pont-à-Mousson; died in Rome.
His father was William Barclay. Received early schooling from Jesuits. John
defended his father's work, *De potestate Papae*, which denied the temporal
jurisdiction of the pope over princes. This led to a prolonged controversy, in
which his known opponents were Robert Bellarmine and another Jesuit,
Andreas Eudaemon Joannes. His works include a commentary on the
Thebais of Statius (1601), and:
Euphormionis Lusinini Satyricon
Sylvae (1607), poems
Apology (1611), an apology for the *Satyricon*.
Paraenesis ad sectarios (1617)
Argenis (1621), his greatest work.

JOHANN GERHARD (1582-1637). Lutheran divine, born in Quedlinburg. He died in Jena. Studied philosophy at Wittenberg. He started theological studies but changed to medicine and finally back to theology. In 1616 he became professor of theology at Jena, where the remainder of his life was spent. During his lifetime he received repeated calls to almost every university in Germany (e.g. Giessen, Altdorf, Helmstädt, Jena, Wittenberg), as well as to Upsala in Sweden. He wrote:

Commentarius in harmoniam historiae evangelicae de passione Christi (1617)

Commentarius super priorem D. Petri epistolam (1641)

Commentaries on Genesis (1637)

Commentaries on Deuteronomy (1650)

Confessio Catholica (1633-1637), on the Augsburg Confession.

Loci communes theologici (1610-1622)

Meditationes sacrae (1606)

GEORG GUTKE (ca. 1590-1634), rector in Berlin. Advocated a 'gnostology' or 'noology' or universal knowledge derive from the 'nous,' which was to be the epistemological and methodological foundation of the individual sciences. Wrote:

Habitus primorum principiorum seu intelligentia (Berlin, 1625)

Logicae divinae seu peripatetici libri duo (Cologne, 1631)

CHRISTOPH SCHEIBLER (1589-1653), professor in Giessen. Called the 'protestant Suarez.' Interpreted Arstotle in the manner of the Spanish scholastics. Wrote:

Opus metaphysicum, 2 vols. (Giessen, 1617, 1622)

DANIEL STAHL (1589-1654), professor at Jena. Wrote:

Metaphysica (Frankfurt, 1652)

Institutiones metaphysicae (Jena, 1664)

DANIEL CRAMER (1568-1673), for a time professor in Wittenberg. A rigid follower of the Aristotelian philosophy. Wrote:

Isagoge in metaphysicam Aristotelis (Wittenberg, 1594)

VALENTIN FROMM (1601-1679). Wrote:

Gnostologia h. c. Doctina generalia totius philosophiae fundamenta methodice ... pertribens (Wittenberg, 1631)

XCVI. THOMAS HOBBES

THOMAS HOBBES (1588-1679). Born at Westport; attended Oxford and later was a tutor there. He was of a timid nature. Travelled abroad, where he met Descartes, Gassendi, and Galileo. His great interest was in physical science, he believed sense to be a prime factor in subjective experience. He attempted to explain society and man in the same manner that nature was explained, thus making natural science the foundation of all our knowledge of existence. He is called the founder of English psychology and sociology. Wrote:

The Leviathan; or the matter, form and power of a commonwealth, Ecclesiastical and civil

The Elements of Law, natural and politique

De corpore politico

Decameron physiologicum

Behemoth

XCVII. DUTCH SCHOOL OF LOGIC

FRANCO PETRI BURGERSDIJCK (1590-1629). Born at Lier near Delft. Student at University of Leyden and studied theology at Samur, where he became a professor of philosophy at an early age. After five years he returned to Leyden where he accepted the chair of logic and moral philosophy, and afterward that of natural philosophy. Died at Leyden. Wrote:

Institutionum logicarum libri duo (London: R. Danielis, 1680), translated into English 'by a gentleman' under the title of *Monitio logica, or An abstract and translation of Burgersdicius his logick* (London: R. Cumberland, 1697)

Idea philosophiae moralis (1644)

ADRIANUS HEEREBOORD (1614-1659). Taught at Leyden by Jean de Raey, who combined Aristotelian and Cartesian philosophies. Heereboord wished to bring about an accord between the Cartesian philosophy and the Bible. Leaned toward Spinoza. Wrote:

Hermeneia logica (new edition; London: R. Danielis, 1680)

SLEKERUS, teacher of Jungius.

B. JUNGIUS. Born in Rostock. Pupil of Slekerus. Studied the metaphysics of Suarez.

[158]

XCVIII. JANSENISM AND PORT ROYAL

CORNELIUS JANSEN (1585-1638); bishop of Ypres, and father of the religious revival known as Jansenism. Entered Louvain in 1602. Debated between Jesuit or scholastic party and the followers of Michael Baius who were Augustinian in their thought. He finally attached himself to the latter group, in which he found a like-minded friend in Du Vergier de Hauranne. He went to study the early Fathers with Du Vergier in Paris. In 1616 he returned to Louvain, where he took charge of the College of St. Pulcheria, a hostel for Dutch students of theology. Among his works are:

Augustinus, a treatise on the theology of St. Augustine.

Mars gallicus (1635)

JEAN DU VERGIER DE HAURANNE (1581-1643). Abbot of St. Cyran, father of the Jansenist revival in France. Studied theology at the Flemish university of Louvain. Became involved in the conflict of the Jesuit party and the followers of Michael Baius, at Louvain. Here he met Cornelius Jansen, exponent of the Augustinian party of Baius. After becoming Abbot at St. Cyran he attempted to reform Catholicism on Augustinian principles. He was a vigorous opponent of the Jesuits. His works are:

Question royale (1609)

Petrus Aurelius (1633)

BLAISE PASCAL (1623-1662), born at Clermont Ferrand. Was a French religious philosopher and mathematician. He and other members of his family became Jansenists. His sister joined the Jansenist group at Port Royal. Pascal himself lived much at Port Royal and observed its rules but never became one of its solitaries. Pascal attempted by his writing to defend Jansenism. He did this at the request of Arnauld, head of Port Royal, who had been condemned by the Sorbonne in 1655 for heretical doctrine. Among Pascal's writings are:

Nouvelles experiences sur le vide

Discours sur les passions de l'amour

Pensées sur la religion (Paris, 1669)

Entretrien avec M. de Saci (ca. 1655), concerning Epictetus and Montaigne.

Les provinciales ou lettres écrites par Louis de Montalte à un provincial de ses amis, avec les notes de Guill. Wendock [*Nicole*] (Cologne, 1657), known simply as the *Provinciales*, or the *Lettres provinciales*. This work was directed against the Jesuits because of their opposition to Jansenism.

JACQUELINE PASCAL (1625-1661), sister of Blaise Pascal. She was an infant prodigy. In 1646 through the influence of her brother, she was converted to Jansenism and in 1652 took the veil. In this capacity she was instrumental in the conversion of Blaise. She opposed the consent of the nuns to the condemnation of Jansenism by the Papal Bulls but finally approved.

ANTOINE ARNAULD (Le grand Arnauld; 1612-1694). Studied theology at the Sorbonne. Came under the influence of Du Vergier, who drew him in the direction of Jansenism. His book, *De la fréquente Communion* (1643), which endeavored to make the ideals and aims of his belief clear to the public, caused a great stir, and he remained in seclusion for twenty years as a result. In 1655 he was expelled from the Sorbonne. He was later welcomed, and again persecuted, in France. He spent most of his time in controversy with the Jesuits and Calvinists. The more prominent of his writings are:
Letters à un duc et pair (Paris, 1656), concerning Jesuit methods in the confessional.
La Perpétuité de la foi de l'Eglise touchant l'Eucharistie (Paris, 1664), against the Calvinists, written with cooperation of Nicole.
Art de penser, commonly known as the *Port Royal Logic*.

ANGELIQUE ARNAULD (1591-1661), sister of Antoine Arnauld. Made abbess of Port Royal at the age of eight. In 1608 she started to reform her convent according to the original Rule, but coming under the influence of Du Vergier in 1623, she changed to a Jansenistic mode of thought.

PIERRE NICOLE (1625-1695), a distinguished French Jansenist. Studied theology at Paris. Entered into relation with the Jansenists at Port Royal. He worked with Arnauld at Port Royal. His letters, *Les imaginaires* attacked the Jesuit attitude toward Jansenism. Other works are:
Les visionnaires (1666)
Essais de morale, on practical Christianity.

PASQUIER QUESNEL (1634-1719). French Jansenist theologian. Graduated at the Sorbonne in 1653 and joined the French Oratory in 1657. His Jansenist sympathies caused his banishment from Paris in 1681. After Arnauld's death in 1694 he was generally recognized as the leader of the Jansenist party. He wrote:
Reflexions morales sur le Nouveau Testament, which explained the ideals of the Jansenist party and became the object of Jesuit attacks.

CLEMENT XI (1649-1721). Pope from 1700-1721. In 1713 he issued the bull *Unigenitus,* condemning 101 Jansenistic propositions taken from Pasquier Quesnel's *Reflexions morales.* Certain bishops rejected this bull and a new party division resulted, which prolonged the controversy.

XCIX. BOUHOURS

DOMINIC BOUHOURS (1628-1702), S.J., born in Paris. Joined the Jesuits in 1644. Became professor of humanities at the Jesuit college in Paris, then of rhetoric at Tours. Took an active part in the war of pamphlets between the Jesuits and the Jansenists. Among his very numerous writings are:
Les entretiens d'Ariste et d'Eugene (Paris, 1671)
Pensées chrétiennes pour tous les jours du mois (Paris, 1672)
La manière de bien penser dans les ouvrages d'esprit (Paris, 1687)

C. RENÉ DESCARTES

RENÉ DESCARTES (1596-1650). He studied at the Jesuit college of La Flèche, one of the most famous schools of the time. Descartes may be classified as a philosopher and a scientist. In 1619 he felt a strong urge to restore human knowledge, which was in a state of decadence; for him this mission took on quite a mystical character. He said there was no problem so evident or so certain that it cannot be controverted. Therefore the first problem was to discover a new method. Descartes' great faith in mathematics led him to search for some incontrovertible premise. Starting from the fact of his thinking, and thus of his own existence, he went rapidly to the existence of God and the reliability of the senses. His definition of soul as thinking substance and body as extended substance led to the need of some bridge between the two. Animal spirits in the region of the pineal gland, which is the location of the soul, was his solution of the problem. He wrote:
Discours de la méthode (1637)
Meditationes de prima philosophia (1641)
Principia philosophiae (1644)
Passions de l'ame (1649)
Le Monde, this work had been completed in 1633, but the condemnation of Galileo frightened Descartes who preferred to avoid all collision with ecclesiastical authority.
Recherche de la verité

Regulae ad directionem ingenii
Description du corps humain

CI.   CIRCULATION OF THE BLOOD

WILLIAM HARVEY (1578-1657), born at Folkestone, England. In 1593, he entered Caius College, Cambridge, and three years later he took his B.A. degree. Soon after, he went to study medicine at Padua under Fabricius and Julius Casserius. In 1602, he became a doctor of medicine. Harvey returned to London, and in 1607 he was admitted to the Royal College of Physicians. In 1616 he first brought forth his view upon the movements of the heart and blood. His practice increased, and among his patients was the lord chancellor, Francis Bacon. In 1618 he was appointed the head physician to King James I. He travelled much in his life, and enjoyed great success both abroad and at home. In 1654 he was elected president of Caius College, Cambridge. Harvey's greatest contribution to the world was his discovery of the circulation of the blood.

Among his predecessors in the study of the vascular system, Galen was the first to propound anything of importance and usefulness to Harvey. He discovered that the arteries carried blood as well as air. Jacobus Sylvius (1478-1555; *In Hipp.* and *Gal. phys. partem anatom. isagoge*) described the valves of the veins. Vesalius (*De humani corporis fabrica*, 1542) determined that the septum between the right and left venticle was complete, but he could not deny the invisible pores mentioned by Galen. Servetus, in his *Christianismi restitutio* (1553), concludes that there is a communication in the lungs by which blood passes from the pulmonary artery to the pulmonary vein. He was the true predecessor of Harvey in physiology. Renaldo Columbus (*De re anatomica*, 1559) denies the muscularity of the heart, yet correctly teaches that blood passes from the right to the left ventricle, not through the septum, but through the lungs. Fabricius described the valves more perfectly than had Sylvius. Caesalpinus (*Quaestiones peripateticae*, 1571) followed Servetus and Columbus, being the first to use the term 'circulation.' He is given credit by many for having discovered the circulation of the blood, yet he seems to have had no original views on the subject. The way then to Harvey's great work had been paved by the discovery of the valves in the veins by Sylvius and Fabricius, and the discovery of the lesser circulation by Servetus.

Harvey found that the heart is muscular, and that its regular contraction drives the blood forward. He gives an account of the course of the blood from the right to the left side of the heart through the lungs. He determined that the blood is driven out through the arteries and returns through the veins. He considered the arterial blood as providing nourishment for the body, while that of the veins is impure. He wrote:

Exercitatio anatomica de motu cordis et sanguinis (Frankfort-on-the-Main, 1628) in which the circulation of the blood is propounded.

Exercitationes duae anatomicae de circulatione sanguinis, ad Johannem Riolanum, filium, Parisiensem (Cambridge, 1649)

Exercitationes de generatione animalium, quibus accedunt quaedam de partu, de membranis ac humoribus uteri, et de conceptione (London, 1651)

Anatomia Thomae Parr, published in the treatise of Dr. John Betts, *De ortu et natura sanguinis* (London, 1669)

CII. OCCASIONALISM

ARNOLD GEULINCX (1624-1669). Born at Antwerp. Studied philosophy and medicine at the university of Louvain, where he remained as a lecturer for several years. Having given offence by his unorthodox views, he left Louvain and took refuge in Leyden, where he appears to have been in the utmost financial distress. He entered the Protestant church, and in 1663, through the influence of his friend Abraham Heidanus he obtained a poorly paid lectureship at the university. He died at Leyden. His most important works, published posthumously, are:

Metaphysica vera (1691)

Philaretus (1675)

Physica vera (1688)

Logica restituta (1662)

Annotata in Principia philosophiae R. Cartesii (1691)

Ethics. The first tract of this work is a study of what he termed the cardinal virtues. By these he did not mean prudence, temperance, justice, and fortitude. Virtue according to him is the love of God and of reason. The cardinal virtues are the properties of virtue which immediately flow from its very essence and have nothing to do with anything external. These properties are diligence, obedience, justice, humility.

NICOLAS MALEBRANCHE (1638-1715), was born at Paris. Although deformed and constitutionally weak, he was educated for the priesthood at the

Sorbonne and joined the congregation of the Oratory in 1660. In 1699 he was elected to the Academy of Sciences. Philosophically he developed occasionalism almost to the point of pantheism; he himself remarked that the difference between himself and Spinoza was that he taught that the universe was in God and that Spinoza said that God was in the universe. Said one body cannot act upon another. By a similar argument he attempted to prove that body cannot act upon mind. Wrote:

De la recherche de la vérité (1674)

Conversations métaphysiques et chrétiens (1677)

Traitè de la nature et de la grâce (1680)

Méditations chrétiennes et métaphysiques (1683)

Traité de morale (1684)

Entretiens sur la métaphysique et sur la religion (1688)

Traité de l'amour de Dieu (1697)

Entretiens d'un philosophe chrétien et d'un philosophe chinois sur l'existence et la nature de Dieu (1708)

TABLE OF UNIVERSITIES

The principal Universities of Europe before 1600, with approximate dates of founding and names of founders.

Aberdeen	1494	Bishop William Elphinstone
Alcala	1510	Cardinal Jimenes de Cisneros
Arezzo	1355	Charles V
Basel	1460	Pope Pius II
Bologna	ca. 1158	Frederick Barbarossa
Bordeaux	1441	Pope Eugenius IV
Bourges	1463	Jacques Coeur by order of Louis XI, and Pope Pius II
Caen	1432	Henry VI of England
Cambridge	1284	Hugh de Balsham
Coimbra	1290	Diniz I of Portugal and Pope Nicholas IV
Cologne	1388	The Town Council and Pope Urban VI
Copenhagen	1475	Christian I and Pope Sixtus IV
Cracow	1364	Casimir the Great
Dillingen	ca. 1551	Cardinal Otto Truchsess von Waldburg
Douai	1561	Philip II of Spain
Erfurt	1389	Adolf of Nassau
Ferrara	1391	Pope Boniface IX
Florence	1348	Republic of Flora and Pope Clement III
Freiburg	1455	Archduke Albrecht VI of Austria and Pope Callistus III
Genoa	1471	Bartolomeo Bianco
Glascow	1450/1451	William Turnbull, Bishop of Glasgow, and Pope Nicholas V
Granada	1531	Charles V and Pope Clement VII
Graz	1585	Archduke Karl von Steiermark and Pope Gregory XIII
Heidelberg	1385	Rupert I of Wittelsbach and Pope Urban VI
Helmstedt	1576	Duke Julius
Ingolstadt	1458/1472	Louis the Rich, Duke of Bavaria, and Pope Pius II
Königsberg	1544	Albert I, Duke of Prussia
Leipzig	1409	Friedrich & Wilhelm, Landgraves of Thuringia, and Pope Alexander V

Leyden	1575	Prince William (the Silent) of Orange
Louvain	1425	Duke John IV of Brabant and Pope Martin V
Macerata	1540	Pope Paul III
Mainz	1477	Archbishop Diether von Isenberg
Marburg	1527	Philip the Magnanimous
Montpellier	1289	Pope Nicholas IV
Nancy	1572	Pope Gregory XIII
Nantes	1460	Pope Pius II
Naples	1224	Frederick II
Orleans	1306	Pope Clement V
Oviedo	1568/1608	Fernando Valdez, Archbishop of Seville
Oxford	1249	Archdeacon William of Durham
Padua	1222	A colony of professors from Bologna
Paris	1208	Pope Innocent III
Pavia	1361	Galeazzo II and Charles IV
Perugia	1308	Pope Clement V
Pisa	1343	Pope Clement VI
Prague	1345	Pope Clement VI and Charles IV
Rome		
Roman Academy	ca. 1480	Pomponio Laeto
Roman College	1553	St. Ignatius Loyola
Scotist College	1625	Lucus Wadding
St. Andrews, Scotland	1411	Bishop Wardlaw
Salamanca	1243	St. Ferdinand III
Salerno	ca. 1220	Frederick II
Seville	1254	Alphonso the Wise
Sienna	1275/1285	The Commune of Sienna
Toulouse	1229	Raymond VIII
Trier	1473	The City of Trier
Tübingen	1477	Count Eberhard
Upsala	1477	Archbishop Jakob Ulfsson and Pope Sixtus IV
Valence	1452	Dauphin Louis (Louis XI)
Valencia	1246	Jaime I, the Conqueror, and Pope Innocent IV
Valladolid	1346	Alfonso XI and Pope Clement VI
Vienna	1365	Rudolf IV, Duke of Austria, and Pope Urban V
Wittenberg	1502	Frederick the Wise
Würzburg	1402	John I of Egloffstein, Bishop of Würtzburg, and Pope Boniface IX

BIBLIOGRAPHY

The general reference works which were found most useful, in addition to the standard encyclopedias in the various languages of Europe, are *The Catholic Encyclopedia*, 17 volumes (New York, 1913-1922) ; *Dictionnaire de théologie catholique* (Paris, 1909-　) ; *Realencyclopädie für protestantische Theologie und Kirche*, 24 volumes (3rd edition; Leipzig, 1896-1913) ; *Lexikon fur Theologie und Kirche*, 10 volumes (Freiburg i B: Herder, 1930-1938) ; Hugo Hurter, S.J., *Nomenclator literarius theologiae catholicae*, 5 vols. (3rd edition; Innsbruck, 1903-1913) ; *Friedrich Ueberwegs Grundriss der Geschichte der Philosophie*, 5 volumes (12th edition; Berlin: E. S. Mittler und Sohn, 1923-1928), vol. II edited by Bernard Geyer, and vol. III edited by Max Frischeisen-Köhler and Willy Moog; Gaston Sortais, *Histoire de la philosophie ancienne* (Paris; P. Lethielleux, 1912) ; Maurice De Wulf, *History of Mediaeval Philosophy*, 2 vols. (London: Longmans, Green & Co. Ltd., 1926).

Following is a bibliography of useful works. The principle of selection was that they deal *extensively* with one or more *groups* of thinkers. The listing of works which are either too general or which deal with a single individual would have made the bibliography too cumbersome.

Robert Bellarmine, *De scriptoribus ecclesiasticis cum adiunctis indicibus undecim, et brevi chronologia ab orbe condito usque ad annum MDCXII.* (Cologne: Bernardus Gualtherus, 1613)

Hilaire Belloc, *Characters of the Reformation,* (New York: Sheed and Ward, 1937)

Josef Bohatec, *Die cartesianische Scholastik in der Philosophie und reformierten Dogmatik des 17. Jahrhunderts,* I. Teil, (Leipzig, 1912)

Émile Bréhier, *La philosophie du moyen âge,* (Paris: A. Michel, 1937)

Henri Bremond, *Histoire littéraire du sentiment religieux en France,* 4 vols. (Paris, 1916-1919). English translation under title of *A Literary History of Religious Thought in France,* 3 vols. (New York: Macmillan, 1928-1936)

Eloy Bullón, *Los precursores españolas de Bacon y Descartes,* (Salamanca, 1905)

Jacob Burckhardt, *The Civilization of the Renaissance in Italy,* (London: Swan Sonnenschein and Co., 1904)

BIBLIOGRAPHY

E. A. Burtt, *The Metaphysical Foundations of Modern Physical Science, a historical and critical essay,* (New York: Harcourt, Brace and Co., 1925)

Henri Busson, *Les sources et le développement du rationalisme dans la littérature française de la Renaissance (1533-1601)* (Paris, 1622)

Henri Busson, *La pensée religieuse française de Charron à Pascal,* (Paris: Vrin, 1933)

Florian Cajori, *A History of Mathematics,* (2nd edition; New York: Macmillan, 1926)

E. T. Campagnac, *The Cambridge Platonists,* (Oxford University Press, 1901)

R. W. Carlyle and A. J. Carlyle, *A History of Mediaeval Political Theory in the West,* 6 vols. (Edinburgh: William Blackwood and Sons. Ltd., 1922-1936)

Ernst Cassirer, *Das Erkenntnisproblem in der Philosophie und Wissenschaft der Neueren Zeit,* 3 vols. (2nd edition; Berlin: Bruno Cassirer, 1911-1920)

Ernst Cassirer, *Individuum und Kosmos in der Philosophie der Renaissance* (Leipzig, 1927)

Benedetto Croce, *I predicatori italiani del seicento e il gusto spagnolo,* (Naples, 1899)

Benedetto Croce, *La Spagna della vita italiana durante la rinascenza* (Bati, 1917)

Pierre Duhem, *Le système du monde,* 5 vols. (Paris: Hermann, 1913-1917)

William Archibald Dunning, *A History of Political Theories,* 3 vols. (New York: Macmillan, 1930)

Adolf Dyroff (editor), *Renaissance und Philosophie. Beiträge zur Geschichte der Philosophie.* 13 vols. (Bonn. a. Rh.: Peter Hanstein, 1908-1916)

Franz Kardinal Ehrle, S.J., *Die Scholastik und ihre Aufgaben in unserer Zeit,* (Freiburg i. B.: Herder, 1933)

Johann E. Erdmann, *Grundriss der Geschichte der Philosophie,* 2 vols. (Berlin: Wilhelm Hertz, 1869-1870)

Karl Eschweiler, 'Die Philosophie der spanischen Spätscholastik auf den deutschen Universitäten des siebzehnten Jahrhunderts,' *Spanische Forschungen der Görresgesellschaft,* First series, vol. I (Münster i. W.; Aschendorff, 1928), pp. 251-325.

BIBLIOGRAPHY

Rudolf Eucken, *Beiträge zur Einführung in die Geschichte der Philosophie* (Leipzig: Dürr, 1906)

Allan P. Farrell, S.J., *The Jesuit Code of a Liberal Education,* (Milwaukee: Bruce Publishing Co., 1938)

Fernando de Córdoba y los origenes del renacimento filosófico en España (episodio de la historia et la lógica) por D. Adolfo Bonilla y San Martín . . . y D. Marcelino Menéndez y Pelayo (Madrid: V. Suarez, 1911). Appendix contains the Latin text of Fernando's *De artificio* and his *In De animalibus Alberti libro praefatio.*

J. Neville Figgis, *From Gerson to Grotius, 1414-1625* (Cambridge Unviersity Press, 1923)

J. Neville Figgis, *The Theory of the Divine Right of Kings,* (Cambridge University Press, 1896)

Jac. Freudenthal, 'Spinoza und die Scholastik,' *Philosophische Aufsätze Eduard Zeller gewidmet,* (Leipzig, 1887), pp. 83-138

Otto Gierke, *Political Thories of the Middle Ages,* (Cambridge University Press, 1900)

Étienne Gilson, *La liberté chez Descartes et la théologie,* (Paris: F. Alcan, 1913)

Christian D. Ginsburg, *The Kabbalah, its Doctrines, Development and Literature,* (London: George Routledge and Sons, Ltd., 1925)

Marcellino Gutierrez, O.S.A., *Luis de León y la filosofia Española del siglo XVI* (Madrid, 1891)

F. J. C. Hearnshaw, *The Social and Political Ideas of Some Great Mediaeval Thinkers,* (London: George G. Harrap and Co., Ltd., 1923)

J. Huizinga, *Herbst des Mittelalters, Studien über Lebens—und Geistesformen des 14. und 15. Jahrhunderts in Frankreich und in den Niederlanden,* (3rd edition; Stuttgart: Alfred Kroner, 1938)

Isaac Husik, *A History of Mediaeval Jewish Philosophy,* (New York: Macmillan, 1930)

Paul Janet, *Histoire de la science politique dans ses rapports avec la morale,* 2 vols. (Paris: F. Alcan, n. d.)

Rufus Jones, *Spiritual Reformers of the 16th and 17th Centuries,* (New York: Macmillan, 1914)

BIBLIOGRAPHY

C. von Kaltenborn, *Die Vorläufer des Hugo Grotius*, (Leipzig, 1848)

Kurd Lassivitz, *Geschichte der Atomistik*, (Hamburg, 1890)

A. G. Little, *The Grey Friars in Oxford*, (Oxford: Clarendon Press, 1892)

Michele Losacco, *Storia della dialettica* (Firenze: L. S. Olschli, 1922)

L. Mabilleau, *Étude historique sur la philosophie de la renaissance en Italie* (Paris, 1881)

L. Mabilleau, *Histoire de la philosophie atomistique*, (Paris, 1895)

Joseph Maréchal, S.J., *Précis d'histoire de la philosophie moderne*, vol. I, (Louvain: Museum Lessianum, 1933)

G. Meerssemann, O.P., 'Les origines parisiennes de l'albertinisme colonsis,' *Archives d'histoire doctrinale et littéraire du moyen âge*, VII, (Paris, 1932), 121-142

Marcelino Menéndez y Pelayo, *Historia de las ideas estéticas an España*, 9 vols. (Madrid: A. P. Dubrull, 1884-1891)

Marcelino Menéndez y Pelayo, *La Ciencia Española*, 3 vols. (Madrid, 1915-1918)

C. Michalski, *Les courants philosophiques à Oxford et à Paris pendant le XIVe siècle*, (Cracow, 1922)

Perry Miller, *The New England Mind, The Seventeenth Century*, (New York: Macmillan, 1939)

Robert v. Nostiz-Rieneck, S.J., 'Leibniz und die Scholastik,' *Philosophisches Jahrbuch*, VII (1894), 54-67.

John Owen, *The Skeptics of the French Renaissance*, (London: Swan Sonnenschein and Co., 1893)

E. Allison Peers, *Studies of the Spanish Mystics*, 2 vols. (London: Sheldon Press, 1927-1930)

Peter Petersen, *Geschichte der Aristotelischen Philosophie im Protestantischen Deutschland*, (Leipzig: Felix Meiner, 1921)

Frederick J. Powicke, *The Cambridge Platonists*, (Cambridge, Mass.: Harvard University Press, 1926)

Carl von Prantl, *Geschichte der Logik im Abendlande*, 4 vols. (Leipzig: S. Hirzel, 1855-1870)

BIBLIOGRAPHY

A. Renaudet, *Préréforme et humanisme à Paris pendant les premières guerres d'Italie (1494-1517)*, (Paris, 1916)

Fritz, Rintelen, 'Leibnizens Beziehungen zur Scholastik,' *Archiv für Geschichte der Philosophie*, XVI, (1903), 157-189, 307-334.

Otto Ritschl, *Die Geschichte der dogmatischen Theologie in den protestantischen Kirchen*, 4 vols. (Leipzig, 1909)

G. Ritter, 'Studien zur Spätscholastik. I. Marsilius von Inghen und die okkamistische Schule in Deutschland. II. Via antiqua und via moderna auf den deutschen Universitäten des XV Jahrhunderts.' *Stizungsberichte der Heidelberger Akademie der Wissenschaften*, Phil.-hist. Klasse, 1921, 4. Abh.; 1922, 7 Abh.

Heinrich Ritter, *Geschichte der Philosophie*, 12 vols. (Hamburg, 1829-1853)

Heinrich Ritter, *Die christliche Philosophie nach ihrem Begriff, ihren äusseren Verhältnissen und in ihrer Geschichte bis auf die neuesten Zeiten*, 2 vols. (Göttingen, 1858-1859)

Ralph Roeder, *The Man of the Renaissance. Four Lawgivers: Savonarola, Machiavelli, Castiglione, Aretino.* (New York: The Viking Press, 1935)

Knorr Baron von Rosenroth, *Kabbala denudata*, 2 vols. (Vol. I: Sulzbach, 1677-1678; vol. II: Frankfort a. M., 1684). English translation by S. L. MacGregor Mathers (London: Kegan Paul, Trench, Trubner and Co., Ltd., 1938)

Gerardus Schneemann, S.J., *Controversiarum de divinae gratiae et liberique arbitrii concordia initia et progressus*, (Freiburg i. B.: Herder, 1881)

Heinrich Schreiber, 'Die Bibliothek der ehemaligen Mainzer Kartause,' *Zentralblatt für Bibliothekswesen*, Beiheft 60, (Leipzig: Otto Harrassowitz, 1927)

Gerard Smith, S.J. (editor), *Jesuit Thinkers of the Renaissance*, (Milwaukee: Marquette University Press, 1939)

Carlos Sommervogel, S.J., *Bibliothèque de la Compagnie ed Jésus*, (new edition, 9 vols.; Paris: Alphonse Picard, 1890-1900). Cf. also E. M. Rivière, S.J., *Corrections et additions à la Bibliothèque de la Compagnie de Jésus* (Toulouse, 1911)

Henry Osborn Taylor, *Thought and Expression in the Sixteenth Century*, 2 vols. (2nd edition; New York: Macmillan, 1930)

BIBLIOGRAPHY

Lynn Thorndike, *Science and Thought in the Fifteenth Century*, (New York: Columbia University Press, 1929)

Lynn Thorndike, *History of Magic and Experimental Science*, vols. 3 and 4. (New York: Columbia University Press, 1934)

Giuseppe Toffanin, *La fine dell'umanisimo*, (Turin, 1920)

Giuseppe Toffanin, *Storia dell'umanisimo*, (Naples, 1933)

Marguerite Tollemache, *Spanish Mystics*, (London, 1886)

John Tullach, *Rational Theology and Christian Philosophy in England in the Seventeenth Century*, 2 vols. (1872)

Emil Weber, *Die philosophische Scholastik des deutschen Protestantismus im Zeitalter der Orthodoxie*, (Leipzig, 1907)

Emil Weber, *Der Einfluss der protestantischen Schulphilosophie auf die ortho-dox—lutherische Dogmatik*, (Leipzig, 1908)

Carl Werner, *Franz Suarez und die Scholastik der letzten Jahrhunderte*, 2 vols. (Regensburg: G. J. Manz, n. d.)

Carl Werner, *Geschichte der apologetischen und polemischen Literatur der christlichen Theologie*, 5 vols. (1861-1867)

Carl Werner, *Die Scholastik des späteren Mittelalters*, 4 vols., (1881-1887)

Otto Willmann, *Geschichte des Idealismus*, 3 vols., (third edition; Braunschweig: Friedrich Vieweg und Sohn, 1907)

A. Wolf, *A History of Science, Technology, and Philosophy in the 16th and 17th Centuries*, (New York: Macmillan, 1935)

Maurice de Wulf, *Histoire de la philosophie en Belgique*, (Brussels, 1910)

INDEX

INDEX

Ellinger, A., 62
Engelcke, H. A., of Rostock, 150
Erasmus, Desiderius, 54
Estella, Diego de, 131
Eustacchi, Bartholommeo, 78

Faber, Jacobus, 62
Faber, Jacobus, Cusanus School of, 62
Faber, Johannes, de Werdea, 38
Fabri, Johannes, 92
Fabricius, Franz, 112
Fabricius, Hieronymus, 78
Falconi, Juan, 132
Farel, Wilhelm, 83
Faventinus, Benedictus Victorius, 39
Feltre, Vittorino da, 40
Fenner, Dudley, 115
Feribrigus, Richard, 10
Ferrarensis, Franciscus Sylvester, 71
Ficino, Marsilio, 36
Fisher, St. John, 57
Fludd, Robert, 144
Fonseca, Pedro da, 105
Fonseca, Cristobal de, 137
Fotherby, Martin, 137
Foucher, Simon, 156
Fracastoro, Girolamo, 79
Franck, Sebastian, 48
Frankenburg, Abraham von, 144
Fraunce, Abraham, 116
Freigius, Thomas, 112
Frischlin, Nicodemus Philipp, 113
Fromm, Valentin, 157
Fusterer, Johannes der, 14

Galileo Galilei, 151
Gallés, Francisco, 100
Gardiner, Stephen, 57
Gassendi, Opponents of, 149
Gassendi, Pierre, 147
Gataker, Thomas, 142
Gavardi, Federico Nicoli, 155
Gaza, Theodorus, 40
Geist, Marcellus, of Atzenheim, 30
Gelnhausen, Johannes de, 32
Gennadius, Georgius Scholarius, 40
Gentili, Alberico, 124
George of Brussels, 38
Gerard of Calcer, 20
Gerard of Elten, 29
Gerhard, Johann, 157
German Logicians, 119
Gerson, John, 7
Gerson, Levi Ben, 23
Gesner, Konrad, 78

Geulincx, Arnold, 163
Giese, Tidemann, 60
Gilbert, William, 144
Giles, 6
Giles of Viterbo, 52
Glisson, Francis, 137
Goclenius, Rudolph, 118
Goës, Emanuel de, 106
Gonzago, Cardinal Ercole, 90
Goorle, David van, 146
Gracian, Balthazar, 101
Gracian, Jeronimo, 128
Granada, Luis de, 134
Granger, Thomas, 117
Gregory of Valencia, 108
Greve, Henry, 50
Greville, Robert, 138
Groote, Geert de, 13
Gropper, John, 89
Grotius, Hugo, 125
Guarinus of Verona, 27
Guido, 11
Gutke, Georg, 157

Hamilton, Patrick, 66
Hardewyk, Gerhard, 52
Harvey, William, 162
Heereboord, Adrianus, 158
Hegius, Alexander, 54
Heidelberg, At The University of, 19
Heidelberg Graduates in Arts, 29
Heinsius, David, 143
Heliocentric Universe, 150
Helmont, Franz Mercurius van, 62
Helmont, Johannes Baptista van, 62
Henry VIII, King, 56
Henry of Gorkum, 28
Henry of Hainbuch, 18
Henry of Hesse, 20
Henry of Nördlingen, 14
Henry of Odendorp, 7
Henry of Zoemeren, 22
Herbert of Cherbury, 144
Hessels, Johann Heinrich, 91
Heytesbury, William, 9
Hill, Nicholas, 145
Hiquaeus, Antonius, 154
Hobbes, Thomas, 158
Hofmann, Daniel, 140
Holkot, Robert, 4
Hooker, Richard, 125
Hosius, Stanislaus, 90
Hotman, Francois, 127
Humanist Circle of Pope Leo X, 45
Humanists, Early Italian, 1

INDEX

INDEX

INDEX

MEDIAEVAL PHILOSOPHICAL TEXTS IN TRANSLATION

Translation #1 :   "Grosseteste: On Light"
by Clare Riedl-Trans.
This treatise is significant as an introduction to an influential
thinker and man of science of the Middle Ages.

Translation #2 :   "St. Augustine: Against the Academicians"
by Sister Mary Patricia, R.S.M.-Trans.
Augustine aims to prove that man need not be content with mere
probability in the realm of knowledge.

Translation #3 :   "Pico Della Mirandola: Of Being and Unity"
by Victor M. Hamm-Trans.
In this work Pico tried to discover the genuine thought of Plato
and Aristotle on being and unity.

Translation #4 :   "Francis Suarez: On the Various Kinds of Distinction"
by Cyril Vollert, S.J.-Trans.
Suarez propounds his theory on distinctions, a point of capital importance for a grasp of Suarezian metaphysics.

Translation #5 :   "St. Thomas Aquinas: On Spiritual Creatures,"
by Mary C. Fitzpatrick-Trans.
This book falls into two general divisions: an introduction and
the translation from the Latin.

Translation #6 :   "Meditations of Guigo,"
by John J. Jolin, S.J.-Trans.
A series of reflections by Guigo, 12th century Prior of the hermi-
tage Charterhouse.

Translation #7 :   "Giles of Rome: Theorems on Existence and Essence,"
by Michael V. Murray, S.J.-Trans.
An essay dealing with the *a priori* deductions of being and its
conditions.

Translation #8 :   "John of St. Thomas: Outlines of Formal Logic"
by Francis C. Wade, S.J.-Trans.
A standard English translation of the Logic of John of St.
Thomas.

Translation #9 :   "Hugh of St. Victor: Soliloquy in the Earnest Money of the
Soul,"
Kevin Herbert-Trans.
The purpose of the work is to direct the soul toward a true love
of self, an attitude which is identical with a love of God.

Translation #10 :   "St. Thomas Aquinas: On Charity,"
by Lottie Kendzierski-Trans.
This treatise is significant as an expression of St. Thomas' discussion on the virtue of charity in itself, its object, subject, order,
precepts, and principal act.

Translation #11 :   "Aristotle: On Interpretation-Commentary by St. Thomas and
Cajetan,"
Jean T. Oesterle-Trans.
This translation will be of particular value to teachers and students
of logic.

Translation #12 :   "Desiderius Erasmus of Rotterdam: On Copia of Words and
Ideas,"
by Donald B. King and H. David Rix-Trans.
One of the most popular and influential books of the 16th century
is made available here for the first time in English.

Translation #13 : "Peter of Spain: Tractatus Syncategorematum and Selected Anonymous Treatises,"
by Joseph P. Mullally and Roland Houde-Trans.
The first English translation of these tracts now makes it possible for scholars of logic to better appreciate the continuity of Formal Logic.

Translation #14 : "Cajetan: Commentary on St. Thomas Aquinas' On Being and Essence,"
by Lottie Kendzierski and Francis C. Wade, S.J.-Trans.
A basic understanding of the relation between Cajetan and St. Thomas.

Translation #15 : "Suarez: Disputation VI, On Formal and Universal Unity,"
by James F. Ross-Trans.
The study of late mediaeval philosophy and the decline of scholasticism.

Translation #16 : "St. Thomas, Sieger de Brabant, St. Bonaventure: On the Eternity of the World,"
by Cyril Vollert, S.J., Lottie Kendzierski, Paul Byrne-Trans.
A combined work bringing together the writings of three great scholars on the philosophical problem of the eternity of the world.

Translation #17 : "Geoffrey of Vinsauf: Instruction in the Method and Art of Speaking and Versifying,"
by Roger P. Parr-Trans.
This text, of one of the most important mediaeval literary theorists, is here for the first time translated into English.

Translation #18 : "Liber De Pomo: The Apple, or Aristotle's Death,"
by Mary F. Rousseau-Trans.
A significant item in the history of mediaeval thought, never previously translated into English from the Latin.

Translation #19 : "St. Thomas Aquinas: On the Unity of the Intellect Against the Averroists,"
by Beatrice H. Zedler-Trans.
This is a polemical treatise that St. Thomas wrote to answer a difficult problem confronting his times.

Translation #20 : "The Universal Treatise of Nicholas of Autrecourt,"
by Leonard L. Kennedy C.S.B., Richard E. Arnold, S.J. and Arthur E. Millward, A.M.
This treatise gives an indication of the deep philosophical skepticism at the University of Paris in the mid-fourteenth century.

Translation #21 : "Pseudo-Dionysius Aeropagite: The Divine Names in Mystical Theology"
by John D. Jones-Trans.
Among the most important works in the transition from later Greek to Medieval thought.

Translation #22 : "Matthew of Vendôme: Ars Versificatoria (The Art of the Versemaker)"
by Roger P. Parr-Trans.
The text of this, the earliest of the major treatises of the *Artes Poetical* is here translated in toto with special emphasis given to maintaining the full nature of the complete original text.

Translation #23 : Suarez on Individuation
Translation by Jorge J. E. Garcia

MEDIAEVAL PHILOSOPHICAL TEXTS IN TRANSLATION

IN PREPARATION

St. Thomas Aquinas: Questions on the Soul
Translated by James H. Robb

Metaphysical Disputation XXXI (31), De Ento Finito, On Finite Being
Translated by Norman Wells

OTHER RELATED TITLES

The Crusades: A Documentary Survey
    By James A. Brundage

St. Ignatius' Idea of a Jesuit University
    By George E. Ganss, S.J.

Some Philosophers on Education: Papers Concerning Doctrines of Augustine,
    Aristotle, Aquinas and Dewey
    Ed. Donald A. Gallagher

"Active Life" and "Contemplative Life": A Study of the Concepts from Plato
to the Present
    By Sr. M. Elizabeth Mason, O.S.B. and George E. Ganss, S.J.

Giles of Rome: Errores Philosophorum
    Translated by John O. Riedl

The University of Toulouse in the Middle Ages
    By Cyril E. Smith

Jesuit Thinkers of the Renaissance
    Ed. Gerard Smith, S.J.

Averroes' Destructio Destructionum Philosophiae Algazelis in the Latin Version of Calo Colonymos
    By Beatrice H. Zedler